*"I'm not proud of leaving the Leafs this way.
If you'd told me three years ago my career here
would end like this, I'd never have believed it."*
—Darryl Sittler

*"They threw me in (in the trade) because
they didn't think I'd ever be a goalkeeper."*
—Glenn Hall

*"I've been traded, haven't I? If you tell me it's
New York, I'm going to jump out the window.'
Cherry then said to Orr, 'Bob – open the window!'"*
—Phil Esposito

*"What is this, kindergarten or a country club?
When I make a deal, I do what's best for the
hockey club. I don't care who is unhappy."*
—Punch Imlach

*"Mike [Keenan] has told me a lot of things. He has
always told me he loved me and would never trade me."*
—Denis Savard

*"I'm very happy to go to Detroit. I talked with Scotty
Bowman today, and he told me that they traded for
me because they want me to play."*
—Slava Fetisov

The BEST, WORST, and BIGGEST NHL Trades of All Time!

Library and Archives Canada Cataloguing in Publication

Podnieks, Andrew
The Best, Worst, and Biggest NHL Trades of All Time!

ISBN 9781552679173

Moydart Press
www.andrewpodnieks.com

First Printing 2013

Printed and bound in China

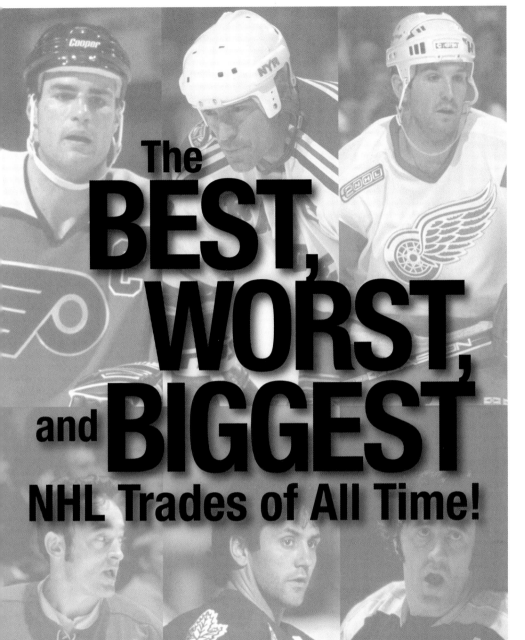

The
BEST,
WORST,
and BIGGEST
NHL Trades of All Time!

ANDREW PODNIEKS & ROB DEL MUNDO

MOYDART

CONTENTS

Trades

OCTOBER 11, 1930

Leafs Acquire King for Life

The Deal [TORONTO MAPLE LEAFS trade **Art Smith, Eric Pettinger, and $35,000** to the OTTAWA SENATORS for **King Clancy.**

"In spite of his relatively small, 154-pound physique, Clancy liked to deliver punishing bodychecks."

THE DIRT At the beginning of the Great Depression, sports were generally the furthest thing from anyone's mind as families struggled to put food on the table. As the 1929-30 NHL season progressed in the wake of the stock market crash, attendance at Ottawa Senators home games was in rapid decline. Indeed, the club was forced to move one of its games to Atlantic City where the Sens played the New York Rangers. Ottawa's 21-15-8 record that year was good for third place in the NHL's Canadian Division, but it was the last time that it finished above .500.

Along with Montreal's Howie Morenz and Boston's Eddie Shore, defenceman Francis "King" Clancy was considered one of the game's most colourful personalities. With the 1930-31 season about to get underway and the financially-strapped Senators no longer able to afford their star blueliner, Clancy, already a two-time Stanley Cup winner, was made available to the highest bidder. The Montreal Maroons had been interested in him for several years, but not at the asking price of $35,000.

Meanwhile the league's other clubs were having their own troubles at the box office, and the Toronto Maple Leafs were no exception. Owner Conn Smythe initially didn't have the funds to obtain Clancy, so he wagered on a race horse that he owned – a filly named Rare Jewel. The horse was victorious, enabling Smythe to meet Ottawa's cash demand for Clancy.

THE DEBATE This transaction was made for purely financial reasons and can't be fairly assessed in terms of each player's on-ice contributions. Defenceman Art Smith played in all but one of the Senators' 44 games that year, while left winger Eric Pettinger was held pointless in the 13 games in which he laced up the skates. Neither player whom Ottawa received in the deal played beyond the 1930-31 campaign.

In contrast, Clancy teamed with Hap Day to form a solid defence pairing for the Maple Leafs. Clancy's first season with Toronto ended with a selection to the NHL's First All-Star team alongside Eddie Shore.

Meanwhile Smythe's vision for his hockey club continued to expand as construction began on the team's new arena, Maple Leaf Gardens. The hockey shrine at 60 Carlton Street opened its doors on November 12, 1931, with the home side dropping a 2-1 decision to the Chicago Black Hawks. Despite the loss, the team posted a 23-18-7 record under coach Dick Irvin. In the 1932 playoffs, the Leafs disposed of Chicago and the Montreal Maroons in the first two rounds, then swept the Rangers in a best-of-five finals series to claim their first Stanley Cup.

/// Did You Know?

No man in NHL history was as active in the game at so many levels as Clancy. After retiring, he became a referee for 15 years and was respected as the best of his era. He later coached the Leafs, and to this day is the only man to play in, coach, and referee an All-Star Game. Even during his playing days he did it all, playing all six positions in a single game on one occasion and playing goal twice when his team's goalie received a penalty and had to go to the box for two minutes.

King of the '67 Cup

Every Leafs fan knows 1967 was the last year the team won the Cup, but few know the vital role Clancy played in the victory. Coach Punch Imlach was brilliant, but he was also dictatorial and often reviled by players. During one crucial stretch of the '66-'67 season, though, Imlach was ordered by doctors to rest, such was the state of his exhaustion. Clancy filled the breach and guided the Leafs to a 7-1-2 record in ten games. When Imlach returned, the coach and his players were revitalized and went on to win their historic Cup.

Clancy was named an All-Star in each of his next three seasons. In spite of his relatively small 154-pound physique, he liked to deliver punishing body-checks, particularly against his rival Shore. By the time "King" retired early in the 1936-37 season, Toronto had played in three Stanley Cup finals, finishing first in the Canadian Division in each of the first three seasons following their 1932 championship.

In 1953, Clancy stepped behind the Leafs' bench to coach the team for three years before becoming the club's assistant general manager. Clancy held the post during Toronto's dynasty years as they won the Stanley Cup four times between 1962 and 1967. He was appointed Leafs vice-president in 1969 and became the right-hand man to eccentric owner Harold Ballard. Clancy continued to be associated with the team until his death on November 8, 1986.

The King Clancy Trophy has been awarded annually since 1988 to "the player who best exemplifies leadership qualities on and off the ice and has made a noteworthy contribution to his community." Clancy was inducted into the Hockey Hall of Fame in 1958.

THE RESULT From Ottawa's perspective, Clancy wasn't the only casualty of the 1930-31 fire sale. Syd Howe, Allan Shields, and Wally Kilrea were sold to the Philadelphia Quakers. The team finished in the basement of the Canadian Division with a 10-30-4 record. The news got worse. The Senators suspended operations the following year, as did the Quakers, so that the teams could get their financial books in order.

Ottawa returned to the NHL in 1932-33 but posted a dismal record of 11-27-10, only to follow with a poor 13-29-6 showing the next season. In both instances the Senators finished with the worst record in the league. The franchise moved to St. Louis in 1934 where it was renamed the Eagles. The move to the "Gateway to the West" didn't change the team's fortunes as it finished 11-31-6, once again dead last in the league's standings.

The team then folded. Ottawa did not see the return of the NHL again until 1992-93 when the new incarnation of the Senators entered the league.

Toronto's fortunes were vastly different. The team flourished under the Clancy-Day pairing and the Kid Line of Joe Primeau, Busher Jackson, and Charlie Conacher providing the offensive punch. Clancy missed a total of just eight games in the six full seasons that he donned a Maple Leafs uniform. His number 7 is co-honoured with another legendary Toronto defenceman, Tim Horton, and both have banners hanging from Air Canada Centre in their honour.

The Maple Leafs and Conn Smythe had the luxury of an arena that would become one of hockey's most famous shrines for 68 years. The Ottawa Senators had neither the rink, nor the fans support, to feasibly compete. Ottawa's loss was Toronto's tremendous gain.

/// King Clancy Night

A proud Irishman, Clancy was given his own special tribute night by Conn Smythe while still a player. On March 17, 1934—St. Patrick's Day, of course!—Clancy was paraded out to centre ice on a sleigh. He was dressed in a large green robe, wore a crown, and held a sceptre. King was given many gifts, and when the game began Clancy continued to wear a green Leafs sweater. The Rangers were the opposition this night and complained the different togs made it difficult to identify him, so Clancy was told to revert to the old Blue and White.

OCTOBER 3, 1934

Impossible—Morenz Leaves Habs!

The Deal [CHICAGO BLACK HAWKS trade **Lionel Conacher, Leroy Goldsworthy, and Roger Jenkins** to the MONTREAL CANADIENS for **Howie Morenz, Lorne Chabot, and Marty Burke.**

"Neither Goldsworthy nor Jenkins played enough with Montreal to make a long-term impact, but neither did Morenz, Chabot, or Burke with the Black Hawks."

THE DIRT When a superstar becomes so iconic for a team, it's almost impossible to imagine him wearing a different sweater. Seeing Wayne Gretzky in a Los Angeles uniform or Bobby Orr donning the colours of Chicago seems so out of place.

Decades before the Great One left Edmonton, or Number 4 left Boston, Montreal Canadiens legend Howie Morenz was traded from the team with which he is not only closely associated but truly immortalized. From the moment that he entered the NHL in 1923-24, Morenz dominated the game with his blinding speed, creative passing, and thunderous slapshot. Morenz and Montreal were one and the same.

Nicknamed "The Mitchell Meteor" or "The Stratford Streak," Morenz, incredibly, finished among the top eleven scorers in each of the first ten seasons of his career. He won the league's scoring title in 1927-28 and 1930-31, also taking home the Hart Trophy in both years and adding a third NHL most valuable player award in 1931-32. He was part of three Stanley Cup-winning teams with the Habs and was the most electrifying player in the sport.

By comparison, his eleventh season, 1933-34, was not a happy one. Injuries took their toll. Fans at the Montreal Forum booed the three-time All-Star centre. Morenz's 21 points were his lowest total since his rookie season, and his output of eight goals was a career low.

Meanwhile the Chicago Black Hawks were crowned Stanley Cup champions in the spring of 1934. As the following season approached, the team was looking for a trading partner. Chicago needed to replace goaltender Chuck Gardiner, who had suddenly passed away from a brain hemorrhage just months after celebrating a Cup triumph.

THE DEBATE Included in the package to Montreal was goalie Lorne Chabot, a former Stanley Cup winner for Toronto and the man called upon to replace Gardiner for the Black Hawks. Chabot set a career high for victories in his first year in Chicago, winning 26 games. However, he lost the starting job to Mike Karakas the following year and finished his career playing for the Montreal Maroons and New York Americans.

Also going to the Windy City was Marty Burke, a defenceman called "husky" and "hard-hitting." Burke was a mainstay of the Black Hawks' blue line for three seasons before returning to Montreal in 1937-38.

Lionel Conacher—celebrated as Canada's athlete of the half-century—was one of the players that the Canadiens received in return for Morenz. A hard-hitting, punishing defenceman, Conacher was eventually inducted into the halls of fame of hockey, football, and lacrosse, as well as Canada's Sports Hall of Fame.

But Conacher never played a game for the Habs. Instead, he was dealt along with future NHL scoring champion Herb Cain to the Montreal Maroons for the rights to defence prospect Nels Crutchfield. Sadly, Crutchfield's potential was never realized. After playing 41 games in 1934-35, Crutchfield suffered injuries in a car accident in the summer that ended his hockey career.

/// Did You Know?

Although Lionel Conacher was inducted into the Hockey Hall of Fame in 1994, hockey might well have been the sport at which he was least accomplished. Indeed, he was amateur boxing champion of Canada as a light-heavyweight. He was considered one of the country's top lacrosse players and led the Toronto Argonauts to the 1921 Grey Cup. He won an International League championship with the Toronto Maple Leafs baseball club, and he won the Memorial Cup before winning the Stanley Cup twice. Incredibly, he was named both top athlete and top football player of the first half of the 20th century.

Right-winger Leroy Goldsworthy had also been a star pitcher in the Northwestern Baseball League. He was praised by Chicago Black Hawks coach and general manager Tommy Gorman as a strong forechecker instrumental in the team's Stanley Cup championship. Goldsworthy played 80 games in two seasons with the Canadiens, registering 35 goals and 55 points. He continued to build his reputation as a fine defensive player with both the Boston Bruins and New York Americans after moving on from the Habs.

Defenceman Roger Jenkins suited up for the Canadiens for 45 games in 1934-35 before moving to Boston. A journeyman, he played for the Habs, Maroons, and New York Rangers in 1936-37 before returning to Chicago the following year to win a second Stanley Cup.

As for Morenz, his time in Chicago was short-lived. Although he produced 34 points in his first season with the Black Hawks, he never regained the form that made him the superhero that he was with the Canadiens. Midway through the 1935-36 season, he was dealt to the Rangers. The following year, he returned to the place where his Hockey Hall of Fame career began.

THE RESULT The late 1930s and early '40s were dark days in the history of the Canadiens' franchise. Aside from a productive 1936-37 campaign in which the Habs finished first in the Canadian division and advanced to the semi-finals, they had a run of misery from 1933-34 to 1941-42 during which they either missed the playoffs or were eliminated in the first round. And, when their local rivals, the Maroons, won the Stanley Cup in 1935, the Canadiens were relegated to being the second best team in Montreal.

Neither Goldsworthy nor Jenkins played enough with Montreal to make a long-term impact, but neither did Morenz, Chabot, or Burke with the Black Hawks.

It was the second part of the deal that worked against Montreal due to unfortunate circumstances, namely the transaction that sent Conacher and Cain to the Maroons for Crutchfield. Cain eventually went on to stardom with Boston, winning a scoring title in 1943-44 and becoming the first player in NHL history to break the 80-point mark in a season. He finished with 36 goals and 46 assists.

Morenz's playing career, and ultimately his life, came to a tragic end during his return to the Canadiens. On January 28, 1937, in a game against Chicago, he suffered a broken leg. Morenz died weeks later due to heart failure. His funeral was held at centre ice of the Montreal Forum where thousands of mourners came to pay their respects.

MAY 18, 1939
Five for One for Sweeney

The Deal [TORONTO MAPLE LEAFS trade **Buzz Boll, Busher Jackson, Doc Romnes, Jim Fowler, and Murray Armstrong** to the NEW YORK AMERICANS for **Sweeney Schriner.**

"The real key to the deal for the Americans was Armstrong, who was a throw-in to complete the trade."

THE DIRT Both the Toronto Maple Leafs and New York Americans had mediocre years in 1938-39, finishing with losing records in third and fourth place, respectively, in the seven-team NHL. The Leafs were seven years removed from their first Stanley Cup win while the Americans had finished above .500 only twice in their 14 seasons of existence.

General managers Conn Smythe and Red Dutton decided to shake up their rosters. The Leafs received Schriner, who had been one of the few stars on the Americans. The 26-year-old, Russian-born left-winger won the Calder Trophy in 1935 and had been the league's scoring champion in both the 1935-36 and 1936-37 seasons, the latter culminating in a selection to the Second All-Star Team. Schriner was just three points shy of repeating the feat the following year – before the trade – finishing in second place to Montreal's Toe Blake.

Going to New York was one of the most popular left-wingers in Toronto history in Jackson. Skating on the Kid Line with Joe Primeau and Charlie

Conacher, Jackson consistently finished among the NHL's top scorers, leading the league in points in 1931-32 en route to a Leafs' Stanley Cup title.

Jackson had been named an All-Star five times, but after registering 40 points in 1936-37, his production declined in each of the following two seasons as he recorded 34 and then 27 points. Also, Smythe was embittered with the fan favourite due to Jackson's partying lifestyle and drinking habits.

Buzz Boll suffered a knee injury prior to the start of the 1938-39 season and played only eleven games for the Leafs that year. Armstrong saw limited action in Toronto, playing only a dozen games over two seasons with the team while spending most of his time with Toronto's farm club in Syracuse.

Two of the other players in the deal were of little consequence. Doc Romnes ended up playing just 15 games for the Americans, recording just one assist. Fowler, a defenceman, was used only periodically by the Leafs, moving back and forth between Toronto and Syracuse, and being used occasionally as a forward. Fowler never played a game for New York.

THE DEBATE Schriner was a consistent producer for the Leafs, but he played in the shadow of Toronto stars Syl Apps and Gordie Drillon. In 1940-41, Sweeney earned 38 points in 48 games, marking the only one of his six seasons with the Leafs in which he finished in the top ten in scoring.

The 1942 Leafs team became immortalized in hockey history during the Stanley Cup finals. Trailing 3-0 in the best-of-seven series against Detroit, Hap Day took the risky move of benching veterans Drillon and Bucko MacDonald in

/// Did You Know?

Murray Armstrong was the first NCAA coach to actively recruit Canadians, offering scholarships and luring top players from north of the border in what today is a common practice. He coached University of Denver for 21 years after his playing days and won five national championships.

favour of Don Metz and rookie Gaye Stewart. With goaltender Turk Broda leading the way, Toronto rallied to win the next four games to become the first team in the major North American pro sports to win a championship after trailing by a deficit of three games to none.

Schriner won another Stanley Cup with the Leafs in 1945 and retired after the following season. He was inducted into the Hockey Hall of Fame in 1962.

Jackson had two seasons in New York which were average by his standards, finishing with 20 and 26 points in 1939-40 and 1940-41, respectively. The real key to the deal for the Americans was Armstrong, who was a throw-in to complete the trade. In his first season in New York, he played alongside his Leafs teammate Jackson and also Lorne Carr. A native of Manor, Saskatchewan, Armstrong had 16 goals and 36 points in the 1939-40 season to finish tenth in the NHL scoring race, a surprising and impressive contribution, to say the least.

Boll recovered nicely from his knee injury suffered in his last year with the Leafs. He missed only two games in three seasons with the Americans, collecting a respectable 41 points in 94 games played.

THE RESULT The Leafs had Schriner in the lineup for six seasons, and he contributed to Stanley Cup championships in both 1942 and 1945. Although Schriner never came close to winning a scoring title in Toronto, he earned 37 points in 26 games in 1944-45. The pro-rated average would have placed him third in NHL scoring had he played a full season that year.

Even at the time of the trade, the future of the Americans was bleak. The 1940-41 campaign saw the team finish with a terrible 8-29-11 mark. Once Canada entered the Second World War, many of the team's players enlisted in the military and were unavailable to play. Compounding matters, the "Amerks" were mired in huge financial debt, forcing manager Mervyn "Red" Dutton to sell many of his best players.

The team was renamed the Brooklyn Americans in 1941-42 but couldn't officially move to the New York borough because of the unavailability of an

The Nickname

As a teenager, David Schriner very much admired a baseball player named Bill Sweeney. Schriner played in the style of Sweeney and was soon called Li'l Sweeney by his friends. He liked the reference so much he refused to answer anyone who addressed him as David. In time, the "Li'l" was dropped and David became Sweeney.

arena. The Americans continued to play out of Madison Square Garden, clawing their way to a 16-29-3 finish. Although they had doubled their win total from the previous season, they still finished last in the league's standings. It was the final season for Brooklyn. The team suspended operations for the duration of the war but was never reinstated by the league once peacetime resumed.

Jackson was reunited with his brother, Art, in Boston, while Boll also became a Bruin in the Dispersal Draft. Armstrong committed to military service in Regina, playing one season for the Regina Capitals of the Saskatchewan Senior Hockey League. Armstrong's NHL career resumed with the Detroit Red Wings, where he played for three seasons.

Had it not been for the late inclusion of Armstrong, the deal would have ended up lopsided in Toronto's favour. In the end, such was not the case.

JANUARY 25, 1940

Accommodating a Legend

The Deal [BOSTON BRUINS trade **Eddie Shore**
to the NEW YORK AMERICANS for **Ed Wiseman and $5,000.**

"Don Cherry, who played under Shore in Springfield for four years, called him 'the Darth Vader of hockey.'"

THE DIRT Eddie shore was the dominant defenceman of his era. Immediately upon his entry into the NHL with the Boston Bruins, in 1926, Shore established himself as the most feared blueliner in the game. The man nicknamed "The Edmonton Express" not only pulverized opposing players with crushing bodychecks, he also had an immense skill set to complement his physical play. Between 1930-31 and 1938-39, Shore was named to the First All-Star Team seven times and the Second All-Star Team once.

Shore was also an entrepreneur. During the summer of 1939, just months after winning his second Stanley Cup with Boston, Shore purchased controlling interest of the Springfield Indians of the American Hockey League. As the 1939-40 season opened, he declared his intent to withdraw from the NHL to play in Springfield.

Bruins coach general manager Art Ross was understandably unwilling to lose the services of his star rearguard for nothing. The GM and his star player reached an agreement in which Shore played home games in Springfield, 150 kilometres from Boston, and also in Bruins home games in emergency situations.

But neither party was completely satisfied as it did no good service to either man or either team. Finally, Ross granted Shore's desire to be traded, and the star defenceman was shipped off to Red Dutton's New York Americans. Shore played for New York only at home, and he was permitted to play in Springfield as long as there was no conflict between the Americans and Indians schedule.

On March 9, 1940, the 38-year-old Shore played against his ex-Boston teammates for the first time. New York won that game, 4-2. The Americans made the playoffs for a third consecutive season but bowed out in the quarter-finals to Detroit.

Boston finished first in the regular season on the strength of the contributions of the Kraut Line – Milt Schmidt, Woody Dumart, and Bobby Bauer – who were also the top three scoring leaders. The Bruins were ousted by the eventual Stanley Cup champion New York Rangers in the semi-finals.

THE DEBATE Right-winger Ed Wiseman – described in the *New York Times* as a "no better than average hockey player" – was a solid addition to Boston's lineup. During his first half-season with the Bruins, Wiseman picked up eight points in 18 regular season games. The best was yet to come.

The following year, the Bruins once again vaulted to the top of the NHL's standings, cruising to a 27-8-13 mark. Wiseman registered 16 goals and 24 assists. His 40 points were the best on the team and eighth-best overall in the league. Teammate Bauer finished with one fewer point, while Schmidt and Roy Conacher were just two points in arrears. Wiseman, a Regina native, scored six times in eleven playoff games and Boston went on to win the Stanley Cup, sweeping Detroit in the finals.

Wiseman's next season turned out to be his last one in the NHL. He collected 12 goals and 34 points, and the Bruins won their first playoff round versus the Black Hawks before bowing to the Red Wings. Like many Canadian players, Wiseman left hockey to serve in the military. He was stationed with the Royal Canadian Air Force in Saskatoon.

The Ace Bailey Incident

In a home game against Toronto on December 12, 1933, Shore was knocked to the ice. He was so incensed he tore after Ace Bailey, whom he mistakenly thought had doled out the check. Shore tossed Bailey from behind, and the Leafs star hit his head on the ice, falling unconscious. Bailey needed three life-saving operations before he could return to Toronto, his career unequivocally finished. On February 14, 1934, the Leafs hosted a game against the best of the rest of the NHL, and when Bailey shook Shore's hand during player introductions, the Gardens shook with appreciation of the gesture.

Shore left the NHL after the 1939-40 season, having played just ten games with the Americans, collecting five points and nine penalty minutes along the way. The Americans were on the verge of financial ruin and lasted just two more years in the league, winning only 24 of a possible 96 games over the final couple of seasons.

In Springfield, Shore played three more seasons, amassing 145 penalty minutes in 106 games. He also carved his reputation as a merciless owner, reviled by many around the AHL. His practices were strict; his criticism of his players was biting. Don Cherry, who played under Shore in Springfield for four years, called him "the Darth Vader of hockey." A ruthless dictator, Shore was eventually forced out of the ownership group with the Indians. But he left his legacy by mentoring future coaches such as Cherry, Floyd Smith, and long-time Ottawa 67's coach Brian Kilrea. Nevertheless, the Eddie Shore Award is presented annually to the best defenceman in the American Hockey League.

Shore won the Lester Patrick Award in 1970 in recognition of his outstanding contributions to hockey in the United States. He had been inducted into the Hockey Hall of Fame in 1947.

THE RESULT Art Ross emerged as a victor in this trade, obtaining the best available value in return for a player who no longer wanted to be with the Bruins, or the NHL for that matter. Shore played in only ten NHL games after his departure from Boston. Wiseman collected 82 regular season points in just under two-and-a-half seasons with the Bruins.

The 1941 Stanley Cup championship was the last one in Beantown for 29 years before Shore's successor as hockey's most iconic defenceman, Bobby Orr, ended the drought with his famous leaping goal against St. Louis in 1970. Had Shore not purchased the Indians and stayed committed to the Bruins, there would have been no reason to trade him.

But that was Shore, eccentric to the point where legendary stories are told at the mention of his name. He reportedly fired two publicity directors in Springfield who refused to help him clean the ice at the end of a game. He knocked out a 220-pound concession worker who said something he didn't like. He made the players change light bulbs at the rink.

It was Shore's way or no way. His time in Boston was effectively finished from the moment that he put the ink to the paper to buy the Indians. Receiving Wiseman, plus $5,000, was more than the Bruins could have hoped to get in return.

SEPTEMBER 10, 1943

Greatest Swindle Ever?

The Deal [TORONTO MAPLE LEAFS trade **Frank Eddolls** to the MONTREAL CANADIENS for **Ted Kennedy**.

"Kennedy last played a full season in 1954-55, when he won the Hart Trophy as the league's most valuable player."

THE DIRT On June 7, 1940, a trade between archrivals Toronto and Montreal saw promising defenceman Frank Eddolls – a Memorial Cup champion with Oshawa – go to the Maple Leafs for Joe Benoit.

Eddolls turned pro in the summer of 1941, playing for the Hershey Bears and collecting 19 points in 54 games in his AHL rookie season. The following year he enlisted in the Royal Canadian Air Force, playing hockey with the air force team in the Quebec Senior Hockey League and winning the most valuable player award. But in the summer of 1943, Eddolls suffered a bruise in a lacrosse game and aggravated a knee injury he had suffered five years earlier. Doctors performed surgery, and his hockey career was in jeopardy.

Meanwhile Ted "Teeder" Kennedy was a Canadiens prospect who had played junior hockey in Montreal but returned to his home in Port Colborne, Ontario after feeling homesick. Former NHL player Nels Stewart was coaching a senior team in the area and offered to mentor the 16-year-old centre. Stewart recommended to the

Leafs that they try to acquire the youngster.

While Conn Smythe was overseas during the war, Leafs acting general manager Frank Selke dealt Eddolls back to Montreal for Kennedy, but the transaction was met with Smythe's wrath because Smythe had not been advised of or given authorization to make the trade. Selke was accused of trying to undermine Smythe's authority, causing an irreparable rift between the two men. Eventually Selke joined the Habs.

THE DEBATE The trade wildly exceeded Toronto's expectations. Kennedy scored 49 points in as many games during his rookie season of 1943-44. In addition to his skill, he had a strong work ethic that endeared him to his teammates. Kennedy bolstered his production by five points the following season but saved his best work for the playoffs.

In 1944-45, the powerhouse Canadiens were heavy favourites to repeat as Stanley Cup champions. Montreal boasted the Punch Line of Elmer Lach, Rocket Richard, and Toe Blake, who were the top three scorers in the league. That season, Richard made history by becoming the first player to score 50 goals in 50 games.

But the Habs' top forward unit was neutralized by a line of Kennedy, Bob Davidson, and Mel Hill, and Montreal was stunned in the semi-finals in six games. The battle for the Stanley Cup came down to a seven-game series between Toronto and Detroit. Toronto defenceman Babe Pratt provided the heroics by scoring the winning goal in the final game, won by the Leafs, 2-1. Kennedy finished the playoffs with seven goals and nine points in 13 games.

Two years later, Kennedy posted his first 60-point season. This time, the Leafs faced the Canadiens in the finals, and Teeder scored the Stanley Cup-winning goal in the sixth game. It marked the first of three consecutive Cups for Toronto, the first dynasty in NHL history.

In 1948, at age 22, Kennedy was named captain of the Leafs, replacing the retiring Syl Apps. He went on to score a remarkable nine goals and 14 points in eleven playoff games as the Leafs defended their championship. The following year, the Maple Leafs became the first team in NHL history to win three championships in a row. Toronto claimed four Stanley Cups between 1945 and 1949, and Kennedy was the team's leading playoff scorer in each of those years.

A fifth title came in 1951 when the Leafs and Habs dueled in a classic five-game final series during which every contest was decided in overtime. Bill Barilko's famous overtime winner at 2:53 of the fourth period clinched Toronto's fifth Cup in seven years.

Kennedy last played a full season in 1954-55, when he won the Hart Trophy as the league's most valuable player. By the time he retired, he had played 696 regular season games in a Leafs uniform, registering 560 points. He established himself as a playoff performer with 60 points in 78 post-season games, including a team record 23 points in the finals. One of the greatest players to put on a Maple Leafs sweater, Kennedy was a three-time Second Team All-Star and was inducted into the Hockey Hall of Fame in 1966.

Eddolls played just three seasons in Montreal. He appeared in 43 games in his rookie season of 1944-45, collecting 13 points. But his playing time was drastically reduced in his sophomore year when veteran Ken Reardon returned to the team after serving in World War II. Eddolls played just eight regular season games in 1946 but was part of the team that won the Stanley Cup. He suited up for just six games for the Habs in 1946-47.

THE RESULT The transaction was undoubtedly won by the Leafs, hands down. Prior to the start of the team's 75th anniversary season in 2001-02, Kennedy was named one of the 25 greatest all-time Leafs in a list compiled by a panel of hockey experts. The man called "Teeder" was only the second Toronto player to win the Hart Trophy, following Babe Pratt's honours in 1943-44.

In an unfortunate coincidence for the Habs, they dealt Eddolls as part of another lopsided trade against them. Eddolls' time in Montreal came to an end when he was dealt along with Buddy O'Connor to the New York Rangers for Hal Laycoe, Joe Bell, and George Robertson.

Both new Rangers thrived in New York. O'Connor won the Hart Trophy in 1948, while Eddolls enjoyed five strong years with the Blueshirts, getting the nod as captain in 1950-51. The Rangers came within one goal of winning the Stanley Cup in 1950, only to lose in Game 7 on an overtime marker by Detroit's Pete Babando.

The 1951 Habs team that lost to the Leafs and Barilko certainly could have used either Kennedy, or O'Connor, in their lineup.

Did You Know?

The most famous fan of the Original Six era was surely John Arnott. A season's-ticket holder at Maple Leaf Gardens, he adored Ted Kennedy and was famous for his loud screams of, "C'mon Teeder!" during stoppages in play. Such was the respect Kennedy held for Arnott for all those years of vocal support that on Arnott's death, Teeder acted as a pallbearer at the funeral.

NOVEMBER 2, 1947

Bentley the Best Player in Deal

The Deal [TORONTO MAPLE LEAFS trade **Gus Bodnar, Bud Poile, Gaye Stewart, Bob Goldham, and Ernie Dickens** to the CHICAGO BLACK HAWKS for **Max Bentley and Cy Thomas.**

"With a trio of all-star centremen in Bentley, Apps, and Kennedy, the Leafs cruised to a second consecutive Stanley Cup."

THE DIRT By 1947, the Toronto Maple Leafs had won their second Stanley Cup in three seasons and had two of the best centres in the league in Syl Apps and Ted Kennedy. But Conn Smythe needed a succession plan for Apps' impending retirement scheduled for the end of the 1947-48 campaign.

Smythe looked to Chicago where Max Bentley was the star forward on a sub-standard team. The Black Hawks finished in the basement of the league's standings the previous year with a meagre 19-37-4 record.

Bentley was the two-time defending Art Ross Trophy winner. Together with his brother Doug, and Bill Mosienko, they formed "The Pony Line," each of the three finishing among the NHL's top nine scorers in 1946-47. But while the Black Hawks could find the net – second only to Toronto in goals scored that year – they were terrible in their own end of the rink. Chicago's 274 goals against was by far the worst in the six-team league, allowing 81 more pucks to get past their goaltenders than Detroit, second worst in that dubious category.

Adding to Chicago's misfortune was an ankle injury to Mosienko that occurred during the All-Star Game prior to the start of the year. The Black Hawks began the 1947-48 season by losing their first six games.

In his initial pitch to obtain Bentley, Smythe offered Chicago general manager Bill Tobin the entire newly-formed forward line nicknamed "The Flying Forts" that was made up of Bodnar, Poile, and Stewart. Defenceman Dickens was also included in the proposal. After further negotiating, the additions of Goldham and Thomas from both sides completed the deal.

Bentley was initially heartbroken at the news of no longer having the opportunity to play with his brother. Chicago coach Johnny Gottselig was reluctant to split up the siblings, but he conceded that the Black Hawks had no other tradable assets and something needed to be done to turn around what looked to be another disastrous season.

THE DEBATE The five-for-two swap sent both teams further in the directions they had been travelling the previous years. With a trio of all-star centremen in Bentley, Apps, and Kennedy, the Leafs cruised to a second consecutive Stanley Cup. Toronto finished first in the regular season with a 32-15-13 record, then disposed of Boston in five games in the semi-finals before a sweep of Detroit in the finals to complete their dream season. Bentley collected 48 points in 53 games in the regular season and added eleven points in Toronto's nine post-season games.

When Apps retired, Cal Gardner filled his vacated position at centre. The Leafs struggled in the 1948-49 campaign but managed to finish fourth and earn the final playoff spot with a losing record at 22-25-13. But they surprised their critics by claiming a third straight Stanley Cup, achieving the feat against the same opponents – in identical series scores – as the previous playoff year, taking five and four games to defeat the Bruins and Red Wings, respectively. Another championship, the last of Bentley's career, came in 1951 as Bill Barilko launched his name into folklore with his overtime goal.

Conversely in the Windy City, the downward spiral continued for the Black Hawks. In the 12-year span from 1946-47 to 1957-58, Chicago missed the playoffs eleven times and finished last in the league standings on nine occasions.

Bodnar had the longest tenure of any of the five players that the Black Hawks received. He played for the team for seven years and finished his career with Boston. On March 23, 1952, in a game against the New York Rangers, teammate Bill Mosienko set an NHL record for the fastest hat trick—three goals in 21 seconds. Bodnar assisted on all three of Mosienko's tallies, establishing the mark, of course, for the fastest trio of assists.

Poile finished tied with Bentley for fifth in NHL scoring in 1947-48 as both men recorded 52 points. Early the following year Poile accompanied George Gee in a trade to Detroit for Jim Conacher, Bep Guidolin, and Doug McCaig.

Stewart trumped both Bentley and Poile in scoring during the 1947-48 season, finishing with 54 points for fourth place in the league. Goldham was a durable defenceman, playing all 60 games in 1948-49, and missing just three of the 70 league games the next year. Stewart and Goldham were dealt to Detroit in July 1950 in a massive nine-player deal that also saw Metro Prystai and goalie Sugar Jim Henry become Red Wings. Going to Chicago were Harry Lumley, Don Morrison, Jack Stewart, Al Dewsbury, and Pete Babando, who three months earlier became the first player in NHL history to score a Game 7 overtime Stanley Cup-winning goal.

Like Goldham, Dickens missed little playing time, playing in all but one of Chicago's games during his four-year tenure with the club. After the 1950-51

///Clan Bentley

Max was one of 13 children and five brothers who played hockey. His father was the mayor of Delisle, Saskatchewan, and the family included Doug and Reg, teammates in Chicago, as well as Roy and Wyatt. Max and Doug are both in the Hockey Hall of Fame.

season, Dickens retired at the age of 29. Cy Thomas, meanwhile, a Chicago rookie at the time of the deal, played just eight games in a Maple Leafs uniform, spending much of the season with Toronto's minor league affiliate in Pittsburgh.

THE RESULT Usually the team that wins a trade is the one that receives the best player. The acquisition of Bentley by the Leafs is a prime example of this tenet. Bentley neither was named to the end of year All-Star Team, as he had twice achieved in Chicago, nor won another scoring title, but he filled a need that the Leafs knew they would require attention once Apps retired. Bentley was sold to the New York Rangers prior to the start of the 1953-54 season, his last in the NHL.

The forwards that Toronto gave up, plus their two rookie defencemen, were expendable. Given the Leafs' success and the Black Hawks failures in the years following the trade, few would argue against Smythe being the clear winner.

/// Did You Know?

While most fans believe Maurice Richard had his best chance to win the Art Ross Trophy in 1954-55, the year he was suspended, he actually had a better chance in 1946-47. Richard had 45 goals and 71 points that season, but on the final day of the schedule Max Bentley surpassed him, finishing with 72 points to become only the third player in league history to repeat as scoring champion. Charlie Conacher and Sweeney Schriner had both achieved the double in the previous decade.

AUGUST 20, 1951

Red Wings Fire Sale During Dynasty

The Deal [DETROIT RED WINGS trade **Jim McFadden, George Gee, Max McNab, Jimmy Peters, Sr., Clare Martin,** and **Rags Raglin** to the CHICAGO BLACK HAWKS for **$75,000 and future considerations (Hugh Coflin).**

"The transaction did not reverse the Hawks' fortunes, and they finished last in the standings all but one of the next six years."

THE DIRT Detroit won the Stanley Cup in 1950 and followed up with a first-place finish in the NHL standings the following season. By the summer of 1951, Red Wings general manager Jack Adams had decided that he wanted to call up some younger players from the team's farm club in Indianapolis.

Black Hawks' coach Ebbie Goodfellow was looking to strengthen Chicago's defence which had surrendered a porous 280 goals in 1950-51. Upgrades on the blue line and also at the centre position were desperately coveted. Thus, this trade featured three centremen: Gee, McFadden, McNab, and two defencemen: Martin and Raglin. Five of the six players who came to the Windy City were veterans, the youngster Raglin the lone exception.

The trade marked the largest cash deal in league history at the time, more than doubling the amount – $35,000 – that Toronto paid to purchase King Clancy from Ottawa in 1930.

Of all the players involved in this mega-swap, McFadden had the highest profile, having won the Calder Trophy in 1947-48. In that season, the rookie played in all of Detroit's 60 games, registering 48 points to finish eleventh in scoring.

In Detroit, GM Adams continued to build his team around the nucleus of Gordie Howe, Ted Lindsay, Sid Abel, Red Kelly, and Terry Sawchuk. Goodfellow believed that the deal would increase Chicago's goal total by 60 or 70, hoping that Gee and Peters – linemates as Red Wings – would continue to have the same chemistry.

THE DEBATE On the production side of the scoreboard, the Black Hawks experienced the opposite effect to that which Goodfellow had hoped. In fact, Chicago scored a league low 158 goals in 1951-52, a decrease of 13 from the previous season. The team gave up "only" 241 goals as opposed to 280 the year before, but the total was still the worst of the six-team league as Chicago slumped to its third consecutive last-place finish.

The team was granted a reprieve from the basement in 1952-53 when McFadden led the team in scoring with 44 points, good for a tie for tenth overall in the league. Chicago finished fourth in the standings to earn a first-round playoff matchup against the Montreal Canadiens. The Black Hawks took a 3-2 series lead before the Habs roared back to take the next two games, staving off the upset. Rocket Richard and Bernie Geoffrion then led the ousting of Boston in five games in the finals. The

/// Gee Willikers

George Gee's finest moment in the NHL surely came on April 23, 1950, at the end of Game 7 of the 1950 Stanley Cup finals. That year marked the first time the Cup was won in OT of the final game, the most dramatic situation possible. Playing for the Red Wings, in a game against the Rangers, Gee lined up for a faceoff in the New York end. He motioned winger Pete Babando to get into position, then won the draw back to Babando who wired a shot past goalie Chuck Rayner for the Cup-winning goal in a 4-3 victory. Games 2 and 3 of that series were played in Maple Leaf Gardens because the circus had booked those dates in New York. The Rangers, meanwhile, had won games 4 and 5 in overtime.

poor Black Hawks then returned to the cellar for each of the next four seasons.

McFadden played two full seasons for Chicago, earning 78 points in 140 games. He played 19 games in 1953-54 before joining the minor league Calgary Stampeders of the WHL to close out his pro career that ended in 1957.

Peters' numbers in his first two years with the Black Hawks were almost identical to McFadden's: 77 points in 139 games. Midway through the 1953-54 campaign he was traded back to the Red Wings for future considerations. At season's end, he retired from the NHL but played for two more years across the border with a senior team, the Windsor Bulldogs.

Gee posted relatively good statistics in three seasons with Chicago, picking up 46 goals and 114 points to go along with 197 penalty minutes while missing only three out of 210 games. He joined Peters in Windsor in 1954-55.

Raglan's time with Chicago was brief. He played parts of just two seasons before becoming a minor-league player for the rest of his career. Martin played even fewer games for the Black Hawks, and the team sold him to the New York Rangers in December 1951.

McNab was forced to miss the 1951-52 season because of back surgery and never again returned to NHL form. He played the last seven years of his professional career with New Westminster of the WHL. McNab later took his talents from the rink to the boardroom where he became first a WHL and later an NHL executive. He served as the general manager of the Washington Capitals from 1975-76 until 1981-82.

THE RESULT Chicago received very limited upside from the six players it received in the deal. The transaction did not reverse the Hawks' fortunes, and they finished last in the standings all but one of the next six years. As well, they were $75,000 lighter in the wallet.

Jack Adams had the assets to replace the outgoing Red Wings, most notably a pair of future Hockey Hall of Fame members, Alex Delvecchio and Marcel Pronovost. Delvecchio, a 19-year-old rookie, earned a spot with the big club and played the first season of a 24-year career in 1951-52. He held the record for most games played with one club (1,549) before the mark was surpassed by Nicklas Lidstrom, also with Detroit, in 2012.

Pronovost played his first full season in Detroit in 1951-52 after splitting his time the previous year between the Red Wings and Indianapolis. He earned four consecutive All-Star selections between 1958 and 1961.

Adams had suggested that the Maple Leafs follow his strategy of recalling younger players. Conn Smythe was not in a hurry to heed his counterpart's advice. "He talks about bringing up younger players," said Smythe. "We've brought up young players every year since The Kid Line in 1929. However, it'll probably wind up being known as the Adams system. I'm glad to see that Adams, after 30 years, is getting into the Smythe system."

Smythe ended up eating his words as the Red Wings reeled off three more Stanley Cup victories between 1952 and 1955.

JUNE 3, 1955
Sawchuk Not Untouchable

The Deal [DETROIT RED WINGS trade **Terry Sawchuk, Marcel Bonin, Lorne Davis,** and **Vic Stasiuk** to the BOSTON BRUINS for **Gilles Boisvert, Real Chevrefils, Norm Corcoran, Warren Godfrey,** and **Ed Sandford.**

"The Wings discovered they had two big goalies,
a luxury which no club can afford."
—Milt Dunnell

THE DIRT The Montreal Canadiens set a precedent in 1934 by dealing away their franchise star, Howie Morenz. From then on, no player could be considered 'untradeable.'

From the moment he first stepped on the ice in Detroit, Terry Sawchuk established himself as a goaltender upon which to build a foundation for Stanley Cup glory. His winning the Calder Trophy as the league's best rookie was only a foreshadowing of things to come. The Winnipeg native backstopped the Red Wings to Stanley Cup victories in 1952, 1954, and 1955. In each of those years, Sawchuk won the Vezina Trophy, then presented to the goalie who allowed the fewest goals during the regular season.

Sawchuk was named a First Team All-Star in each of his first three seasons, earning Second Team All-Star nods in the two years to follow. Five years into his NHL career, Sawchuk appeared to be invincible.

But Jack Adams was enamoured by a young goalie in Detroit's farm system named Glenn Hall, who played in the minors for the Edmonton Flyers of the WHL. Hall had played two games for Detroit during the 1954-55 season, winning both games and stopping all but two of 61 shots. Adams had decided to put all his trust in Hall, even as the Wings were hoisting their fourth Cup in six years.

"Sawchuk's ticket at Detroit already had been written, with the destination left blank," wrote Milt Dunnell of the *Toronto Star*. "When Terry was 'rested' at the end of the season, it was just a question of when and where." Noting that Hall's emergence made Sawchuk 'expendable' in management's eyes, Dunnell wrote: "Terry won his own chance in the big league the same way. He filled in for Harry Lumley, now with the Leafs. The Wings discovered they had two big goalies, a luxury which no club can afford. Soon Lum was on his way."

THE DEBATE   In Boston, Sawchuk's time was forgettable. In Bruins' victories, he sparkled, posting nine shutouts in 1955-56. But Boston had nothing close to the firepower that Sawchuk had enjoyed in front of him in Detroit when Gordie Howe and Ted Lindsay led the most potent attack in the league. The Bruins scored a league-worst 147 goals and both the team, and Sawchuk, finished with won-loss records eleven games below .500.

With his confidence waning and self-doubts about his own ability lingering, Sawchuk walked out on the Bruins, and the game, in January 1957. He returned to the NHL in the summer and was traded back to Detroit for Johnny Bucyk and cash.

The prize in the trade for Boston was Vic Stasiuk. Playing on the Uke Line with Johnny Bucyk and Bronco Horvath, Stasiuk scored no fewer than 19 goals in each of his first five seasons for the Bruins, including a career-best 29 in 1959-60. In January 1961, Stasiuk was traded back to Detroit along with Leo Labine for Gary Aldcorn, Tom McCarthy, and Murray Oliver.

After coming to Boston, right-winger Davis spent most of his time in the AHL in Hershey and Providence, playing only a handful of games for the Bruins over five seasons. Bonin played one season for the Milt Schmidt-coached squad before returning to Quebec. He was picked up by Montreal in the 1957 Inter-league Draft and played in his hometown for five seasons.

Detroit's return in the transaction was measured almost solely by the presence of Godfrey. A hard-hitting defenceman, Godfrey became a mainstay on the Red Wings blue line for seven seasons during which he missed just 17 games. He registered 103 penalty minutes in 1956-57 to rank among the NHL leaders in that category. Godfrey returned to Boston in the 1962 Intra-league Draft but was re-acquired by Detroit the next season for Gerry Odrowski. Godfrey's second time around with the Red Wings was less eventful; he split his time between Detroit and the minor leagues towards the end of his career.

In addition to Boston's need for a goalie in 1955, another big factor in the trade was the puzzling animosity of the Bruins' fans towards Sandford. A consistent performer who had a career playoff year in 1953 with eleven points in as many games – including eight goals – Sandford needed a fresh start. He played only four games in Detroit before being dealt to Chicago for Metro Prystai.

Chevrefils was labeled one of his former team's best shooters prior to arriving in Detroit. He played 46 games for the Red Wings but found his way back to Boston in January 1956 when he and Jerry Toppazini were traded for Murray Costello and Lorne Ferguson.

Boisvert, a goalie, and Corcoran, a centre, were career minor-league players who played a combined five games for Detroit.

///// Rookie of Many Years

Sure, Terry Sawchuk was the Calder Trophy winner with Detroit in 1950-51 for his brilliant rookie season, but previous to that he was rookie of the year in two other leagues! He was top rookie with Omaha in the USHL in 1947-48 and top rookie again with Indianapolis in the AHL in 1948-49. In '50-'51, Sawchuk played in all 70 games for Detroit, won a league-best 44 games, and posted a league-best eleven shutouts. GM Jack Adams was so smitten with Sawchuk that he traded starting goalie Harry Lumley to make way for the 20-year-old Sawchuk.

THE RESULT The performance of Stasiuk compares well to that of Godfrey as each player made strong contributions to his new team at his respective position.

Detroit didn't miss Sawchuk in net as Hall had two fantastic years in the Red Wings goal. However, the Red Wings didn't receive the return that would be expected for a franchise goalie, let alone when the team gave up three additional players, including Stasiuk. No one could know that Sawchuk would leave the Bruins a year and a half later.

Adams, unimpressed with Hall's performance in the 1957 playoffs, re-acquired Sawchuk when the netminder came out of retirement. The player whom Detroit gave up was Bucyk. So in a broader perspective, Boston received two-thirds of a potent scoring line—Bucyk and Stasiuk—plus two players of little impact, while giving up Godfrey, a pair of role players, and a pair of minor-league players.

The Bruins received great return but not enough to keep them out of last place for the next several years.

JUNE 10, 1957
Prospect Bucyk the Price for Ukey

The Deal [DETROIT RED WINGS trade **Johnny Bucyk** and **cash** to the BOSTON BRUINS for **Terry Sawchuk.**

"The deal to acquire Sawchuk for nothing more than a young prospect was described by Milt Dunnell in the Toronto Star *as a 'fire sale.'"*

THE DIRT In January 1957 legendary goaltender Terry Sawchuk walked out on the Boston Bruins and said that he had "quit hockey for good," citing nervous tension as his reason. Sawchuk had started his career with Detroit in 1950-51 winning the Calder Trophy as the league's best rookie. In each of his first five seasons in the league, he posted no fewer than nine shutouts a year, blanking the opposition 56 times over that stretch. He proceeded to win the Stanley Cup three times with the Red Wings before being dealt to Boston in a four-for-four player swap following the 1954-55 championship season.

But age 27 Sawchuk succumbed to the pressure that he put on himself to excel and left the Bruins in mid-season. By the time he changed his mind and returned to the game in June, Red Wings general manager Jack Adams was willing to take a risk and re-acquire the netminder whom he had traded two years earlier. Adams had soured on Glenn Hall because Sawchuk's replacement, who played in all of Detroit's 70 games in 1956-57 en route to a first place regular season finish, had a subpar showing in the playoffs as the Wings were ousted in five games by Boston.

Meanwhile, the Montreal Canadiens were embarking on a dynasty of their own, having won the first two of what eventually became five consecutive Stanley Cups, in 1956 and '57. Adams hedged his bets that Sawchuk would return to the form that he displayed during his first stint in Detroit and lead the Red Wings to challenge the Habs as the NHL's dominant team.

Boston's asking price for Sawchuk was Bucyk, a 22-year-old left winger with two seasons of NHL experience under his belt. An undisclosed amount of cash also went to Boston. The deal to acquire Sawchuk for nothing more than a young prospect was described by Milt Dunnell in the *Toronto Star* as a "fire sale." He added that the Bruins would have scoffed at the proposition a year earlier when the goalie's trade value was much higher.

THE DEBATE Bucyk went on to have a prolific 21-year career with Boston. He spent the early part of his time in a Bruins uniform playing on the "Uke Line" along with Bronco Horvath and Vic Stasiuk, two other stars of Ukrainian heritage. But despite personal success, Bucyk toiled on a team that was devoid of any other star players. From 1959-60 until 1966-67—the latter being Bobby Orr's rookie year—Boston failed to qualify for the playoffs, finishing last in the NHL six times. The arrival of future Hall of Famers Orr, Phil Esposito, and Gerry Cheevers

Bucyk a Hall of Famer

Detroit gave up more than it knew for re-acquiring Sawchuk. Bucyk may have been young and inexperienced, but when he joined the Bruins he quickly became a star with staying power. He scored at least 20 goals 16 times, including his final year in the NHL at age 42, and had his best season when he was 36 years old, recording 116 points. Bucyk was captain, Cup champion, and all-time team scorer. Had Jack Adams known this in 1957, would he still have traded the prospect for Sawchuk?

changed the team's fortunes. Bucyk found himself playing on an elite team as Boston claimed the Stanley Cup in 1970 and again in 1972.

The man called "Chief" had a career year in 1970-71 scoring 51 times. Upon his retirement in 1978, Bucyk established the Boston franchise mark of 545 career goals. His career total of 1,369 points as a left winger served as the league's all-time record until the milestone was broken by Luc Robitaille in 2004.

Sawchuk's second time around with the Red Wings was solid, yet not as dominant when measured against the first five years of his career during which he was a First or Second Team All-Star on each occasion. He played an additional seven seasons in Detroit from 1957-58 to 1963-64 and was twice named a Second Team All-Star. But the Red Wings couldn't wrestle any Stanley Cups away from either the Canadiens or the Maple Leafs during this period.

Detroit left Sawchuk unprotected in the Dispersal Draft of 1964, and he was claimed by Toronto. At age 37, he started the sixth game of the 1967 Cup finals against the Habs. George Armstrong's empty-net goal sealed a 3-1 victory and Stanley Cup for a Leafs squad dubbed as the 'Over-the-Hill Gang' because so many of the teams' players were in their late thirties or early forties It was the last game played in the six-team era of the NHL.

Sawchuk played the next season with the expansion Los Angeles Kings. He then joined Detroit for a third appearance before being dealt to the New York Rangers before the start of the 1969-70 season. On May 31, 1970, Sawchuk passed away from internal injuries that he had sustained in a fight with teammate Ron Stewart a month earlier.

THE RESULT Adams' roll of the dice did not work out in his favour. During his second tenure with Detroit, Sawchuk was not excellent, but still a high-quality goaltender. Adams' mistake was in not retaining Hall—who had already proven himself worthy of the starting job with the Red Wings—and who soared to stardom after arriving in Chicago.

Sawchuk Returns

The second go 'round in Detroit for Sawchuk lasted seven years, but these were not the same as the glory days of shutouts and Cup wins. Whereas his last five years the first time saw Sawchuk post a GAA below 2.00 every season, the second stint saw his GAA never go lower than 2.64. Double-digit shutout seasons gave way to three or four, and victories went from the forties to mid-twenties. In 1964, the Wings left him unprotected in the Waiver Draft, an unthinkable consideration a decade earlier. But the resilient goalie was claimed by the Leafs and still had one more Cup in his tired and aged body, in 1967.

The Detroit teams of the early 1960s had limited regular-season success but made a pair of consecutive surprise runs to the Cup finals in 1963 and 1964. The latter year is best known for the heroics of Leafs defenceman Bob Baun. With Detroit poised to win the Stanley Cup on home ice in the sixth game, the game went into overtime. Baun, who had cracked a bone in his ankle midway through the third period, came off the Leafs bench to slap the game-winner past Sawchuk. The series returned to Maple Leaf Gardens for the deciding seventh game, won by Toronto.

Bucyk was a consistent scorer in Boston, reaching the 20-goal mark on 16 occasions. He also holds the team's Iron Man record of 418 consecutive games played. He retired as the Bruins all-time leader in games played, assists, and points, milestones which have since been surpassed by Ray Bourque. Bucyk's number 9 is retired by the team, and he was an inductee into the Hockey Hall of Fame in 1981.

JULY 23, 1957

Lindsay Punished for PA Efforts

The Deal [DETROIT RED WINGS trade **Ted Lindsay** and **Glenn Hall** to the CHICAGO BLACK HAWKS for **Johnny Wilson, Forbes Kennedy, Hank Bassen,** and **Bill Preston.**

"They threw me in (in the trade) because they didn't think I'd ever be a goalkeeper."
—Glenn Hall

THE DIRT During his Hockey Hall of Fame career, no player was a greater agitator than "Terrible" Ted Lindsay. A tenacious grinder and determined scorer, Lindsay maximized his 5'8" physique to wage battles against the league's toughest opponents, including Rocket Richard. Lindsay played most of his career on the "Production Line" with Gordie Howe and Sid Abel.

His nine career All-Star selections at left wing are second only to Bobby Hull. Lindsay won the scoring title in 1949-50 with his linemates Abel and Howe finishing second and third, respectively. That season ended with the Red Wings winning the Stanley Cup. Detroit claimed three more titles in 1952, 1954, and 1955.

In 1956-57, Lindsay registered a career-high 85 points, finishing four points back of Art Ross Trophy winner Howe. Away from the rink, however, Lindsay was concerned about player benefits such minimum rookie salaries and a pension fund. He and Canadiens defenceman Doug Harvey were instrumental in attempting to organize a National Hockey League Players' Association.

Furious at the attempt by the players to gain more control and dictate working conditions, the owners took their own measures to disband the newly-formed union before it ever got off the ground. Howe was intimidated away from committing to the cause, creating a long-term rift between him and his best friend, Lindsay.

Leafs' defenceman Jimmy Thomson, one of the union's leaders, was summarily traded by Toronto owner Conn Smythe to Chicago. The same fate befell Detroit's All-Star left winger Lindsay. Red Wings' general manager Jack Adams exiled Lindsay, along with goalie Glenn Hall, to Chicago, which had finished last in the NHL standings for a fourth year in a row.

"It got to the point where I couldn't take it anymore," said Lindsay after the trade. "A series of rumours about my attitude, as well as derogatory remarks about myself and my family showed me that the personal resentment of the Detroit general manager toward me would make it impossible for me to continue playing hockey in Detroit."

THE DEBATE Lindsay played three seasons in Chicago, scoring as many as 58 points in 1958-59, but never approaching his best numbers that he registered in Detroit. He retired for four years before making one final return to the Motor City in 1964-65 to end his career.

The greater acquisition by the Black Hawks was Hall, who, unlike Lindsay, flourished in the Windy City. "They threw me in (in the trade) because they didn't think I'd ever be a goalkeeper," said Hall. "Teddy and I went to Chicago, and it was probably the best thing that ever happened to me."

The 1959-60 season was the breakout year for Hall's teammate Bobby Hull, who won the Art Ross Trophy by scoring 81 points. The following season, a Chicago team that included Hall, Hull, Stan Mikita, and Pierre Pilote ended the Black Hawks' 22-year Stanley Cup drought.

Hall played ten years with Chicago, earning five First All-Star Team selections and three to the Second Team. Picking up from his final two seasons in Detroit during which he never missed a game, Hall played in each of the Black Hawks' games including the first 12 outings of the 1962-63 season, establishing a mark of 502 consecutive games played by a goaltender. This, unquestionably, is a record that will never be broken.

Wilson was an Iron Man of his own, playing 580 games in a row at left wing. His acquisition by the Red Wings in the Lindsay trade was Wilson's second stop in Detroit. He put up modest numbers – 67 points in two full seasons – before being traded once again, to Toronto, in 1959, in a deal to get Barry Cullen.

Kennedy, a fierce checker, contributed far more penalty minutes than points to the scoresheet. In a little more than two seasons with Detroit, Kennedy racked up 292 minutes in penalties in 147 games and registered 53 points. Over the next two years, he spent his time in the minor leagues before being traded to Boston for Andre Pronovost, a journeyman left winger.

Kennedy's last career NHL game came as a member of the Maple Leafs, and he left swinging – literally. With Toronto on the wrong end of a 10-0 demolition by Boston in the opening game of the 1969 playoffs, the game turned nasty. Leafs defenceman Pat Quinn was already a marked man for crushing Bobby Orr earlier, but then Kennedy ended up brawling with the entire Bruins team and even some Boston Garden fans. He was assessed eight penalties in the affair, setting a league record. A four-game suspension ensued, effectively ending his career after the Leafs were swept in the first round.

Goaltender Bassen did not have an immediate impact with Detroit. He played for three different minor league teams – Seattle, Springfield, and Vancouver – in each of the next three seasons before finally making his Red Wings debut in 1960-61. Having to play second fiddle to Terry Sawchuk, and later Roger Crozier, Bassen split his time between Detroit and the minors. His final season came with Pittsburgh in 1967-68.

THE RESULT The resentment felt by Adams towards Lindsay combined with his underestimation of Hall came back to haunt the Red Wings. Sawchuk was more than adequate in the Red Wings net, but he never regained the form of his peak years when he first played with Detroit between 1950 and 1955.

Despite the initial failed attempt by Lindsay to unionize the players, the NHLPA was re-established once and for all in 1967. The player benefits enjoyed by today's members are a direct result of Lindsay's efforts.

In 2010, the trophy formerly known as the Lester B. Pearson Award was renamed after Lindsay. It is presented annually to the outstanding player in the league as voted by the members of the NHLPA.

Integrity Ted

Fierce and combative, Ted Lindsay was respected by all, not only for his play on ice but for his efforts off ice. The Hockey Hall of Fame waived the five-year waiting period to induct him in 1966, but when Lindsay found out that the induction ceremonies were an all-male affair, he took a stand. His wife had made countless sacrifices over his two decades in the game, and if she weren't allowed to attend, he wasn't going either. The Hall refused to bend, and Lindsay, true to his word, stayed home. A year later, the Hall opened the ceremonies to women.

FEBRUARY 10, 1960

Red Starts Second Career Up Front

The Deal [DETROIT RED WINGS trade **Red Kelly**
to the TORONTO MAPLE LEAFS for **Marc Reaume.**

"I thought my hockey days were over. When I started playing in the league, I thought, 'If you have a ten-year career, that's a long career.'" —Red Kelly

THE DIRT The first half of the 1950s was dominated by the Detroit Red Wings, who won four Stanley Cups in six seasons between 1950 and 1955. The last half of the decade belonged to the Montreal Canadiens, who took home an unprecedented five straight championships beginning in 1956.

As the 1959-60 season progressed, the decline of the Red Wings was evident. At the 50-game mark, Detroit was a respectable 20-19-11 but was being outclassed by Montreal who boasted a mark of 32-9-9. Dickie Moore was the two-time defending Art Ross Trophy winner while Jean Béliveau, Henri Richard, and Bernie Geoffrion were elite players during the Habs' dynasty.

By the first week of February 1960, the relationship between defenceman Red Kelly and management was irreparably strained. Unknown to the booing fans who believed his play had slipped dramatically, Kelly had been playing with a broken foot. The ailment was divulged only to the top brass within the organization. On February 5, the Red Wings traded Kelly along with Billy McNeill to the Rangers for Eddie Shack and Bill Gadsby.

But both Kelly and McNeill refused to report to New York. Rather than move to the last place team in the NHL, Kelly retired. "I thought my hockey days were over," said Kelly. "When I started playing in the league, I thought, 'If you have a ten-year career, that's a long career.' I played twelve and a half years and thought, 'That's it. Now I gotta earn a living.'"

The league was forced to rescind the trade. But just ten days later, Toronto coach and general manager Punch Imlach persuaded Kelly to end his retirement and join the Maple Leafs. A subsequent deal sent Marc Reaume to Detroit for Kelly's rights. NHL president Clarence Campbell initially declared the trade illegal but eventually relented.

THE DEBATE Imlach moved Kelly into the centre position, which was a huge transition and a stroke of genius. Kelly had excelled as a defenceman during his entire career with the Red Wings that lasted nearly 13 seasons. An All-Star on the blue line for eight consecutive years between 1950 and 1957, Kelly was the first ever recipient of the James Norris Memorial Trophy, first awarded to the league's best defenceman in 1954.

In his second game with the Leafs, Kelly faced his former team for the first time, centering a line between Frank Mahovlich and Gerry Ehman. Toronto won handily, 7-1. Indeed, Kelly and his left-winger Mahovlich formed a dangerous tandem. In 1960-61, Mahovlich netted 48 goals while Kelly collected 50 assists. Both figures established new career highs in each player's respective category. At season's end, Kelly was named the winner of the Lady Byng Trophy as the league's most gentlemanly player for the fourth time in his career.

The following year saw the Leafs earn the first of what turned out to be four Stanley Cups in the next six years. That year, 1962, also marked the first year that Kelly served as a Member of Parliament. Incredibly, he represented the region of York West while still continuing to play hockey. His election forced him to take weekly flights to Ottawa. Kelly retired from politics three years later to concentrate on the Leafs full time.

Entering Canada's centennial year, 1967, the Canadiens were the two-time defending champions, taking over from the Leafs who had won the previous three Cups. Toronto – buoyed by aging veterans such as Kelly, Tim Horton, Terry Sawchuk, and George Armstrong – spoiled Montreal's plans to host hockey's Holy Grail in the Quebec pavilion of Expo '67 and won the Stanley Cup in a six-game finals series. The triumph marked the last game of the NHL's pre-expansion era and also the final game of Kelly's playing career.

Kelly moved behind the bench, coaching in Los Angeles and Pittsburgh before coming to Toronto in 1973. Two years later, he famously inspired "pyramid power" among a lineup that included Darryl Sittler, Borje Salming, and Lanny McDonald, placing pyramids under the team's bench in an attempt to draw inspiration and physical strength. Consecutive playoff exits at the hands of Philadelphia in 1976 and 1977 brought Kelly's coaching career to a close.

Reaume had been praised by Imlach as a player ready to fill in whenever any one of the Leafs' top four defencemen—Tim Horton, Allan Stanley, Carl Brewer, or Bob Baun—was unavailable. "I know that Reaume will be a help to Detroit," said Imlach at the time of the trade. "He'll be happy to get a chance to play regularly. I'll say this about Reaume; he's the best fifth defenceman in

Kelly Does It All

The list of accomplishments attached to the name Red Kelly is amazing. He was the first defenceman to score 100 career goals, even though he was hardly famed for his offense. He won the Norris Trophy once and the Lady Byng Trophy four times, one of only two defencemen ever to be named the most gentlemanly player (Brian Campbell of Florida won in 2011-12). He won the Cup with two different teams at two different positions, was inducted into the Hockey Hall of Fame and was a Member of Parliament. He coached Los Angeles and, more famously, the Leafs.

the NHL and that's why I didn't worry, well not very much, when one of our other defencemen was injured."

Reaume, however, was plagued with injuries during his tenure in Detroit. The blueliner played only 47 games in the Motor City before being dispatched to the Hershey Bears of the AHL. Reaume won the Eddie Shore Award in 1962-63 as the AHL's best defenceman. He was an All-Star on several minor-league teams but played only 30 more NHL games in his career, in Montreal and Vancouver.

THE RESULT   One of the most lopsided deals in NHL history was consummated because Red Wings general manager Jack Adams had alienated one of his star players and was forced to part with an eight-time All-Star for virtually nothing.

The move to centre paid dividends for Kelly and also for the Leafs, whose strength up the middle with Kelly, Dave Keon, and Bob Pulford was the class of the league.

In 1969 Kelly became only fourth player in history to have his traditional five-year waiting period for induction into the Hockey Hall of Fame waived. His number 4 is co-honoured by the Leafs with along with Hap Day. Kelly won the Cup four times with Detroit as a defenceman and four more with the Leafs as a centre, a unique accomplishment in hockey. He is also the only player in league history to have won the Cup eight times without having played for the Montreal Canadiens.

JUNE 13, 1961

Harvey Proves Habs Wrong

The Deal [MONTREAL CANADIENS trade **Doug Harvey** to the NEW YORK RANGERS for **Lou Fontinato.**

"On the surface, it makes the Rangers 15 per cent stronger than they were last season and the Canadiens 15 per cent weaker. If the Canadiens want to help the Rangers, I say they've done it." —**King Clancy**

THE DIRT Only a select few players in the history of hockey have had the impact on his position as Doug Harvey did as a defenceman with the Montreal Canadiens. Possessing incredible skill at both ends of the ice, Harvey claimed the Norris Trophy in seven out of eight years beginning in 1955, and he was an All-Star for eleven years in a row starting with the 1951-52 season. All but one of his All-Star selections were on the First Team.

But there were intangibles working against Harvey. In 1957, he and Ted Lindsay led the players' charge to form the first National Hockey League Players' Association. The owners not only stifled the union but retaliated by trading away the most vocal noisemakers. Lindsay and Jimmy Thomson were moved to last-place Chicago by the Red Wings and Maple Leafs, respectively. Harvey wasn't jettisoned immediately, but he was blacklisted.

Also, Harvey – according to his biographer William Brown, author of "Doug: The Doug Harvey Story" – suffered from an undiagnosed bipolar disorder. The malady was accompanied by heavy drinking.

But on the ice, Harvey was still the best blueliner in the game. Leafs' executive King Clancy offered his opinion on the trade to the Rangers to Dink Carroll of the *Montreal Gazette*: "On the surface it makes the Rangers 15 per cent stronger than they were last season and the Canadiens 15 per cent weaker. If the Canadiens want to help the Rangers, I say they've done it. The Rangers ought to have the best power play in the league next season. You can imagine what it will be like with Harvey and Andy Bathgate on the points."

THE DEBATE Harvey joined the Rangers not only as a star player but as the team's head coach, and he produced immediate results. The 1961-62 team finished fourth with a 26-32-12 record, earning its first playoff berth in four years. The Rangers were bounced in the semi-finals by the Maple Leafs in a six-game series in which the home team won every game. (Toronto played four games at home because of the circus at Madison Square Garden.)

Proving that Montreal had given up on him too quickly, Harvey was once again named to the First All-Star Team while also bringing home another Norris Trophy. It was the final time in his career that Harvey won either award. No player has won the Norris in consecutive years with different teams.

Harvey gave up the coaching reins a year later and concentrated solely on being a player for two more seasons with the Rangers. Fourteen games into the

The Pre-Orr Orr

Doug Harvey was called the Bobby Orr of his era anachronistically. It was a way to try to explain where Orr came from or how Harvey played, even though the two were very different. Harvey was sensational at carrying the puck up ice instead of passing it ahead to forwards right away. But he never had ambitions to go end-to-end á la Orr. It was his way of controlling play, avoiding danger inside his own blue line, and waiting to get the forwards involved in the offense in the centre-ice area.

1963-64 season, however, Harvey retired from the NHL and happily spent his time in the minor leagues. He had a two-game appearance with Detroit in 1966-67, then joined the Kansas City Blues of the CHL the following year. Harvey retuned to the NHL for the 1968 playoffs, playing for the expansion St. Louis team that was swept in the finals by none other than his old team, Montreal. He played in all 70 games for St. Louis in 1968-69, the last year of his NHL career.

Lou Fontinato was the polar opposite to Harvey. Fontinato was a physical, temperamental defenceman who won a Memorial Cup with the Guelph Biltmore Mad Hatters in 1952. His defence partner, Harry Howell, went on to play with the Rangers, as did teammates Andy Bathgate and Dean Prentice. He earned the nickname "Leapin' Louie" for leaping every time he was whistled for a penalty.

The 6'1" native of Guelph, Ontario, joined the Rangers full-time in 1955-56, playing in all 70 games and leading the NHL with 202 penalty minutes. For a player who liked to rough up the opposition, Fontinato was incredibly durable, not missing a game in three seasons between 1955-56 and 1956-58, and finishing first in penalty minutes at the end of the third season with 152.

However, his physical style of play finally caught up to him in a game against Detroit on February 1, 1959. In a continuation of a long-running feud with Gordie Howe, Fontinato squared off in an infamous fight against "Mr. Hockey." Howe not only broke Fontinato's nose but also dislocated his jaw and took out several of his teeth.

After arriving in Montreal, Fontinato picked up from where he left off in New York, making frequent trips to the sin bin. For the third time his career, he led the league in penalty minutes in 1961-62. Unfortunately, his playing days ended abruptly on March 9, 1963, in a game versus the Rangers. Fontinato missed a check on Vic Hadfield and crashed headfirst into the boards, breaking his neck. He was paralyzed for a month but made a recovery. His playing days, though, were over.

THE RESULT Harvey's final All-Star selection and Norris Trophy both came in his first year as a Ranger, showing his critics in Montreal that he could still dominate the blue line just as effectively while playing on an inferior team. The Blueshirts returned to the playoffs with Harvey both on the ice and behind the bench, turning the transaction clearly in New York's favour, even with Harvey staying for just over one more year after the 1961-62 season.

Fontinato contributed more with his fists than he did with his stick, compiling 308 penalty minutes in 117 games played with the Habs, while scoring just four goals and 25 points.

After a four-year Stanley Cup drought, the Canadiens were champions once again in 1965. The roster had two physical defencemen in Ted Harris and Terry Harper as well as enforcer John Ferguson, proving that Fontinato was effectively replaceable in the wake of his unfortunate injury.

Whatever animosity was held by the Montreal organization towards Harvey followed him for decades after the trade. Harvey's number 2 wasn't retired by the Habs until 1985, nearly a quarter-century after he last skated for the team.

JUNE 4, 1963

Habs Ruthless, Trade Plante

The Deal [MONTREAL CANADIENS trade **Jacques Plante, Don Marshall,** and **Phil Goyette** to the NEW YORK RANGERS for **Gump Worsley, Dave Balon, Leon Rochefort,** and **Len Ronson.**

"He's the best goalie I've ever had and close to the best I've ever seen. But that doesn't say he can run the hockey club." —Frank Selke

///

THE DIRT The Montreal Canadiens' dynasty of the late 1950s set a standard so high that any result other than a Stanley Cup championship was unacceptable. In 1962-63, the Habs' regular-season record of 28-19-23 was respectable but good enough only for third place. The team had finished on top of the NHL standings in each of the previous five seasons. In the playoffs, Montreal was handily bounced in the semi-finals in five games, Toronto sailing to a 5-0 win in the clinching game at Maple Leaf Gardens. The Cup drought for the *bleu, blanc, et rouge* was extended to three years, a seeming eternity for Toe Blake's team.

On a drive to a meeting in Montreal, Jacques Plante turned on the radio and was shocked to hear a news report that he had been traded to the New York Rangers. He pulled over to the curb in stunned silence, feeling betrayed by the team that he had idolized his entire life—and led to six Stanley Cup victories, six Vezina Trophies, and one Hart Trophy while wearing their colours.

"It was like telling me my wife had died," said Plante in a *Montreal Gazette* article that was published the following day.

Habs managing director Frank Selke explained the reasoning behind the deal that had sent shockwaves throughout the league. "We got rid of Plante because we couldn't depend on him anymore. Toe Blake couldn't have taken much more without punching him on the nose. He's the best goalie I've ever had and close to the best I've ever seen. But that doesn't say he can run the hockey club." Selke also said that Plante's issues were "more mental than physical," perhaps a passing reference to Plante's hypochondria which caused him to develop various ailments on game days when, in management's eyes, he simply didn't feel like playing.

In the days after the trade, Red Fisher wrote in the *Montreal Star* that, "Plante was the scapegoat for the Canadiens' fall to third place. The front office wanted to make an example of a big player to wake up the rest."

THE DEBATE Coming over from New York was goalie Gump Worsley, the Calder Trophy winner in 1952-53, who was frequently left to his own devices on a terrible Rangers team. Once asked which NHL team gave him the most trouble, Worsley answered "the Rangers." He called the trade "good for me and my family," adding, "If I do my job right, it won't be any different."

Plante the Pioneer

Jacques Plante was not just a great goalie; he changed the game in many ways. For starters, he was the first goalie to come out of his net and play the puck with the purpose of controlling play and starting a rush up ice by preventing the other team from maintaining puck possession. He was also the first goalie to raise his arm to indicate to his defenceman that an icing call was in effect. And, most significant, he defied coach Toe Blake by wearing a goalie mask even after his injuries had healed following Andy Bathgate's famous shot that hit him in the face. Indeed, Plante had an 18-game winning streak with the mask, lost one game when Blake insisted he wear it, and then put it back on for good. Winning was Plante's proof of the mask's success, and not even Blake could argue that.

Worsley appeared in only a handful of games in 1963-64, playing on just eight occasions. But his playing time increased as he formed a strong tandem with Charlie Hodge. In 1964-65, Montreal returned to glory, winning the first of four Stanley Cups in five years. Worsley, a member of each of those championship teams, also enjoyed personal success. He was an All-Star Team selection in 1966 and 1968 and shared the Vezina Trophy with Hodge in 1965-66, winning the same award with Rogie Vachon two years later.

In Manhattan, Plante had two unhappy years, posting a combined record of 32-53-12 as the Rangers missed the playoffs both times. He retired from hockey in 1965 but resurfaced three years later in St. Louis before moving to Toronto, and then Boston, to end his career.

The Rangers received a productive centre in Phil Goyette, who scored at least 60 points in three of his six seasons in New York, finishing eighth in NHL scoring in 1966-67, the last pre-expansion season. On June 10, 1969, Goyette was traded to St. Louis for a first-round draft pick that turned out to be Andre Dupont.

Don Marshall didn't register point totals as high as Goyette, but he could be relied upon for about 20 goals a season. He missed only four games in his first six seasons in New York. His last season with the club was in 1969-70. The Buffalo Sabres claimed him in the Expansion Draft prior to the start of the next season.

The supporting cast the Canadiens received along with Worsley was unimpressive. Dave Balon was a decent role player, scoring at least 40 points in each of his first two years in a Habs uniform. He lasted a total of four seasons in Montreal and then joined the Minnesota North Stars. Balon returned to the Rangers for a second stint, collecting a career-high 70 points in 1969-70.

Leon Rochefort played only 40 games with the Canadiens between 1963 and 1967, spending the bulk of his time over that four-year stretch with the Quebec Aces of the AHL. After the 1966-67 season, during which he registered 16 points in 27 games, Rochefort was claimed by Philadelphia in the Expansion Draft. He played for six different teams over the last eight years of his career.

Len Ronson never played for the Habs and spent all but 18 games of his 16-year professional career in the minor leagues, 13 of which came in 1960-61 with the Rangers, before the trade. He surfaced to play five games with the Oakland Seals in 1968-69.

THE RESULT The transaction proved to be a renaissance for Worsley, who went from being shell-shocked between the pipes in the Rangers goal on a regular basis to All-Star status and Stanley Cup success in Montreal. After his time with the Canadiens, Worsley ended up with the fledgling Minnesota North Stars, with whom he played from 1970 to 1974 before retiring. He was inducted into the Hockey Hall of Fame in 1980.

Plante was a disappointment in New York, and his surprise retirement in 1965 didn't add to the long-term benefits of the deal. The consistent play of Goyette and Marshall over the next several years saved the trade from being a total bust for the Rangers.

/// The Idiosyncratic Gumper

Gump, or, variably, "the Gumper," had the dubious distinction of following his Calder Trophy season as rookie of the year in the NHL by being demoted to the minors because he wanted a pay raise of $500. He later made his way back to the Rangers, then won the Stanley Cup four times with Montreal in the 1960s, but he retired midway through the 1968-69 season because his extreme fear of flying finally got the better of him. During the Original Six days prior to 1967, of course, teams travelled by train, but with expansion, notably to the west, long trips necessitated the need for plane travel. Worsley finally came out of retirement to play for Minnesota, and continued to play maskless until the final half dozen games of his two-decade career which ended in 1974. He was the last NHL goalie to play without a mask.

FEBRUARY 22, 1964

Huge Deal Helps, Hinders Leafs

The Deal [NEW YORK RANGERS trade **Andy Bathgate** and **Don McKenney** to the TORONTO MAPLE LEAFS for **Dick Duff, Bob Nevin, Arnie Brown, Bill Collins,** and **Rod Seiling.**

"This deal will be great for Toronto as of the moment, and just as beneficial to the Rangers in the future."
—**Muzz Patrick**

THE DIRT The 1962-63 edition of the Toronto Maple Leafs was arguably the best team in franchise history. Loaded with greats such as Frank Mahovlich, Dave Keon, and Johnny Bower, Punch Imlach's crew finished with the best regular season record in the NHL with 82 points. The Leafs lost only two playoff games that spring, defeating Montreal and Detroit on their way to a second consecutive Stanley Cup.

But with 15 games remaining in the 1963-64 season, Punch Imlach made a stunning blockbuster move with New York. Chief scout Bob Davidson was dismayed by the deal, however, because so many young players who were part of the Leafs' championship nucleus were traded.

Rangers general manager Muzz Patrick summed it up nicely. "This deal will be great for Toronto as of the moment, and just as beneficial to the Rangers in the future." Unquestionably, the Leafs were getting an established superstar in Bathgate, who was a four-time All-Star Team selection and the 1959 Hart Trophy winner. He became the highest-scoring player on the Leafs roster at the time of the trade.

///Did You Know?

Rod Seiling played for Canada in two international tournaments, the 1964 Olympics and 1972 Summit Series. In the former, the defenceman was named to the All-Star Team for his outstanding play, but Canada, coached by Father David Bauer, finished fourth after a controversy which decided a tie-break among the second, third, and fourth teams, all of which had ten points. Tournament directors awarded Sweden silver and Czechoslovakia bronze on the basis of overall goals differential, although it had been argued by Canada that the agreement going into the Olympics was that a tie between more than two teams would be broken by goals differential only between those teams tied (which would have given Canada bronze instead of the Czechs). Seiling later played in three games for Canada at the Summit Series.

However, like Patrick, Duff had the foresight to accurately predict the transaction's long-term effects. "It won't look like such a good trade three years from now," said Duff to Jim Proudfoot of the *Toronto Star*. "These other guys will be playing and the fellows Toronto got will be ready to pack it in. I'm sorry to leave for a lot of reasons, but I think I'll get more opportunity to play with the Rangers. They're a young team with a future."

THE DEBATE The Leafs dueled the Canadiens in the 1964 semi-finals, but a hat trick from Dave Keon in Game 7 set up a rematch of the previous year's Stanley Cup showdown against the Red Wings. In Game 6, Toronto trailing 3-2 in the series, the Leafs received an heroic overtime goal from Bob Baun to force a deciding game at Maple Leaf Gardens. The Leafs prevailed 4-0 to earn a third straight championship.

Bathgate and McKenny were big contributors for Toronto on the scoresheet. Bathgate's five goals in 14 games trailed club leader Keon by just two, while McKenny had 12 points in as many games.

However, players such as Keon and George Armstrong later revealed that the "quick fix" Imlach deal was the beginning of a reversal of fortune for the Leafs. "I believe the trade of Bob Nevin and Dick Duff for Andy Bathgate was the start of the slide," said Keon. "If they had stayed, it would not have taken us 14 games to win the Cup. It was hard for Bathgate to play within our system."

Bathgate's time in Toronto was short-lived. After the 1964-65 campaign he was dealt in an eight-player swap with the Red Wings that saw Billy Harris join him in Detroit while Larry Jeffrey and Marcel Pronovost became Leafs.

McKenny scored 19 points in 52 games with the Leafs following the 1964 championship and was claimed on waivers by Detroit the following year.

The young players whom the Leafs surrendered went on to reach their full potential elsewhere. Duff played 43 games for the Rangers before a trade sent him and Dave McCombe to Montreal for Bill Hicke plus a loan of Jean-Guy Morrisette for the remainder of the 1964-65 season. During his five-year career with the Canadiens, Duff – a clutch playoff scorer – won four Stanley Cups to go along with the three championships he earned as a Leaf. He had brief stops in Los Angeles and Buffalo before retiring in 1972. In 2005, Duff was inducted into the Hockey Hall of Fame.

Nevin was appointed team captain soon after joining the Rangers. He was a consistent scorer during a seven-year stay in New York, collecting a career-high 31 goals in 1968-69. In 1970-71, the Rangers won their first playoff series in 21 years, defeating the Maple Leafs in the quarter-finals. New York bowed out in the semi-finals to Chicago in seven games. Nevin finished the post-season with eight points in 13 games. He was traded to Minnesota for Bobby Rousseau a month later.

/// Bathgate's Impressive Résumé

Andy Bathgate was not only inducted into the Hockey Hall of Fame in 1978; he boasts many other awards and honours. He won the Memorial Cup in 1952 with Guelph, played in the NHL for 17 seasons, and had his number 9 retired by the Rangers along with Adam Graves. He won his only Stanley Cup with the Leafs in 1964 and was named MVP of the WHL while playing for the Vancouver Canucks towards the end of his career. This success led Pittsburgh to sign him, where he played his final NHL season. Three years later, he came out of retirement to play briefly for the Vancouver Blazers in the WHA.

Seiling became an anchor on the Rangers' blue line for a decade. His strength was in preventing goals as opposed to scoring them, although he did collect a career-high nine goals and 42 points in 1972-73. Seiling, once an Olympian at the 1964 Winter Games in Innsbruck, Austria, was invited to play for Team Canada in the 1972 Summit Series, playing in three of the eight games.

Brown, like Seiling, was a stay-at-home defender. In his first full Rangers season, in 1964-65, Brown formed a defence tandem with Harry Howell. The pairing flourished for several years, and Howell won the Norris Trophy in 1967. Brown was a constant and consistent player in New York before being dealt to Detroit in 1971.

Collins never played for the Rangers but enjoyed a 768-game career with seven different teams, most notably in Minnesota and Detroit.

THE RESULT   George Armstrong said that the Leafs won the 1964 Stanley Cup "in spite of" the Bathgate trade and not because of it. It was difficult for Bathgate to adapt to the Leafs' team-oriented style of play.

Montreal won the next two championships and was favoured again in 1967 before the 'Over-the-Hill' Leafs pulled off an upset. Almost every hockey fan knows that the 1967 triumph was the last one for Toronto, leading to a drought that extended into the next generation and, indeed, the next century. But the start of the franchise's downfall can be traced back to three years before that last hurrah.

JUNE 11, 1964

Dryden Traded Once—At Age 16

The Deal [BOSTON BRUINS trade **Ken Dryden** and **Alex Campbell** to the MONTREAL CANADIENS for **Guy Allen** and **Paul Reid.**

> *"I thought I had been Montreal property all along."*
> —Ken Dryden

THE DIRT Today's generation of NHL prospects enter the league via the Entry Draft where the lowest-ranked teams have the highest priority of selection in order to maximize parity.

But for most of the pre-expansion era such a draft did not exist. Instead NHL teams held a monopoly on junior players by way of a sponsorship system. The professional club sponsored a group of junior and senior teams in exchange for the rights to those prospects. The highest profile networks were built by Toronto and Montreal. The Maple Leafs had access to St. Michael's College and the Toronto Marlboros. The Canadiens, for instance, had the resources to purchase the entire Quebec Senior Hockey League in order to eventually sign Jean Béliveau of the Quebec Aces.

Once a prospect signed a C-form, he was bound to the parent team and placed on the appropriate junior or minor club for further development until he turned professional. In 1962, Bobby Orr – three weeks shy of his 14th birthday – signed a

C-form to play with the Oshawa Generals, who were sponsored by the Boston Bruins.

The disparity between the league's strongest and weakest farm systems was enormous. Between 1942 and 1962, all but one of the 21 Stanley Cup championships over that period were won by Toronto, Montreal, or Detroit.

The first NHL Amateur Draft was held in 1963, giving all six clubs equal access to players not already signed to C-forms. The following year, Ken Dryden – a goaltender playing with the Junior B Etobicoke Indians in the west end of Toronto – was selected in the third round, 14th overall, by Boston. The netminder indicated that he was leaning towards playing the U.S. college system, an option rarely exercised by NHL prospects in the early 1960s and even more rarely by goalies. He was promptly dealt to Montreal in a swap involving four players selected on draft day.

THE DEBATE None of Campbell, Reid, or Allen ever played an NHL game. However Dryden's story is legendary. Following an outstanding career at Cornell University and a brief stint with the Canadian National Team, Dryden was summoned to the Canadiens to play six games during the 1970-71 regular season. The 23-year-old starred, giving up just nine goals in those outings.

To the surprise of many fans, Dryden was given the starting assignment over veteran Rogie Vachon once the playoffs began. Montreal looked to be overmatched heading into its quarter-finals series against Boston while the Bruins seemed good bets to repeat as Stanley Cup champions, one year removed from Bobby Orr's famous, diving goal. Boston dominated the regular season with 57 wins, setting single-season team records for goals (399) and most 100-point scorers (four). In Phil Esposito, Orr, John Bucyk, and Ken Hodge, the Bruins had the top four point producers in the NHL.

The Bruins were outplayed in the first game, but won 3-1 on a solid performance from goaltender Gerry Cheevers. Coach Tom Johnson had promised backup Eddie Johnston a Game 2 start and stayed true to his word in spite of Cheevers' heroics. Boston built up a seemingly insurmountable 5-1 lead before the Habs roared back with six unanswered goals for the stunning win, the greatest comeback ever in a playoff game.

Game 2 was a turning point in a series eventually won by Montreal in seven games. Dryden continued to hold the fort as the Canadiens eliminated Minnesota in the semi-finals before facing Chicago for the Stanley Cup. Trailing 2-0 in Game 7, Montreal got a huge break when Jacques Lemaire's long shot from centre ice eluded Tony Esposito to help spark a Canadiens' rally. Montreal capped off an unlikely championship with a 3-2 win. Dryden played in every minute of the Habs' post-season and was named the Conn Smythe Trophy winner as the most valuable player in the playoffs.

Dryden was given the mantle as the Habs' starting goalie the next year and again didn't disappoint, posting a 39-8-15 record with eight shutouts. Indeed, his rookie season was so impressive that he won the Calder Trophy, an unprecedented victory for a player coming off a Smythe Trophy win.

In the September 1972 Summit Series, Dryden and Esposito shared duties for Team Canada. On home ice at the Montreal Forum, the Soviets stunned the Canadians, 7-3. But Canada found its stride in Moscow as Dryden earned wins in both Game 6, and then Game 8, when Paul Henderson scored his way into hockey history.

Dryden was the mainstay behind the Canadiens' crease during the team's dynasty in the late 1970s that included another Stanley Cup in 1973 plus four consecutive championships between 1976 and 1979. Coached by Scotty Bowman

Did You Know?

Ken Dryden was one of three goalies to play for Canada at the 1969 World Championship in Stockholm, Sweden. He, Wayne Stephenson, and Steve Rexe played under coach Jackie McLeod as Canada finished fourth in the six-team tournament. Dryden was invited to the team after finishing his fourth and final season with Cornell. The Big Red won the NCAA championship in 1967, and Dryden posted an astonishing record of 76-4-1 in 81 career games. Just four years later, he led Montreal to an improbable Cup victory.

and boasting the likes of Guy Lafleur, Steve Shutt, Larry Robinson, and Bob Gainey, the Habs rewrote the record book. The 1976-77 edition of the team was practically invincible, posting an astounding 60-8-12 record while losing only once in 40 games on home ice.

Dryden retired permanently at the end of the 1979 season. His post-hockey achievements are well-known. He wrote one of hockey's defining books "The Game," served as Canada's Minister of Social Development, and was president of the Maple Leafs. He was inducted into the Hockey Hall of Fame in 1983.

THE RESULT The Amateur Draft was intended to support the weaker teams such as Boston. The anonymity of all four teenaged players involved in the swap made it impossible to predict such a one-sided result. But although the Bruins failed to make the playoffs between 1960 and 1967, they became a powerhouse when Orr and Esposito rose to prominence.

Dryden later admitted that he knew nothing about the trade until a decade later. "I thought I had been Montreal property all along," he said.

/// Summit Series

It was the best of times and worst of times for Dryden in September 1972. The star Montreal goalie had a rough series but was good when it mattered most. He and Tony Esposito each played four of the eight games. Dryden played in game one, the shocking 7-3 win by the Soviets in Montreal. He didn't play again until game four, but this was a humbling 5-3 loss, in Vancouver, which saw the team booed off the ice. Dryden next played in game six, a crucial 3-2 win and certainly his best game of the series. He then sat for game seven and was back in goal for the ultimate contest. Although he allowed five goals, Canada scored six thanks to the efforts of Paul Henderson in the final minute. It wasn't vintage Dryden, or vintage Canada, for that matter, but goalie and team won when history was being made.

MAY 15, 1967

Bruins Fleece Hawks to Get Espo

The Deal [CHICAGO BLACK HAWKS trade **Phil Esposito, Ken Hodge,** and **Fred Stanfield** to the BOSTON BRUINS for **Gilles Marotte, Pit Martin,** and **Jack Norris.**

"We hated to give up Marotte, a promising, tough, young defenceman, but we had to give up something to get what we wanted." —Milt Schmidt

THE DIRT The 1966-67 season was over, and as the NHL was ending its glorious Original Six era and heading to a doubling of teams to 12, two of the old guard pulled off a mammoth trade that affected both franchises for years to come. The deal came at the trade deadline, May 15 being the final day for player transactions until June 5, draft day, when 12 teams would be involved.

Although the magnitude of the trade was shocking, what was even moreso was the fact that Chicago had finished first in the standings with 94 points while the Bruins had finished dead last with only 44 points. Indeed, the team's records were nearly revered in every area. The Hawks posted a 41-17-12 record while the Bruins were 17-43-10. Chicago scored 264 goals and allowed 170 while the B's scored 182 and allowed 253. Chicago had the top two scorers in the game. Stan Mikita won the Art Ross Trophy with 97 points while Bobby Hull was second with 80. No Bruins player was even close.

But while the Hawks made it to the playoffs for the ninth straight season in

'66-'67, they lost in the semi-finals to the Leafs in six games. The Bruins, on the other hand, missed the playoffs for the eighth straight year, finishing in last place on six occasions during that infamous streak.

THE DEBATE In retrospect it's impossible to understand what Chicago felt it could get out of the deal, but the optics at the time were not as distorted as they became over the ensuing years. Of course, Esposito went on to have a Hall of Fame career with the Bruins, but in his first three seasons in Chicago he scored 23, 27, and 21 goals. At 25 years of age, he seemed to be a steady 20-goal man, nothing more, and his skating was weak. In the 1967 playoffs, he neither scored nor drew so much as a single assist in those six games against Toronto, sealing his fate in the Windy City.

Worse for Chicago, though, Ken Hodge and Fred Stanfield also developed into fine players, notably Hodge who played on a line with Espo and Wayne Cashman, the highest-scoring threesome in the league for several years. Hodge scored 50 goals one year and twice had 105 points in a season while Stanfield had six straight 20-goal seasons with Boston.

Chicago acquired Gilles Marotte, Pit Martin, and Jack Norris. Oddly, time has skewed the trade, for in the spring of '67 it was seen in principle as an Espo-for-Marotte deal. As Boston GM Milt Schmidt noted the day the trade was announced, "We hated to give up Marotte, a promising, tough, young defenceman, but we had to give up something to get what we wanted."

Marotte, 22, was deemed expendable because Bobby Orr had just finished

/// The Goalie

By the time Jack Norris was traded to the Hawks, the goalie had played just 23 NHL games. He appeared in only ten more in Chicago over the next two years and ended his career in the WHA several years later, a throw-in in the deal who played as such.

The Orr Factor

Boston general manager Milt Schmidt showed remarkable vision in orchestrating a trade that made his counterpart in Chicago, Tommy Ivan, look silly. Schmidt knew that in Bobby Orr he had a franchise player, a superstar who could lead his team to the highest heights. But Orr couldn't do it alone; he needed help. Schmidt acquired three forwards at a time when he could laugh and say, 'Why do I need a defencemen? I have Bobby Orr!'

his rookie season in the NHL with Boston and played every bit up to the mammoth expectations with which he entered the league. The Bruins needed some scoring up front to work with Orr and could afford to give up a blueliner.

The middle part of the deal was viewed as Martin going to Chicago while Ken Hodge, another more lanky version of Espo—tall and strong—went to the Bruins. Martin was coming off a season of 20 goals and 42 points with Boston. With Chicago, he had seven seasons of at least 20 goals, building to 90 points in 1972-73, but he was never considered equal to Hodge, who was inestimably more skilled and worked magnificently in the corners to get the puck to Esposito in the slot.

The rear end of the deal paired Stanfield and goalie Jack Norris, but Norris played such a small role in Hawks' history his inclusion is of inconsequential importance. Stanfield went on to be a productive and important contributor to the Bruins for several years.

THE RESULT The one-sidedness of this trade was apparent immediately. The Bruins actually finished ahead of Chicago in 1967-68, posting a 37-27-10 record while the Hawks were 32-26-16. The Bruins nearly doubled their point total from a year ago, going from 44 to 84, while the Hawks fell by 14 and barely made the playoffs.

Worse, Phil Esposito bolted to second in the league scoring with a career best 84 points (including 35 goals) while Ken Hodge had 25 goals and Fred Stanfield had 20. In one fell swoop, Boston added 80 goals to their lineup and made the playoffs for the first time since 1959.

Pit Martin had just 16 goals for the Hawks and Marotte had no goals and only 21 assists. In the playoffs, though, Montreal swept Boston in four games while the Hawks advanced one round after beating the Rangers in six games. The Hawks were, in turn, crushed by the Habs in five games in the semi-finals.

A year later, the Bruins were the ones that won a playoff round while the Hawks failed to qualify at all for the post-season. Another year later, the Bruins were Stanley Cup champions, the highest-scoring team in NHL history, and on their way to the greatest glory.

In the end, Boston got a Hall of Famer for a top-prospect defenceman; a star for a solid forward; and, a reliable scorer for virtually nothing. The Hawks made it to the Cup finals twice in the coming years, losing to Montreal in both 1971 and 1973.

When Esposito arrived in Boston, however, he predicted the team would make the playoffs in his first year, win a round of the playoffs in his second year, and win the Stanley Cup in his third year. Yes, yes, and YES! The Bruins won the Cup in 1970 and again in 1972, giving fans in Boston memories that have endured to this day.

The Hawks continued to ice an excellent team, but the Bruins became champions. No comparison. Chicago general manager Tommy Ivan was fleeced.

/// Did You Know?

They say the team that gets the best player in a trade wins, and Boston surely got the marquee name among the six men who switched teams. Esposito went on to set records for goals in a season (76) and points in a season (152), and by the time he retired in 1981 his 717 career goals was second only to Gordie Howe. He led the league in goals six times, won the scoring title five times, and claimed the Hart Trophy and Lester B. Pearson Award twice each.

MARCH 3, 1968

Big M, Nerves and All, Sent to Wings

The Deal [TORONTO MAPLE LEAFS trade **Frank Mahovlich, Pete Stemkowski, Garry Unger,** and **the rights to Carl Brewer** to the DETROIT RED WINGS for **Norm Ullman, Paul Henderson, Floyd Smith,** and **Doug Barrie.**

"Mahovlich was the type of player who needed positive reinforcement... But Imlach's harsh treatment of him...had the opposite effect."

THE DIRT The Maple Leafs' dynasty of the 1960s included four Stanley Cup wins in six years led by Frank Mahovlich as their top left-winger. A native of Timmins, Ontario, "The Big M" made an immediate impact with the team by scoring 36 points in 67 games in his rookie season of 1957-58. That year he was named the Calder Trophy winner while Bobby Hull of Chicago was runner-up.

In 1960-61, Mahovlich had a breakthrough season, collecting 48 goals in the first 56 games of the year. With 14 games remaining, it appeared all but certain that he would reach the 50-goal plateau, becoming the first player since Maurice Richard 16 years earlier to do so. A late season scoring drought, however, kept him from achieving the milestone. Nevertheless, Mahovlich's 84 points were good enough for third place in league scoring, trailing only Bernie Geoffrion and Jean Béliveau.

Mahovlich scored at a point-per-game clip over the dozen games that the Leafs played in their 1962 Stanley Cup playoff run. His aggressive play was also evident as he led the league with 29 penalty minutes during that playoff year. Toronto capped off a run of three consecutive championships ending in 1964, adding a fourth title in 1967 before the league expanded from six to 12 teams.

While Mahovlich was an integral part of the Leafs' success, his relationship with coach and general manager Punch Imlach was tumultuous. A contract dispute in 1962 almost resulted in Mahovlich being sold to Chicago for the unheard of sum of $1 million. Imlach also often accused his star forward of not putting forth his best effort. In 1964-65, Mahovlich suffered a bout of depression thanks to Imlach's coaching, missing eleven games that season.

Early in the 1967-68 season, Mahovlich was hospitalized once again with stress-related problems. Imlach decided to pull the trigger on a blockbuster deal with Detroit. Asked if he thought he'd be happier in Detroit, Mahovlich replied. "I guess we'll just have to wait and see. Maybe I'm just not a happy guy."

THE DEBATE A rejuvenated Mahovlich had a career year in his first full season with the Red Wings in 1968-69. Playing on a line with Gordie Howe and Alex Delvecchio, Mahovlich set new personal standards with 49 goals and 78 points. Two years later, his situation got even better. On January 13, 1971, Mahovlich was traded to Montreal for Guy Charron, Bill Collins, and Mickey Redmond. Playing on the same team as his younger brother, Peter, he won another two Stanley Cups. Mahovlich joined the WHA in 1974-75, playing two years each in Toronto and Birmingham before ending his pro career.

The Red Wings received a versatile centre in Pete Stemkowski, whose line with Bob Pulford and Jim Pappin led the 1967 playoffs in scoring during the Leafs' last Stanley Cup run. Stemkowksi played for two years in Detroit plus ten games in 1970-71 before being shipped to the Rangers on Hallowe'en for defenceman Larry Brown. With the Blueshirts, Stemkowski had a career year in 1973-74, scoring 70 points in 78 games. After seven years in New York, Stemkowski played one season with the Kings before hanging up his skates.

Garry Unger, the third player to go Detroit in the deal, had played just 15

Graceful or Lazy?

Frank Mahovlich was unquestionably one of the finest players of his era, but to many he could have or should have been even better. Fans said he skated effortlessly down the left wing, while critics said the same thing. The former suggested elegance and a natural gift; the latter suggested a lack of all-out effort. Despite his size, speed, and skill, though, he never hit the 50-goal mark for a season, even though he came tantalizingly close on two occasions. In 1960-61, with the Leafs, he finished with 48 after enduring a terrible drought over the last dozen games of the season. In 1968-69, playing on a line with Gordie Howe and Alex Delvecchio, he made it to 49. Howe also never hit 50 despite retiring as the greatest goalscorer in the game's history.

games for the Leafs. Once establishing himself as a full-time player, he proved durable beyond comprehension, playing in a record 914 consecutive games with Detroit, St. Louis, and Atlanta. The Blues were the team with which Unger enjoyed success after the Red Wings traded him and Wayne Connelly for Red Berenson and Tim Ecclestone on February 6, 1971. Unger enjoyed back-to-back seasons in 1974-75 and 1975-76 in which he topped the 80-point mark.

Carl Brewer, a solid defender on three of the Leafs' Cup-winning teams in the 1960s, was also often at odds with Imlach. In 1965, Brewer quit the Leafs and went back to the University of Toronto to complete his degree. He didn't play in the NHL again until 1969-70 when he registered a career-best 39 points in Detroit to go along with a Second All-Star Team selection. On February 22, 1971, Brewer was dealt to St. Louis for future considerations.

Norm Ullman was the centrepiece of the trade for the Leafs. A two-time All-Star with the Red Wings who led the NHL in goals in 1964-65 with 42, Ullman and Henderson formed a dangerous forward line with Ron Ellis. Indeed, the 1970-71 season was Ullman's most productive year of his NHL career as he finished sixth in the scoring race with 85 points. His first six full seasons in Toronto were solid, but by 1975-76 Ullman – frustrated with his diminishing ice time – left for the WHA.

Known more for his international heroics, Henderson produced consistently for six years in Toronto although he would never be confused with a bona fide all-star. He joined the rival WHA one season before Ullman. Right-winger Floyd Smith scored 59 points in 131 games for the Leafs before being sold to Buffalo on August 31, 1970. Following his playing days, Smith coached Toronto for 68 games in 1979-80.

THE RESULT Mahovlich was the type of player who needed positive reinforcement from Imlach to be motivated. But Imlach's harsh treatment of him – which was resented by almost all of Mahovlich's Leafs teammates – had the opposite effect.

The Leafs received a substantial amount of offence from Ullman, making the transaction at least fair. Mahovlich's two additional Stanley Cups in Montreal came as a result of playing with a far superior supporting cast.

Henderson the Hero

Paul Henderson's trade to Toronto might well have been a blessing in disguise. He had 30 goals in 1970-71 and then a career best 38 in 1971-72. His peak years couldn't have come at a better time or in a better city. In the summer of '72, Team Canada was assembled and practised at Maple Leaf Gardens to prepare for the Summit Series. Had Henderson not been playing right under the noses of management, or had produced such a good year, he might well have never received an invitation to the team, which would have been a shame. He formed the only line that played all eight games as a unit, with Toronto teammate Ron Ellis and young Philadelphia centreman Bobby Clarke, and Henderson was, after Phil Esposito, the best player in the series. Of course, more to the point, he scored the game-winning goals in the final three games, including the series winner at 19:26 of the third period of the last game.

JANUARY 26, 1971

Backstrom Pawn in Pollock's Genius

The Deal [MONTREAL CANADIENS trade **Ralph Backstrom** to the LOS ANGELES KINGS for **Gord Labossiere** and **Ray Fortin.**

"I'm leaving with no hard feelings, but don't think I've short-changed the Canadiens. I've helped them win six Stanley Cups and eight league titles and scored 215 goals." —Ralph Backstrom

THE DIRT A precursor to this transaction occurred on May 22, 1970, and involved the Montreal Canadiens and California Golden Seals. The Canadiens traded winger Ernie Hicke and their first-round selection in the 1970 Amateur Draft, which the Seals used to take Chris Oddleifson, to the Seals for defenceman François Lacombe and the Seals' first-round pick in the 1971 draft.

Initially christened the Oakland Seals in the 1967 six-team expansion, the franchise had losing records in each year of its existence, making the playoffs just twice – in 1969 and 1970. In their first year known as the Golden Seals, 1970-71, California was mired in misery, wallowing in last place at 14-30-3 on January 26. Meanwhile two junior stars were virtually guaranteed to be the first pair of players selected at the draft table at the end of the year. Guy Lafleur was lighting the lamp for the Quebec Remparts while Marcel Dionne was shining for his club, the St. Catharines Black Hawks.

Canadiens general manager Sam Pollock needed a star player to replace Jean

Béliveau, who at age 39 was playing in his final NHL season. Pollock had his sights set on Lafleur, a scoring machine from Thurso, Quebec who was setting junior records. Lafleur eventually finished his final amateur season with 130 goals and 209 points in just 62 games.

The shrewd Pollock knew he need to maximize his chances of ensuring that the Golden Seals finished last, which would secure the first overall selection with the top-round pick that he acquired from California. He found a willing trade partner in the Golden Seals' West Division rival, the Los Angeles Kings – a team whose lead in the standings over California had been trimmed to a just one point by mid-January. Had L.A. finished dead last, Pollock would have the second overall choice and not the first.

THE DEBATE Ralph Backstrom had an illustrious career with the Canadiens. The Calder Trophy winner in 1958-59 as the league's best rookie, the Kirkland Lake native played 13 seasons in a Montreal uniform, winning six Stanley Cups. A consistent 20-goal scorer, Backstrom was used primarily as a checking centre behind Montreal's top two pivots, Jean Béliveau and Henri Richard. But in 1970,

/// Sam Pollock

Sam Pollock is forever connected to the Montreal Canadiens. Indeed, Pollock has his name on the Stanley Cup some nine times in a general manager's career that lasted just 14 years. Pollock also was GM for Team Canada at the inaugural Canada Cup tournament in 1976, but few people know that after he left the Habs he moved to Toronto and was member of the Board of Directors for the Toronto Blue Jays in the early 1990s. He later became chairman and CEO for five years (1995-2000). Paul Godfrey, later president and CEO of the Jays, mourned Pollock when hearing of his death in 2007. "The Blue Jays organization has benefited greatly from his leadership and vision," Godfrey said. "I was honoured to have worked alongside him. Sam brought the same fierce competitiveness and intelligence to baseball that made him a legend in hockey."

Backstrom asked for a trade, indicating his wish to move to a warmer climate. He retired twice during the 1970-71 season prior to the team finally granting his wish in January.

"I want to play, so I'm very happy things have straightened out," Backstrom told the *Montreal Gazette*. "I've worked hard to keep in shape, and I expect to a get a lot of ice time with the Kings. I'm leaving with no hard feelings, but don't think I've short-changed the Canadiens. I've helped them win six Stanley Cups and eight league titles and scored 215 goals."

In the 33 games that he played to close out the season in Los Angeles, Backstrom collected 14 goals and 27 points. More importantly for the Canadiens and Pollock, the Kings posted a record of 11-17-5 the rest of the way; not spectacular, but good enough for a ninth-place finish in the overall standings.

Neither Labossiere nor Fortin ever played for the Habs, but it didn't matter. The Golden Seals ended the season at 20-53-5, last place in the 14-team league. Pollock's plan worked to perfection, and Montreal gained the first choice of available superstars at the draft. The Habs selected Lafleur, who had just won the Memorial Cup with the Remparts. The rest, as they say, is history.

Lafleur had a Hall of Fame career in Montreal, igniting the passion of fans at the Forum with his explosive speed down the right wing and dangerous slapshot. While he was an adequate contributor in each of his first three years with the Habs, 1974-75 was the year that Lafleur vaulted into the category of superstars. Breaking the 50-goal plateau and 100-point barrier for the first time, he earned the first of what would be six consecutive First Team All-Star selections at right wing.

Between 1974-75 and 1979-80, Lafleur scored at least 50 goals and 119 points in each season, winning three Art Ross Trophies in a row from 1976-78. The Canadiens formed a powerful dynasty in the late '70s, claiming the Stanley Cup in four consecutive years ending in 1979. Lafleur was the leader on offense, playing on a potent line with Steve Shutt and Jacques Lemaire. Not only would all three players eventually become Hall of Famers, but so did several of their teammates including Bob Gainey, Larry Robinson, and goalie Ken Dryden.

Lafleur announced his sudden retirement in 1984 but returned to the game four years later. He ended his career playing one season with the New York Rangers and two with the Quebec Nordiques.

Backstrom played 172 games with the Kings before being traded to Chicago for Dan Maloney. During his time in California, Backstrom experimented with the first version of inline skates. After he retired from the NHL, he became the founder of Roller Hockey International.

THE RESULT Los Angeles received a player who could help the team earn a respectable place in the standings at season's end. At 33 years old, Backstrom proved that he could still be an effective scorer. While he never scored more than 27 goals or 65 points in a season, he may have evolved into a superstar player on a lesser team had he not played a third-line role behind Béliveau and Richard in Montreal.

The real mismatch lies in the initial 1970 trade between Montreal and California. In Golden Seals' owner Chuck Finley's defence, his team had finished fourth in the West Division and earned its second straight playoff appearance at the time of the deal. But if Finley had had the foresight to see how much California would falter, he likely would have held on to the first-round pick. And Lafleur would have played in California, not Montreal!

/// The Last Years of Ralph Backstrom

After being seconded to Los Angeles in early 1971, Backstrom was here, there, and everywhere. He scored 57 goals with the Kings in two and a half years and played the final 16 games of his NHL career with Chicago. Backstrom then stayed in Chicago, signing with the WHA Cougars in the summer of 1973. He played the final four years of his career in the "other" league, earning a spot on the team that represented the league in the '74 Summit Series against the Soviet Union. Although he won the Stanley Cup six times and played more than 1,000 games in the NHL, he never made the cut for induction into the Hockey Hall of Fame.

MAY 15, 1973
Parent Goes to Broad Street Bullies

The Deal [TORONTO MAPLE LEAFS trade **Bernie Parent** and a **2nd-round draft choice in 1973 (Larry Goodenough)** to the PHILADELPHIA FLYERS for a **1st-round draft choice in 1973 (Bob Neely)** and **future considerations.**

"Parent's play justified the opinion of Philadelphia's scouts and management, who had rated him as one of the four best goalies in hockey."

THE DIRT In January 1971 the Maple Leafs traded Mike Walton and Bruce Gamble to Philadelphia to acquire goaltender Bernie Parent. The swap brought an end to Walton's final tumultuous days in a Leafs uniform where he feuded with coach Punch Imlach and at one point was diagnosed with acute depression. Walton was then immediately shipped to Cup-contending Boston while Parent was given a stall at Maple Leaf Gardens.

Parent replaced Bruce Gamble as Toronto's backup goalie to Jacques Plante, posting a 7-7-3 record in 18 games. The following year Parent assumed the starting role, playing in 47 games to Plante's 34, going 17-18-9 along the way with three shutouts.

The 1972-73 season marked the inaugural year of the World Hockey Association. The rival professional league gained instant credibility when Bobby Hull signed a $1 million contract with the Winnipeg Jets, and dozens of other NHL stars soon followed, lured by higher salaries.

When Parent and the Leafs couldn't reach terms over a reported salary difference of $8,000, the goalie also defected to the WHA, signing a multi-year deal with the upstart Miami Screaming Eagles. However signs of future instability within the new league became evident when the Miami franchise folded before ever playing a game.

Parent then took his talents to Philadelphia where he joined the Blazers, playing in 63 of the team's 78 regular-season games. However, more financial disputes awaited Parent. He played just one game in the playoffs but refused to return to the lineup when Philadelphia refused to maintain a $600,000 bank balance to guarantee his contract.

Prior to the 1973-74 season, Parent was ready to return to the NHL. His wife, who didn't like living in Toronto, wouldn't let him play for the Leafs. General manager Jim Gregory arranged the last-minute trade at the draft.

THE DEBATE Six places after selecting Lanny McDonald with their own 1st-round pick, the Leafs used the draft choice they received from Philadelphia to choose Bob Neely, a tough defenceman from the Peterborough Petes who led the OMHA Junior A league with 304 penalty minutes. Roger Neilson, Neely's junior coach, said of his protégé, "mechanically he can do everything. He can throw a pass as well as anybody, and he can set up plays. But he has a bad temper and this can affect his play. I'm sure however, that the maturity that comes along with pro hockey will make him an excellent player." Neely's career lasted just over four seasons in Toronto, during which time he racked up 264 penalty minutes in 261 games. He was sold to the Colorado Rockies on January 9, 1978.

The Flyers drafted defenceman Larry Goodenough, a blueliner from the London Knights, with the 2nd-round pick previously held by Toronto. On January 20, 1977, Philadelphia sent Goodenough and Jack McIlhargey to Vancouver for Bob Dailey. Goodenough went back-and-forth between the NHL and the minor leagues over his career, posting career numbers very similar to Neely's.

When Punch Imlach traded Lanny McDonald and then Darryl Sittler (above), it marked the end of the era which was the closest the Leafs came to Cup victory since 1967.

*Lanny McDonald was much loved in Toronto but established his legacy in Calgary,
scoring his 500th goal and 1,000th point and winning the Cup in his final season.*

Eric Lindros's refusal to play for Quebec turned out to be the best thing for the Nordiques, as the players the team acquired in a mammoth trade turned out to be the cornerstones of Cup wins in Colorado.

King Clancy was the first top NHL star involved in a blockbuster deal when the Ottawa Senators were forced to sell him to Toronto for the colossal sum of $35,000.

The Philadelphia Flyers had few bona fide offensive stars, but Reggie Leach was certainly at the top of the list after coming over from California.

Chris Pronger was a winner wherever he went, be it St. Louis, Edmonton, Anaheim, or Team Canada.

The Ottawa Senators used their first-round draft choice in 2001 from the Alexei Yashin trade to select Jason Spezza second overall.

Brendan Shanahan's career culminated with Detroit, the team with which he won the Stanley Cup three times—1997, 1998, 2002.

But Parent's play justified the opinion of Philadelphia's scouts and management, who had rated him as one of the four best goalies in hockey. In 1973-74, Parent appeared in 73 games, posted 12 shutouts, and won the Vezina Trophy. Even more impressively, he established a single-season record for wins by a goaltender with 47, a mark that stood for 33 years until Martin Brodeur did one better in 2006-07.

The dream season for Parent continued in the 1974 playoffs as the Flyers became the first expansion team to win the Stanley Cup, defeating the Boston Bruins in the finals. Recording a 1-0 shutout in the decisive sixth game, Parent finished with 12 wins and five losses in the post-season, winning the Conn Smythe Trophy.

Philadelphia repeated as champions in 1974-75 as the Broad Street Bullies and their pugilistic ways were in stark contrast to their hometown motto—"The City of Brotherly Love." Parent recorded 44 wins and once again had a dozen shutouts in the regular season. His goals-against average in the playoffs was a sparkling 1.89 and he won the Conn Smythe Trophy a second straight year while the Flyers defeated the Buffalo Sabres in the finals.

A neck injury limited to Parent to just eleven games the following year. The Flyers advanced to the finals for a third straight time, but the Montreal Canadiens – using a model of speed and skill as opposed to rough, physical play – swept the series in four games to dethrone the Cup champions.

Bernie Parent

"What if" are the two most provocative words in sports. In the case of Bernie Parent, consider that he played junior hockey in Niagara Falls and was property of the Boston Bruins. Parent made his NHL debut with Boston in 1965 and spent two years with the team. In fact, he was teammates with Bobby Orr during Orr's rookie season, 1966-67. But in the summer of '67, when the NHL doubled from six to 12 teams, Parent was left available in the Expansion Draft and the Flyers pounced. The Flyers, too, made a gaffe by trading him to the Leafs, believing Doug Favell was the better man. It was only by luck that Parent wanted out of Toronto and the Flyers were able to get him for nothing more than, as it turned out, Bob Neely.

Over the next three years, Parent logged fewer games while sharing the workload with Wayne Stephenson, his very capable backup. In February 1979, a stick from a New York Rangers player accidentally made its way through the right eye-hole of Parent's trademark mask. The netminder suffered irreparable eye damage on the play, and he was forced to end his career. Parent was inducted into the Hockey Hall of Fame in 1984.

THE RESULT   While Parent became the first Leaf to flee for the WHA in 1972, other Toronto players such as Dave Keon, Norm Ullman, and Paul Henderson soon followed.

Having allowed Parent to walk away, the Leafs turned primarily to Ron Low in goal in 1972-73 before giving Doug Favell and then Wayne Thomas a chance. All three netminders were unimpressive compared to the sensational Parent. Toronto wouldn't obtain another high-calibre goalie again until Mike Palmateer earned the starting job in 1976-77, two years after Parent led the Flyers to consecutive Stanley Cups.

The Leafs had a future Hall of Famer on their roster and let him go for next to nothing.

Bob Neely—First Round Draft Choice

With all due respect to Bob Neely, the Leafs should have done better with a draft choice they acquired from Philadelphia when they traded Hall of Fame goalie Bernie Parent. Neely went 10th overall at the 1973 Amateur Draft but several other players were available with later selections, notably Darcy Rota (13th), Rick Middleton (14th), and Pat Hickey (30th). As it turned out, Neely, a tough defenceman, played parts of five seasons with the Leafs before finishing his career in the AHL. Denis Potvin was the first overall choice that year while the Leafs had an earlier pick of their own, selecting Lanny McDonald fourth overall.

MAY 24, 1974

Cup-bound Flyers Add Rifle

The Deal [CALIFORNIA GOLDEN SEALS trade **Reggie Leach** to the PHILADELPHIA FLYERS for **Larry Wright, Al MacAdam, a 1st-round draft choice in 1974 (Ron Chipperfield),** and **future considerations (George Pesut).**

"Leach's production skyrocketed in his first year in Philadelphia. His output of 45 goals equaled the combined total from his last two years with California."

THE DIRT Reggie Leach, an incredibly talented right-winger, was a junior star in his home province of Manitoba, producing three seasons of 65 goals or more for the Flin Flon Bombers. His hard shot and hometown combined to give him the nickname "Riverton Rifle." He was chosen third overall by the Boston Bruins in the 1970 Amateur Draft but had difficulty finding a spot on a roster that had superstars such as Phil Esposito, Johnny Bucyk, and Ken Hodge. In February 1972, Leach was traded to the Golden Seals in a deal that sent Carol Vadnais to the Bruins.

The 1972-73 season was Leach's first full schedule in California. The team was awful on the ice, winning just 16 out of 78 games and finishing second-last in the overall standings. The only team worse than the Golden Seals was the expansion New York Islanders, who won only a dozen games in their inaugural season. Nevertheless, Leach found the net consistently, collecting 23 goals and 35 points in what was his first of ten consecutive seasons with at least 20 goals.

Leach, however, had developed a reputation for being a problematic personality. Off the ice, he struggled with alcohol abuse. "Reggie was semi out of control, like we all were," said former Seals teammate Walt McKechnie. "He had the skill in Oakland – you could see it on certain nights."

Leach stayed with the Golden Seals for one more year, earning 46 points in 1973-74. At the end of the season, five days after the Philadelphia Flyers won their first Stanley Cup, the Flyers traded for Leach, who was reunited with his former teammate in Flin Flon, Bobby Clarke.

Reflecting on his time in California, Leach said "Looking back, I would do things differently. I was too laid back and never took the leadership in my hands like I did in junior hockey."

THE DEBATE Leach's production skyrocketed in his first year in Philadelphia. His output of 45 goals equaled the combined total from his last two years with California. With future Hall of Famers Clarke, Bill Barber, and Bernie Parent as his teammates, Leach won the Stanley Cup for the first and only time in his career as the Flyers defended their championship in 1975.

The following year, Leach produced one of the finest single-season offensive performances in league history. He led the NHL with 61 goals in 1975-76, setting a franchise record in the process. He was named as a Second Team All-Star at right wing. Leach continued his scoring prowess throughout the playoffs as the Flyers advanced to the finals for the third year in a row. He compiled a ten-game goal-scoring streak to set an NHL playoff record, and tied another record with five goals in one post-season game.

Philadelphia's bid for a third straight Cup, however, was stopped by the Montreal Canadiens in a four-game sweep in the finals. Leach finished the playoffs with an incredible 19 goals, setting another NHL record that has since been tied by Jari Kurri. Although he didn't add another Stanley Cup ring to his mantelpiece, Leach was named the Conn Smythe Trophy as most valuable player in the playoffs, becoming the first non-goalie to win the award on a team that didn't win the Cup.

Over the next three years, Leach posted better-than-average, but not sensational, numbers. He reached the 50-goal mark for a final time in 1979-80 as the Flyers advanced to another Stanley Cup finals series, losing in six games to the New York Islanders. After eight seasons in Philadelphia, Leach signed with Detroit in 1982 to play the final year of his NHL career.

Al MacAdam was part of the Flyers' first Stanley Cup in 1974, but he did not play the required number of games to get his named engraved on the trophy. He suited up for all 80 games in his first year in California, scoring 18 goals and 43 points while developing into a first-line right-winger. The following season, 1975-76, saw the creation of the "3M" line with left-winger Bob Murdoch and centre Dennis Maruk. When the franchise relocated to become the Cleveland Barons in 1976-77, the line remained intact.

The times in Cleveland were unhappy. In fact, MacAdam and a teammate threatened a strike over the owners' inability to meet the players' payroll. The franchise eventually merged with the Minnesota North Stars where MacAdam had his best offensive year, in 1979-80, scoring 42 goals and 93 points. He had two series-winning playoff goals that year – against Toronto and Montreal – capping off the season by winning the Bill Masterton Trophy.

/// Off-ice Battles Bigger

While Reggie Leach had a great shot and was a prolific scorer, his greatest battles weren't with an enemy goalie—it was with the bottle. After retiring, he started a lawn-care business in South Jersey and drank way too much. He ended up broke and divorced, but through his own determination and the help of AA, he has been sober since 1985. Leach met a woman named Dawn and eventually moved to a reservation in Northern Ontario to work with kids at Aundeck Omin Kaning First Nation on Life Choices. He still runs hockey clinics and connects with younger generations through hockey, but Leach is a more content man thanks to a sobriety that has given him new life after the NHL.

Larry Wright played only two games for the Seals, returning to the Flyers the following year where he spent most of the 1975-76 season with the Richmond Robins of the AHL.

California used its 1st-round pick to select Ron Chipperfield, a high-scoring centre with the Brandon Wheat Kings of the WHL. Chipperfield chose to play in the rival WHA over the NHL, playing with the Vancouver Blazers and Calgary Cowboys before becoming the first captain in the history of the Edmonton Oilers.

The Seals also received George Pesut, a defenceman, as future considerations. He played 92 games in two seasons for California registering 25 points and 130 penalty minutes. Pesut played the bulk of his pro career in Germany.

THE RESULT MacAdam was a very good front-line player during his time with his new franchise, even as it relocated to a different city and then merged with another team. But Leach's production makes the Flyers the clear victor in the trade. His 1975-76 campaign in which he became the first 80-goal single-season scorer (regular season and playoffs) in league history ranks among the game's most impressive performances.

George Pesut and the Mystery of Duncan MacPherson

While never amounting to much as an NHLer, Pesut moved to Germany as a player and later stayed on as a coach. He was friends with another player, Duncan MacPherson, who visited him in Nuremberg in the summer of 1989 just before MacPherson had to start as a player-coach with Dundee in the Scottish league. MacPherson borrowed Pesut's car to go snowboarding at the Stubai Glacier Ski Resort in Austria and was never heard from again. His body was found 14 years later in 2003, still perfectly preserved in ice in a crevasse MacPherson had apparently fallen into while skiing on his own.

JUNE 26, 1975

Leafs Give Up on Iron Man Before Game 1

The Deal [TORONTO MAPLE LEAFS trade **Doug Jarvis** to the MONTREAL CANADIENS for **Greg Hubick.**

"Bowman felt that the Petes graduate was NHL-ready after watching him in a pre-season game against Chicago. Jarvis won almost every draw against Stan Mikita."

THE DIRT At a diminutive 5'9", Doug Jarvis didn't appeal to many NHL scouts or executives, least of all those on the Montreal Canadiens who felt he was too small for the league. At the 1975 Amateur Draft, Montreal general manager Sam Pollock used his three selections on Robin Salder, Pierre Mondou, and Brian Engblom, before the Maple Leafs selected Jarvis at the 22nd spot overall.

But Jarvis – who starred for the Peterborough Petes, scoring 133 points in his final junior year – had the attention of Habs coach Scotty Bowman. The Montreal bench boss, who once held the same post with Peterborough, was tipped off by Jarvis' coach Roger Neilson. A friend of Bowman's, Neilson held the opinion that Jarvis had faceoff abilities that could match anyone at the professional level.

The Leafs, meanwhile, were negotiating a trade for Montreal goalie Wayne Thomas because Toronto felt that it needed to replace Doug Favell. An initial proposal for the transaction involving Toronto's first-round pick the next year for Wayne Thomas and defenceman Hubick fell through. Pollock requested an

The first World Juniors

Doug Jarvis played for Peterborough during the 1973-74 season when the first unofficial and invitational edition of the World Junior Championships took place. Hosted by the Soviet Union, Canada's team included few well-known names: Doug Halward, Stan Jonathan, Paul Evans, and Jarvis. Canada finished tied with Finland for second place behind the Soviets, with three wins and two losses in the six-team event played in Leningrad. The Toronto Marlies were supposed to have gone over but the team declined because so many of its best players had signed as underage juniors in the new WHA, notably Marty and Mark Howe and Wayne Dillon.

additional player to replace Hubick, but Leafs general manager Jim Gregory declined. Instead, the transaction was completed on June 17 without the Hubick component. The Habs used the 1976 draft choice to select Peter Lee.

During the Thomas and Hubick negotiations, the Canadiens learned that Jarvis was considering playing for the Houston Aeros of the WHA instead of playing in the Leafs farm system. Bowman once again insisted that Pollock acquire Jarvis. Pollock finally relented, placing a call to Leafs owner Harold Ballard while Gregory was out of town. The Habs GM offered Hubick – then a 23-year-old defenceman playing with the Habs' farm team in Nova Scotia – straight-up for Jarvis.

Ballard accepted the terms. The transaction received scant attention in the Toronto newspapers the following day given that Jarvis hadn't yet played a game or even skated in practice at the Gardens.

THE DEBATE Jarvis was all but certain to start his career in the minor leagues with Montreal, but Bowman felt that the Petes graduate was NHL-ready after watching him in a pre-season game against Chicago. Jarvis won almost every draw against Stan Mikita, a two-time Hart Trophy winner and faceoff specialist himself.

A training camp injury to Jacques Lemaire created the opportunity for Jarvis to start in his first NHL game on October 8, 1975. The centreman was teamed with left-winger Bob Gainey and right-winger Jim Roberts to form a tenacious checking line, while Jarvis and Gainey were considered the Canadiens' top penalty-killing forwards. The unit was spectacular on New Year's Eve 1975 as Montreal and Central Red Army skated to a 3-3 tie at the Montreal Forum in what many historians call 'the greatest exhibition game ever played.'

The Habs toppled the two-time defending champions Philadelphia Flyers to win the 1976 Stanley Cup. Jarvis had 35 regular-season points plus three points in 13 playoff games during his rookie season. More notably, the freshman played in all 80 games, foreshadowing the feat for which he was to become most famous.

Montreal reeled off four consecutive Stanley Cup victories during a powerful dynasty between 1976 and 1979. Under the guidance of Bowman, the team posted an astounding 229-46-45 regular-season record over that time. Nine players who shared in those glory years went on to be inducted into the Hockey Hall of Fame.

Jarvis never missed a game during his seven-year tenure in a Canadiens' uniform. His time in Montreal came to an end in a five-player trade that sent him and future Norris Trophy winner Rod Langway to Washington.

At the end of the 1983-84 season, Jarvis – two years into his career in a Capitals sweater – won the Frank J. Selke Trophy as the league's best defensive forward. Five of the first seven Selke Trophies ever awarded went to either Jarvis or Gainey, the top two penalty-killers on the Habs' dynasty teams from the 1970s.

Jarvis was traded to Hartford for Jorgen Pettersson on December 6, 1985, not having missed any games during his time with the Capitals either. Midway through his second year with the Whalers, Jarvis faced the team with which he had the most success—Montreal—on December 26, 1986. It was Hartford's 33rd game of the season, and most significantly, it was the 915th consecutive game played by Jarvis, breaking the Iron Man record that had been previously held by Garry Unger. Jarvis capped off the season—once again having played in all of his team's games—by winning the Bill Masterton Trophy.

The 1987-88 season in Hartford began with Jarvis, as always, playing the first two games. However, he was scratched by coach Jack Evans on October 11, 1987, one day after playing in his 964th consecutive game. Amazingly, Jarvis never played an NHL game again, finishing his pro career with a 24-game stint with Hartford's AHL farm club in Binghamton.

THE RESULT The forgotten man, Greg Hubick, played in 72 games for the Leafs in 1975-76, scoring 14 points. After that, he spent most of his career playing for Toronto's Central Hockey League affiliate, the Dallas Black Hawks. Hubick also had a brief five-game appearance with the Vancouver Canucks in 1979-80.

The Leafs' primary checking line of the late 1970s consisted of Pat Boutette, Jerry Butler, and Jimmy Jones. The trio was effective, particularly in the 1977-78 campaign when Toronto won 41 games and made a surprise appearance in the semi-finals by eliminating the New York Islanders in the previous series.

Toronto, however, was then swept away by Jarvis and the Habs in four games. The Jarvis trade would not have impacted either that 1978 series or the Canadiens' sweep of the Leafs the following year, but the playoff dominance by the Habs does put an exclamation point on what was unquestionably a lopsided swap.

Greg Hubick's Brief Playoffs

Drafted by Montreal in 1971, Greg Hubick was in no way a part of a great Habs future that included Ken Dryden, Guy Lafleur, and several other future Hall of Famers. Indeed, Hubick's first NHL game came the night of April 19, 1975, game four of the Montreal-Vancouver playoff series (which the Habs won in five games). He was in Scotty Bowman's lineup only because of an injury to Steve Shutt the previous game, and as game four unfolded, he sat at the end of the bench. He had the best seat in the house all game. Finally, with just 16 seconds remaining in the third period and the Habs on their way to a comfortable 4-0 win, Hubick got the nod and skated in his first NHL shift. That summer he was traded, ensuring that he likely had the shortest career in Habs history.

NOVEMBER 7, 1975

Second Blockbuster with Espo

The Deal [BOSTON BRUINS trade **Phil Esposito** and **Carol Vadnais** to the NEW YORK RANGERS for **Brad Park, Jean Ratelle,** and **Joe Zanussi.**

"'I've been traded, haven't I? If you tell me it's New York, I'm going to jump out the window.' Cherry then said to Orr, 'Bob – open the window!'" —Phil Esposito

THE DIRT It was a shocker of a deal that came as a surprise to the two highest-profile components, Phil Esposito – the NHL scoring champion in five of the previous six seasons, and Brad Park – then a five-time All-Star. Teammates, coaches, and ticketholders were stunned. Forty incredulous fans called the league offices asking for official confirmation.

"I was in bed about 8 o'clock this morning, as all little good boys should be," said Esposito the day after the trade. "Don Cherry came to my room and told me. I was crushed," he said. Bobby Orr was also in the room with Esposito and Cherry, the Bruins coach. The two-time Hart Trophy winner recalled saying "'I've been traded, haven't I? If you tell me it's New York, I'm going to jump out the window.' Cherry then said to Orr, 'Bob – open the window!'"

The newest Bruins defenceman Park was equally astonished. "I'm shocked. I had no inkling at all of such a trade and from what I understand, neither did Esposito or Ratelle. It really shook me up. I haven't quite recovered yet."

Rangers general manager Emile Francis made the deal to spark his team. "We were losing without resistance. That made me angry." Two weeks earlier the Blueshirts had suffered three embarrassing losses by scores of 9-1, 7-1, and 7-2 to the Sabres, Islanders, and Flyers, respectively. Esposito, who had just completed his eighth consecutive All-Star season, was acquired to provide that competitive spark.

On the Bruins side, Harry Sinden, Boston's general manager, held a secret that few people knew—Bobby Orr was leaving the team. Knee injuries eventually limited the iconic defenceman to just ten games in 1975-76, so Sinden was trading to replace Number Four.

THE DEBATE Park was initially, and understandably, uncomfortable with the trade. Years earlier, Park had written a book in which he wasn't complimentary to the Boston fans, or their star players Phil Esposito and Bobby Orr. Nevertheless, he reported immediately to the Bruins. "What am I going to do, work in a mine?" he said.

While Bobby Orr was irreplaceable, Park eventually won the adoration of the city that he had once badly criticized. He was named to the first All-Star team at the end of the 1975-76 season, registering 59 points and 118 penalty minutes in 56 games. Park was the finalist for the Norris Trophy, but Denis Potvin of the Islanders took home the hardware after the voting was over.

The following season saw Boston advance to the Cup finals for the fourth time

/// **Trivia Man**

Joe Zanussi was the throw-in in this superstar trade, but he left his mark on the game in several small ways. He was traded by Detroit to the Rangers in 1972 and was later traded to St. Louis by the Bruins for Rick Smith. Zanussi had won the Memorial Cup in 1968 with the Estevan Bruins and was named the CHL's best defenceman for 1970-71 with the Fort Worth Wings. Four years later, he was named best blueliner in the AHL, with Providence, but he was never able to take his game to the highest level. Nonetheless, he remains the "fifth man" in one of the biggest trades of the 1970s.

in eight years. Park and Ratelle and their teammates, however, were swept by the Canadiens as Jacques Lemaire scored the Stanley Cup-winning goal in overtime.

The 1977-78 season was nothing if not an offensive outburst for the Bruins. The team set a league record by having eleven, 20-goal scorers on its roster. Ratelle had 25 while Park netted 22. Boston once again advanced to the finals, taking the powerhouse Habs to six games before losing their bid for the Cup. Park was named an All-Star for the seventh time in his career and, just as happened two years earlier, finished second to Denis Potvin in Norris Trophy voting. Park played with the Bruins until 1983, when he signed as a free agent with Detroit.

Ratelle was also in unchartered territory playing in Beantown. Having starred in New York on the "GAG" line with Rod Gilbert and Vic Hadfield, Ratelle found himself separated from his right-winger Gilbert for the first time in his career. Known for his finesse style of play, Ratelle finished the 1975-76 season with 105 points and was named the Lady Byng Trophy winner. The line of Ratelle, Rick Middleton, and Stan Jonathan was a key component in the Bruins' consecutive appearances in the finals. Ratelle retired after playing 47 games in 1980-81.

In Manhattan, Esposito – much to his chagrin – was named captain immediately upon his arrival. He held the position for two years before Dave Maloney took over the "C" in 1978-79. Esposito was a solid contributor for the Rangers despite not being the dominant scoring leader that he was in Boston.

For four years he averaged just under a point a game and scored at least 34 goals in a season during that stretch, from 1976-77 to 1979-80. The highlight of Esposito's New York career was a surprise run to the Stanley Cup finals in 1979. The Rangers bowed out to the Canadiens in five games. New York would have faced Boston had it not been for coach Cherry's infamous too-many-men penalty in the semi-finals.

Vadnais was a sturdy defenceman with offensive ability. Like Esposito, Vadnais was on the tail end of his career by the time he arrived in New York. His numbers steadily declined after he collected 48 points in his first full year with the Rangers.

In 1982, Vadnais was claimed in the Waiver Draft by New Jersey.

The throw-in in the deal, Joe Zanussi, played 68 games for Boston before being traded to St. Louis for Rick Smith on January 20, 1976.

THE RESULT Sinden's contingency plan for Orr worked to perfection. The legendary Number Four signed with Chicago in 1976. Park immediately took the reins as Boston's top blueliner, while teammate Ratelle contributed more than his fair share of production on the forward unit.

The Bruins made it to the finals twice in the late 1970s following the deal, while the Rangers achieved the feat once. But the era belonged to the unstoppable Canadiens.

Boston has the decided advantage in this trade, but the Rangers didn't get fleeced by any means. It was a rare instance of a blockbuster deal involving big names going both ways, and both teams getting value for their efforts.

/// Esposito Retires Mid-Season

It isn't often that a player of Phil Esposito's stature retires mid-season, but that's exactly what Espo did when he announced that the Rangers game of January 9, 1981, would be his last. He had maintained an impressive scoring pace after coming to the Rangers, but the '80-'81 season was disastrous for the almost 39-year-old. He scored only seven times in the first half of the season and felt he could no longer play at a level that was acceptable to him. "I started losing my enthusiasm," he admitted. That final home game against Buffalo was a celebration. It ended in a 3-3 tie, and Esposito assisted on the first New York goal, by Dean Talafous, the last point of his distinguished career. At the time, he was second only to Gordie Howe for points (1,590) and goals (717).

DECEMBER 29, 1979
Emotional Bottom as Punch Trades Lanny

The Deal [TORONTO MAPLE LEAFS trade **Lanny McDonald** and **Joel Quenneville** to the COLORADO ROCKIES for **Wilf Paiement** and **Pat Hickey**.

"What is this, kindergarten or a country club? When I make a deal, I do what's best for the hockey club. I don't care who is unhappy."
—Punch Imlach

THE DIRT For Leafs fans of a certain age, one moment is forever etched in memory. In game seven of the 1978 quarter-finals against the soon-to-be dynastic New York Islanders, Lanny McDonald – playing with a full shield to guard a broken nose – fired the puck past goalie Chico Resch to send Toronto into the next round. Although the Leafs were no match for Montreal in the semi-finals, a team with McDonald, Darryl Sittler, and Borje Salming on its roster seemed very close to contending for the Stanley Cup all the same.

The team had a setback the following year, winning seven fewer games in 1978-79. That summer of '79, Punch Imlach – the man who guided the franchise to four Stanley Cups in the 1960s – returned to manage the team under owner Harold Ballard. The hiring eventually set the franchise back the better part of an entire generation.

Imlach feuded with his players, most notably captain Darryl Sittler. In one of his first actions as general manager, Imlach told Sittler to refuse an invitation to appear on a popular *Hockey Night in Canada* feature called "Showdown," a popular skills competition filmed in the summer and shown between periods during the hockey season.

The relationship between the two men declined rapidly. Imlach would have loved to trade Sittler, but the captain had a no-trade clause. Out of spite, Imlach shipped off Sittler's best friend on the team, Lanny McDonald. Irate fans immediately flocked to Maple Leaf Gardens in protest. McDonald and Sittler formed one of NHL's most dangerous tandems. Both had represented Canada in the 1976 Canada Cup – won on Sittler's overtime goal – and also finished in the top ten in scoring in 1977-78.

But Imlach defended his controversial move. "What is this, kindergarten or a country club? When I make a deal, I do what's best for the hockey club. I don't care who is unhappy."

McDonald immediately suited up for his new team on the day of the trade as the Rockies hosted the Flyers. He didn't mince words when asked about leaving Toronto. "The whole operation seems to be deteriorating," he suggested. "Instead of building up the players, they're tearing them down. It's not easy to live in that situation, let alone play in it. It's very disappointing after giving seven years of your career. That's the good part about it. I knew I gave my best for seven years. I'm going to do my best for Colorado, and I'm happy as hell to be going to a place that wants me. They've given me a purpose to play the game again."

Number 99

Believe it or not, Wayne Gretzky wasn't the only number 99 when he entered the league in 1979. In fact, the Canadiens of 1934-35 had three players wear the highest possible number—Joe Lamb, Des Roche, and Leo Bourgeault. Then, Wilf Paiement switched to number 99 when he got to the Leafs midway through Gretzky's rookie season, and he wore it for the two years he was with the team. He changed numbers again when the Leafs traded him to Quebec.

Lanny and King

Every hockey fan knows the name Lanny McDonald, and every Lanny McDonald fans refers to him simply as Lanny. But few know that his middle name is King, a name given to him by his father, Lorne, a longtime Leafs fan and great admirer of King Clancy. How appropriate then that when Lanny joined the Leafs he befriended Clancy, and because of his tireless hours and years of charity work McDonald eventually was honoured with the King Clancy Trophy in 1987-88 for his community service. It was the first year of the trophy, given to the league by the Leafs in remembrance of one of hockey's original greats.

THE DEBATE The trade made an immediate impact on the Leafs for all the wrong reasons. Sittler promptly resigned as captain. Other Imlach deals involving Sittler's closest allies soon followed. Dave "Tiger" Williams was traded to Vancouver in February. The Leafs finished five games under .500 in 1979-80 and were easy prey for the Minnesota North Stars in the first round of the playoffs. At the Entry Draft in June 1980, popular goaltender Mike Palmateer was traded to the Washington Capitals.

The next year, the Leafs were the last team to qualify for the 1980-81 playoffs and were embarrassed by the New York Islanders in a three-game sweep. Sittler was eventually, and mercifully, traded to Philadelphia in January 1982. The once-proud franchise was in disarray, and the malaise plagued the team throughout much of the decade. The low point came in 1984-85 when the team posted just 20 wins on its way to a last-place finish in the league's overall standings.

McDonald was a point-a-game producer during his time in Colorado. In his only full season with the team, 1980-81, he scored 35 goals and 81 points. The team struggled at both ends of the ice. Don Cherry, McDonald's first coach with the Rockies, quipped that goaltender Hardy Astrom's biggest problem was "pucks." The season ended with McDonald accepting an invitation to play for Canada at the World Championship. Early in 1981-82, McDonald was traded to his home province of Alberta where he enjoyed his greatest team success with the Calgary

Flames, winning a Stanley Cup in his final career game in 1989.

The Rockies also received a steady defenceman from Toronto in Joel Quenneville. The blueliner stayed with the franchise up to the end of its first year in New Jersey – 1982-83 – when the team relocated to become the Devils. He was traded to Calgary with Steve Tambellini for Mel Bridgman and Phil Russell on June 20, 1983.

In Paiement's first full season with the Leafs, the right-winger posted better-than-average numbers, scoring 40 goals and 97 points in 1980-81. At the 1982 trade deadline he was shipped to the Quebec Nordiques for Miroslav Frycer and a draft pick. Paiement curiously wore number 99 at the same time that Wayne Gretzky was breaking records in Edmonton.

Hickey's time in Toronto was shorter than Paiement's. After playing the 1980-81 campaign in a Leafs uniform, he was dealt to the Rangers just one game into the following season, for a draft pick.

THE RESULT From a Leafs fan's perspective, much has been said and written about the Imlach-Ballard days of the 1980s, and virtually all of the words have been justifiably unkind. Toronto became the perennial laughingstock of the league under an owner who understood little about the game and a general manager whose abilities were rooted in the dictatorial days of the Original Six. Junior prospects refused to play in the once-proud city, and fans attended games at Maple Leaf Gardens wearing paper bags over their heads.

The period of misery was in stark contrast to the vibrant, energetic teams of the late 1970s when McDonald was consistently scoring 40 or more goals and Sittler was collecting 100 or more points. In truth, the decline of the franchise was symbolized by this trade.

NOVEMBER 25, 1981

Flames Get Lanny, Build for Cup Run

The Deal [COLORADO ROCKIES trade **Lanny McDonald** and **a 4th-round draft choice in 1983** (later traded to the New York Islanders–**Mikko Makela**) to the CALGARY FLAMES for **Don Lever** and **Bob MacMillan**.

"I know the players traded away were popular, and I'm not going to try to replace them. I hope the fans take to me the way they took to them."
—Lanny McDonald

THE DIRT The 1980-81 Calgary Flames had finished a successful first year in Alberta after relocating from Atlanta, posting the NHL's sixth-best record at 39-27-14. The team won two playoff rounds, advancing to the semi-finals before losing to the Minnesota North Stars in six games.

The Flames, however, struggled at the start of the 1981-82 season. After 23 games the team had a poor record of 6-12-5. Worse, an appalling road record of 1-8-2, which included a seven-game winless streak away from Stampede Corral, was plaguing general manager Cliff Fletcher's squad.

The Colorado Rockies continued to underachieve as the new season began. Just 20 games into Billy MacMillan's tenure as general manager – having coached the team the previous year – the Rockies had just three wins. The franchise was in its eighth year of existence including the first two seasons in Kansas City, and had qualified for the playoffs only once in its brief history. Prior to the start of the season, Colorado placed Lanny McDonald on the open trade market in the hopes of creating a bidding war for the coveted right-winger.

When the deal was finalized between the Rockies and Flames, the mustachioed McDonald was taken aback. "I was really surprised," he said. "I didn't think I was the problem. I don't agree with the trade. My job now is to come here and do the best I can for Calgary. I know the players traded away were popular, and I'm not going to try to replace them. I hope the fans take to me the way they took to them."

A native of Hanna, Alberta, McDonald had optimistic hopes about playing in his home province. "I'd like to go out a winner this year. This team has the potential to be a winner and I'm not ready to retire for quite a while yet."

Lever was devastated to be leaving Calgary. His wife had been scheduled to join him in Calgary for the first time in the season. She had been tending to the couple's baby who had been born prematurely during the summer. "I really don't know what to say," he said. "I just had my wife coming in. I'm disappointed to be leaving a team that seems to be going somewhere to join a team like Colorado that's starting over again. I knew they were after McDonald, and I knew they'd have to give away a couple of players to get him."

THE DEBATE After McDonald arrived, the Flames played above .500 for the rest of the 1981-82 regular season. But in the playoffs they were swept in the preliminary round by the Vancouver Canucks, a team that went on to the Stanley Cup finals against the New York Islanders.

The 1982-83 season was the most productive year of McDonald's career. Teamed with centre Guy Chouinard, McDonald scored 66 goals and 98 points, surpassing benchmarks that he had set while playing in Toronto when he was a consistent 40-goal scorer. Only Wayne Gretzky, who scored 71 times, had more goals than McDonald that season. At the end of the year, McDonald was named a Second Team All-Star and also won the Bill Masterton Trophy.

While McDonald never reached those totals again, he continued to be a veteran presence as the Flames evolved into a Stanley Cup-contending team, up-

The 'stache

It started as a simple summer effort. McDonald decided to grow a beard knowing he'd have to shave it by the time he went to Leafs' training camp because the team didn't permit full facial hair. But as September neared, he decided to trim it and keep a moustache, and he was soon inspired by the famous lip hair of baseball pitcher Sparky Lyle, famous for maintaining a much-admired variation. McDonald's grew particularly bushy, and it became an important part of his persona to fans in Toronto and later Calgary. Razor companies offered him good money to shave it; he refused. During the Cup playoffs in the 1980s, Flames fans adopted cardboard red 'staches to go along with McDonald's as "playoff beards" became popular. And to this day, Lanny has always continued to be Lanny and has kept the moustache bushy and, as he proudly asserts, well groomed.

setting the powerhouse Oilers in a seven-game series in 1986 before losing to Montreal in the finals.

In 1988-89, McDonald shared the team captaincy with Jim Peplinski and Tim Hunter. The Flames went on to win the Presidents' Trophy and advanced to the Stanley Cup finals for a rematch with the Canadiens three years' previous. The series pitted the runaway top two teams in the NHL against each other. Calgary had earned 117 points in the regular season, two better than Montreal.

The 1989 Cup finals went to a sixth game at the Forum with the Flames holding a 3-2 series lead and having a chance to become the first road team in history to win the Stanley Cup against the Habs in Montreal. With the score tied 1-1 early in the second period, McDonald took a holding penalty. As the Flames finished killing off the power-play, McDonald stormed out of the penalty box and received a cross-ice pass from Joe Nieuwendyk. McDonald rifled the puck past the right blocker of Patrick Roy, scoring what would be the final goal of his career. The Flames prevailed, 4-2, leaving the man with the famous moustache to retire with a Stanley Cup victory, the first of his illustrious career.

Don Lever, was an adequate performer for Colorado, finishing the 1981-82 season with 30 goals combined between two teams and playing in the 1982 All-Star Game. His rights were sold to Buffalo for cash on September 9, 1985.

Bob MacMillan had a career year in 1978-79 with 37 goals and 108 points, but he never reached that stratosphere again, posting average numbers similar to Lever's in Colorado, and then in New Jersey after the franchise was relocated.

THE RESULT The move to the Garden State had little impact on the franchise, newly named the Devils in 1982-83. New Jersey was the doormat of the league, and trading away McDonald certainly didn't help the team's cause, short term or long term. In November 1983, Wayne Gretzky called the Devils a "Mickey Mouse operation" after Edmonton walloped New Jersey, 13-4. Lever was entitled to express his disappointment at moving from a contender to a basement-dweller.

Few pro athletes have had the swansong like McDonald enjoyed in his farewell season, and fewer were as admired and loved by the hometown fans. In 1988-89, McDonald scored his 500th regular-season goal and 1,000th career point before embarking on the Flames' playoff run that ended with a championship. Three years later, in his first year of eligibility, McDonald was inducted into the Hockey Hall of Fame.

Mikko Makela

The 4th-round draft choice that the Flames acquired with McDonald was later traded to the Islanders, who in turn selected Mikko Makela, chosen 65th overall. Makela made his NHL debut with the New York Islanders two years later, but after six years and three teams he headed back to Europe. After helping Finland win silver at the 1992 World Championship and bronze at the 1994 Olympics, he returned to play eleven games with the Bruins in 1994-95. Makela finished his career four years later and embarked on a coaching career which took him to Lethbridge in the WHL as an assistant. Midway through the 2002-03 season he was named head coach, becoming the first European to hold such a position in Canadian junior hockey history.

DECEMBER 2, 1981

McCourt Victim of Free Agency Restrictions

The Deal [BUFFALO SABRES trade **Danny Gare, Jim Schoenfeld,** and **Derek Smith** to the DETROIT RED WINGS for **Dale McCourt, Mike Foligno,** and **Brent Peterson.**

"The NHL and its member clubs knew this rule would discourage other clubs from seeking free agents' services. It denies a player a chance to sign in a free and open market." —Judge Robert DeMascio

THE DIRT Dale McCourt was the highest-touted prospect in hockey by the time his junior career ended. Winning a Memorial Cup with 1976 with the Hamilton Fincups, McCourt was named the tournament's most valuable player. He collected 139 points in 66 regular-season games in back-to-back years ending in 1976-77. He also led the inaugural World Junior Championship with 18 points in ten games for Team Canada. The Detroit Red Wings made McCourt the first overall pick at the 1977 Amateur Draft.

The 1977-78 season marked McCourt's rookie season in the NHL, and the 21-year-old centre played like a veteran, leading the team in goals (33) and points (72). But a turning point in the Falconbridge, Ontario native's career occurred on August 8, 1978. The league awarded McCourt as compensation to the Los Angeles Kings as a result of Detroit's signing free-agent goalie Rogie Vachon.

McCourt refused to go to the Kings, not wanting to play as a third centre behind Marcel Dionne and Butch Goring. Instead, he obtained a court order to allow him to remain in Detroit. Judge Robet DeMascio ruled that the league's agreement regarding free-agent compensation was an illegal restraint of trade. In overturning the arbitration ruling DeMascio said, "We conclude that the NHL and its member clubs knew this rule would discourage other clubs from seeking free agents' services. It denies a player a chance to sign in a free and open market."

Los Angeles general manager Barry Maguire didn't hide his disappointment. When asked if he thought DeMascio was a Red Wings fan, Maguire replied "I don't even think he's a hockey fan."

McCourt continued to play for Detroit, but his actions had alienated many of his pro-union teammates and members. Eventually the Kings traded his rights back to the Red Wings. Over time the case served to force the NHL to change its system of free-agency compensation. Today, compensation for restricted free agents is based on a model on which a number of draft picks are awarded to the team that loses a player, predicated on salary and number of years of experience.

While McCourt was a point-per-game player for four seasons in Detroit, he never developed into a superstar. The grind of the legal battle took away his passion for the sport.

THE DEBATE The trade should have strengthened the Red Wings, which worried many members of their Norris Division rivals, notably the Toronto Maple Leafs. But outspoken Leafs' owner Harold Ballard disagreed with his employees, calling the 22-year-old Foligno the key to the trade. "He's the ace in the hole," said Ballard. "I'd have given all those guys for Foligno by himself. In the long run, I think we'll see that Scotty (Bowman, Sabres coach and general manager) made the right choice."

Ballards words were prophetic. Foligno, who had registered 134 points in his first two seasons in Detroit, fit in with his new team, scoring 51 points in 56 games following the move to Buffalo. A junior standout in his hometown of Sudbury, Ontario, Foligno was a mark of consistency playing in a Sabres uniform. He scored at least 20 goals in each of his first eight seasons with Buffalo, scoring 41 times and adding 39 assists in 1985-86, a career year. On December 17, 1990, Foligno was traded to Toronto for Brian Curran and Lou Franceschetti.

McCourt's production dropped drastically in Buffalo. He recorded just 52 points in 1982-83, well below the standard that he established for himself both as a junior and as a Red Wing. He was signed by the Maple Leafs early into the next season, but McCourt played for just two years in Toronto before ending what was supposed to be a promising career which turned out to be, by contrast, tumultuous.

Brent Peterson was a defensive checking centre whose career with the Sabres lasted for three-and-a-half seasons. His single-season career bests of 13 goals and 37 points were both set in 1982-83. He became a member of the Hartford Whalers after being claimed in the Waiver Draft.

The Red Wings were hoping that Danny Gare would provide the same offensive spark that enabled him to score a combined 102 goals in his previous two seasons in Buffalo, including a league-leading 56 goals in 1979-80. However, back injuries limited his performance. Gare captained Detroit for four years until the 1985-86 season, after which he was forced to retire. He handed the "C" over to a 21-year-old Steve Yzerman.

Quick Work

The Calder Trophy is an award a player has but one opportunity in a lifetime to win. As soon as he starts his second season, he is no longer qualified. And, one record that a player has just one chance at is even more fleeting, yet Gare came incredibly close to equaling what is arguably the hardest "in-game" record to attain—fastest goal from the start of a career. Gare played his first NHL game on October 10, 1974, a home game against Boston. The 20-year-old earned a roster spot in training camp and was on the ice for the opening faceoff of a new season. Just 18 seconds later, he scored, with assists from Craig Ramsay and Don Luce. That incredible goal, however, was three seconds shy of the record set by Toronto's Gus Bodnar in 1943. No one has come closer than Gare since.

Defenceman Jim Schoenfeld, who went on to become an NHL coach with four different teams, played just one full season in Detroit. He was signed as a free agent by Boston on August 19, 1983. Derek Smith retired after the 1982-83 season after scoring 31 points in 91 career games with Detroit.

THE RESULT Two of the most notable athletes to challenge their respective leagues are NHL star Eric Lindros and NFL quarterback John Elway. In 1983, Elway forced the NFL's Colts to trade him to the Denver Broncos after he decided he didn't want to play in Baltimore. Eight years later, Lindros refused to report to the Quebec Nordiques after the Nords had made him the first overall draft choice in 1991. He was subsequently traded to Philadelphia after sitting out a year.

McCourt's circumstances are different in that he didn't challenge the team that drafted him. But like Lindros and Elway, he exercised all available options to determine his playing future. As a result, McCourt's stance paved the way for a newer structure of free-agency compensation that actually benefited players. On ice, though, McCourt had the promise of Lindros and Elway, but fans will never know how great he may have been had circumstances been different.

International Man of Hockey

Dale McCourt was no stranger to international hockey, having played at the World Junior Championship early in his career and then at the senior World Championship in 1979 and 1981. After he left the NHL in 1984, his career was by no means over. He signed with Ambri-Piotta in Switzerland and played for the next seven and a half years, leading the team with such distinction that upon his retirement early in the 1991-92 season the team retired his number 15 sweater. McCourt then became an assistant coach for the Italian national team and in 1998 was named head coach of the Berlin Capitals of the German league, a post he held for the next eleven seasons.

JANUARY 20, 1982

Leadership Link to 1970s Memories
Gone with Sittler

The Deal [TORONTO MAPLE LEAFS trade **Darryl Sittler** to the PHILADELPHIA FLYERS for **Rich Costello, a 2nd-round draft choice in 1982 (Peter Ihnacak)**, and **future considerations (Ken Strong)**.

"I'm not proud of leaving the Leafs this way.
If you'd told me three years ago my career here
would end like this, I'd never have believed it."
—Darryl Sittler

THE DIRT The mid-to-late 1970s were memorable years to be a Leafs fan. With Lanny McDonald, Borje Salming, Ian Turnbull, and captain Darryl Sittler leading the way, the team brought ticket holders to their feet at Maple Leaf Gardens, making it all the way to the semi-finals in 1978.

But the good vibes evaporated with the departure of coach Roger Neilson and the return of dictatorial general manager Punch Imlach. Almost immediately Sittler was at odds with the once-proud bench boss who had held the dual role of coach and general manager for the Leafs during their dynasty in the 1960s. The clash between the two headstrong men came to a head on December 29, 1979, when Imlach traded McDonald—Sittler's best friend and linemate—to the Colorado Rockies.

Sittler, who resigned his captaincy in disgust as a result, was immovable because of a no-trade clause in his contract negotiated by Leafs owner Harold Ballard. But one-by-one, Imlach traded away Sittler's closest allies on the team. Soon after the McDonald trade, Tiger Williams was jettisoned out of town. Mike

Palmateer and Laurie Boschman were also moved elsewhere in the months that followed.

The Leafs, then in turmoil, were swept in the playoffs in consecutive years in 1980 and 1981, even as Sittler resumed his post as captain in the latter year. Despite the setback, as the 1981-82 season started, Sittler remained open to continuing to play for the only NHL team he'd known, provided that his salary of $195,000 was increased closer to the $300,000 figure that Salming was earning. When the request was rebuffed by Imlach, Sittler demanded a trade.

The move didn't happen right away. In fact, mental exhaustion forced Sittler to leave the team on January 5, 1982. Just over two weeks later, his wish to be traded from Toronto was granted. "I'm not proud of leaving the Leafs this way," he said. "If you'd told me three years ago my career here would end like this, I'd never have believed it. But I guess at some point, after seeing what happened to guys like Normie Ullman, Dave Keon, and Ron Ellis, I began to prepare myself mentally for the possibility that it would happen to me."

THE DEBATE The departure of Sittler from Toronto marked the end of the tenure of one of the most popular players ever to put on a Leafs uniform. Sittler, the 1st-round draft pick from the London Knights in 1970, had a forgettable rookie season during which a wrist injury limited him to just 49 games.

It took until his third year in the NHL, 1972-73, for Sittler to find his offensive flare, which he did by scoring 29 goals and 77 points. Three years later, he was named team captain at age 25, taking the leadership reins from Leafs legend Dave Keon, who left the team and league for the WHA.

The calendar year of 1976 saw Sittler accomplish a trio of incredible feats. On February 7, 1976, in a game versus Boston at Maple Leaf Gardens, practically every puck that Sittler touched turned into a goal. He scored six times and added four assists in an 11-4 victory to set a record for points in a single game by one player.

The Leafs faced the Philadelphia Flyers in the playoffs that year. Game six was a near encore of his February performance as Sittler scored five goals to tie the league record for most goals in a playoff game. As if the year couldn't get any better, he scored the winning goal for Canada in the inaugural Canada Cup, beating Czechoslovakia goalie Vladimir Dzurilla in overtime.

Sittler was named a Second Team All-Star in 1977-78 while finishing third in NHL scoring and posting a career-best 117 points. The Leafs' upset of the New York Islanders, sealed with McDonald's overtime winning goal in game seven, turned out to be the defining moment of the decade for the franchise.

By the time he left Toronto, Sittler was the club's all-time leader in goals (389) and points (916). His first full year with the Flyers was a productive one as he collected 83 points in 80 games in 1982-83. Sittler spent one more year in Philadelphia before a trade sent him to Detroit for Murray Craven and Joe Paterson on October 10, 1984. After playing 61 games for the Red Wings that season, Sittler retired.

The Leafs used the second-round pick to draft Peter Ihnacak, a playmaking centre who had won a silver medal with Czechoslovakia at the 1982 World Championships. Ihnacak found chemistry with countryman Miroslav Frycer and established a rookie club record by scoring 66 points in 1982-83. Over parts of eight seasons with the Leafs, Ihnacak scored 267 points in 417 games.

The End is Nigh for Sittler

Being traded from Toronto to Philadelphia was difficult enough for Sittler, who played only two and a half seasons with the Flyers, but what was worse was his treatment by general manager Bobby Clarke at the end of Sittler's tenure. The Flyers were prepared to call a news conference before the start of training camp for the 1984-85 season to announce that Sittler was to be the new team captain, but Clarke, the new GM, instead told Sittler he'd been traded to Detroit. "Clarke can't come close to realizing how much he hurt me, and my family, that day," Sittler later wrote in his autobiography. Sittler played one uninspired season with the Wings, managing only eleven goals in 61 games, and then retired. He was only 34 years old and had several years of hockey left in him, one would think, and his career goals total of 484 was painfully short of the magical 500 plateau.

Rich Costello played only 12 games over two seasons for the Leafs, while the future considerations turned out to be Ken Strong, whose Toronto career outlasted Costello's by a mere three games.

THE RESULT The Leafs received decent production from Ihnacak, but the Czechoslovakian forward wasn't going to reverse the fortunes of a dismal team all by himself. Ihnacak was sixth on the Leafs in scoring with 44 points in 1984-85, the year that Toronto finished last overall in the NHL.

Sittler's Flyers never won a playoff round, although the former Leafs captain did accept invitations to play for Canada at the World Championships in both 1982 and 1983, scoring eleven points in 20 games over two tournaments.

While the post-trade point totals are comparable—Ihnacak's 267 to Sittler's 205—nothing compensates for the intangible loss of the Leafs parting ways with one of the greatest players in their history.

/// Strong Hockey

Ken Strong was the "future considerations" in the Sittler trade. Strong played just 15 games with the Leafs during a mostly AHL career, but in 1987 he moved to Austria to continue playing. He became an Austrian national and appeared in 1994 and 1995 World Championships as well as the 1994 Olympics for Austria. While Strong was barely on the hockey radar in Canada, he scored an amazing 318 goals and 343 assists in 372 league games in Austria. He later turned to coaching and created the Strong Hockey Academy, a training centre in Toronto to develop all aspects of the game, from skating and shooting, to skills, techniques, and physical development off ice.

SEPTEMBER 9, 1982
Langway Too Good to Sit

The Deal [MONTREAL CANADIENS trade **Rod Langway, Doug Jarvis, Craig Laughlin,** and **Brian Engblom** to the WASHINGTON CAPITALS for **Ryan Walter** and **Rick Green.**

"The pressure won't be as great, and while I know I'm going to a team that hasn't made the playoffs, what I have to do is help the team make it."
—Rod Langway

THE DIRT As the 1982-83 season began, the Habs were three years removed from their last Stanley Cup and had suffered consecutive first-round playoff exits in each of the previous two seasons. For a franchise as proud as the Canadiens, such results were not acceptable. The blockbuster deal was announced by Montreal general manager Irving Grundman who simply stated, "you have to give up players in order to get quality players."

Of the four skaters leaving the Canadiens, defenceman Rod Langway was the likeliest candidate to be dealt. Unhappy with his salary, Langway had threatened to walk out of training camp if he wasn't either traded or offered a renegotiated contract. "It's a whole different game down there," he said of Washington, after the swap. "The pressure won't be as great, and while I know I'm going to a team that hasn't made the playoffs, what I have to do is help the team make it."

At the time of the transaction Langway's defence partner, Brian Engblom, was considered the better defenceman. Coming off a Second Team All-Star selection,

Engblom was also a member of the Team Canada 1981 Canada Cup team that lost in the final game to the Soviet Union. A critical column by Red Fisher in the next day's edition of the *Montreal Gazette* appeared under the headline "Canadiens gave up far too much by letting Engblom go."

"I'm shocked," said Engblom. "It's strange. A lot of players on our club were unhappy. They did a lot of complaining in the off-season. I didn't say a word. Guess who goes!?"

The focal point of the deal for Montreal was Ryan Walter, who had finished the previous season with a career-high 37 goals and 87 points. Walter was entering his fifth season in the NHL and had never scored fewer than 56 points in any year. Grundman believed that Walter would add even more spark to an offense that had scored 360 goals in 1981-82, the third best total in the league.

THE DEBATE The trade paid immediate dividends for the Capitals, and not from the defenceman that they had anticipated. While much of the attention was focused on Engblom at the beginning of the year, it was Langway who was at the forefront as the season progressed. Using his tremendous size and strength, Langway patrolled the Washington blue line on the way to a Norris Trophy and First Team All-Star selection. He became the first American player to be recognized as the NHL's top defenceman.

More importantly for the Capitals, they qualified for the playoffs for the first time in franchise history after eight consecutive years of futility. In 1983-84, Langway

Walter and the Women

Ryan Walter went from being a player to being a broadcaster to being an assistant coach in Vancouver, but after he was fired from the Canucks he became head coach of Canada's national women's team for the 2011 Women's World Championship. Canada won silver that year after a heart-breaking loss to the United States in overtime. Canada twice trailed in the game and lost in extra time after Hilary Knight pushed home a loose puck for the 3-2 win.

defended his Norris Trophy, becoming the first repeat winner of the award since Denis Potvin claimed back-to-back honours in 1977-78 and 1978-79.

Langway played a total of eleven seasons in Washington, serving as team captain in each of those years. Cartilage damage in his knees limited him to just 21 games in 1992-93, the final year of his career. Langway was inducted into the Hockey Hall of Fame in 2002.

Engblom's first season in a Capitals uniform, 1982-83, ended with 27 points in 73 games and an invitation to play for Team Canada at the World Championship. On October 18, 1983, just six games into the following year, he was traded again, this time with Ken Houston to Los Angeles for Larry Murphy, another future of Hall of Fame defenceman to arrive in Washington.

Doug Jarvis was primarily a faceoff specialist and penalty killer throughout his career. He never missed a game in seven full seasons in Montreal. The Iron Man streak continued in Washington where he played more than three seasons before being traded to Hartford for Jorgen Pettersson, on December 6, 1985.

Craig Laughlin posted average numbers during a five-and-a-half year stint in Washington, scoring a career-high 30 goals in 1985-86. He was traded to Los Angeles for Grant Ledyard on February 9, 1988.

The Canadiens never received the output from Walter that they had anticipated. He recorded a very respectable 29 goals and 75 points in 1982-83, his first year in Montreal. Although he never approached those numbers for the remainder of his career, he was able to win a Stanley Cup in 1986 thanks to rookie goaltender Patrick Roy who backstopped the Habs to an unlikely championship. On July 26, 1991, Walter signed with Vancouver as a free agent.

Rick Green played seven years in Montreal, including the Cup-winning season of 1986. A stay-at-home, physical defenceman, Green played in the shadows of Larry Robinson and Chris Chelios but made his contributions by clearing opposing players from in front of his net. He briefly retired in 1989 before making a comeback in the NHL with stops in Detroit and Long Island.

THE RESULT The deal was made one month after David Poile's appointment as Washington's general manager. "I have a mandate to bring this team into the play-offs," he said. Poile was true to his word. In each of the eleven years that Langway anchored the blue line, the Capitals made a post-season appearance.

Walter and Green were serviceable players who were fortunate to win a Stanley Cup because of Roy's heroics. But the trade remains one of the most lop-sided deals ever. The Capitals would have been clear winners had they received only Langway. In getting Engblom, however, Washington obtained an asset that they eventually used to get Murphy, who was an elite defenceman of his own, collecting 81 points in 1986-87.

Adding an Iron Man in Jarvis and a utility player in Laughlin were significant bonuses to Washington's addition of a franchise defenceman and made the deal even more one-sided as a result.

First Taiwanese NHLer

Rod Langway's place of birth is typically listed as Maag, Formosa, but there is more to those words than meets the eye. MAAG is actually an acronym (not a city) for Military Assistance Advisory Group, American soldiers who went to other countries to help train local military. Formosa is the old name for what is currently called Taiwan, the chain of islands in East Asia. Langway's father served overseas, which is how Rod came to be born so far away from the hockey world, but he was raised in the more traditional Randolph, Massachusetts. Rod actually attended the University of New Hampshire on a football scholarship, hockey not being his best sport until his late teens, but he eventually made it to the NHL through most unconventional means.

JUNE 6, 1986

Canucks Let Neely Bloom with Bruins

The Deal [VANCOUVER CANUCKS trade **Cam Neely** and **a 1st-round draft choice in 1987 (Glen Wesley)** to the BOSTON BRUINS for **Barry Pederson**.

"It's a new challenge to be going to a team like Vancouver. I hope I can get a tradition and a new attitude going, but I'm not going to turn the franchise around by myself." —Barry Pederson

THE DIRT After a surprise run to the Stanley Cup finals in 1982, the Vancouver Canucks struggled through the rest of the decade. The team suffered first-round exits in each of the next two playoffs, then missed the post-season altogether in 1984-85. They saw playoff hockey once again the following year but were ripe pickings for the Edmonton Oilers, losing the Smythe Division semi-finals in 1986 in a three-game sweep in the best-of-five.

Vancouver general manager Jack Gordon was in desperate need of a top-line centre. The Canucks had scored just 282 goals in 1985-86, the third-lowest output in the NHL. Patrik Sundstrom, the highest scoring centre on the team, had just 18 goals.

The Canucks focused on Barry Pederson of the Boston Bruins, who had played his junior hockey in British Columbia, with the Victoria Cougars. A 1st-round draft choice of the Bruins in 1980, Pederson set a club record by scoring 44 goals in his rookie year, 1981-82, and was runner-up to Dale Hawerchuk in the Calder Trophy voting.

With Rick Middleton at his right wing, Pederson scored at an incredible rate in Beantown, posting totals of 107 and 116 points in his second and third years in the league, respectively. But in 1984-85, he was diagnosed with a serious tumour and had to have a large portion of his shoulder muscle removed. He was held to just 22 games, and his playing career was jeopardized.

Pederson recovered to play in all but one of the Bruins' games the next season, scoring 29 goals and 76 points. Unable to reach terms of a new contract with Boston, however, he found himself returning west. "It's not a real surprise," he said. "We knew something might happen when the Bruins only offered me a one-year contract. I wanted at least a four-year deal. It's a new challenge to be going to a team like Vancouver. I hope I can get a tradition and a new attitude going, but I'm not going to turn the franchise around by myself."

THE DEBATE Cam Neely was a 1st-round pick of the Canucks at the 1983 NHL Entry Draft less than a month after he won a Memorial Cup with the Portland Winter Hawks. A native of Comox, B.C., he made it into the Vancouver lineup as an 18-year old, scoring 31 points in 56 games in his rookie season. He missed just 15 games over the next two seasons, posting 39- and 34-point campaigns in 1984-85 and 1985-86, respectively, despite seeing limited ice time.

Injury, not Lack of Skill, was Pederson's Undoing

The curious aspect of this trade is that Pederson was at one time as good a young player as any in the NHL. In his first three full seasons with the Bruins, he had 92, 107, and 116 points, superstar numbers by any measure. Had the Canucks acquired him after the last of these seasons, in 1984, it would have been a trade that made sense. But Pederson had serious shoulder surgery, missed the better part of an entire year, and came back to post a more modest total of 29 goals and 76 points in 79 games. Clearly he was still a fine player, but clearly he had not returned to his form prior to the shoulder troubles. Indeed, that's why GM Harry Sinden traded him, and to get Neely and a high draft choice was icing on the cake in this lop-sided deal.

The Trade Kept on Giving for Boston

Consider this. The Bruins acquired Neely and a 1st-round draft choice, whom they used to select Glen Wesley. During Wesley's seven years with the Bruins, the team went to the Cup finals twice, only to lose to Edmonton both in 1988 and 1990. The Bruins later traded Wesley in 1994 for three 1st-round draft choices—in 1995, 1996, and 1997—and used those selections to acquire Kyle McLaren (1995), Jonathan Aitken ('96), and Sergei Samsonov ('97). While Aitken never amounted to much, Samsonov was a Calder Trophy winner and McLaren had a decent career before contract demands forced the Bruins to trade him to San Jose. Wesley, meanwhile, eventually won a Cup, with Carolina in 2006, and the Hurricanes later retired his number 2, which he wore for ten of 20 NHL seasons. The defenceman finished with 1,457 regular-season games to his credit.

When the trade was announced, Neely said, "After the last couple of years, I wanted to prove to people that I could play. Now I guess I'll have to do it in Boston."

Neely's arrival in Beantown coincided with immediate team success. He scored 72 points in 1986-87, nearly doubling his previous career-best single-season total. The next year Neely topped the 40-goal mark for the first time, finishing with 42 goals on the way to being named a Second Team All-Star. Boston advanced to the Stanley Cup finals, and Neely led the league in the playoffs with 71 shots on goal in 23 games. However, Wayne Gretzky and Mark Messier had the last laugh as the Edmonton Oilers claimed the Cup in a convincing four-game sweep.

Neely set career marks with 55 goals and 92 points two years later and went on to register 28 points in 21 games during the 1990 playoffs. Once again the Oilers and Bruins met in the Cup finals, Edmonton prevailing in five games. At the end of the year, Neely earned his second career All-Star selection.

In 1990-91, Neely registered 50 goals for the second year in a row, but he suffered a devastating injury in game three of Boston's playoff series versus Pittsburgh when Ulf Samuelsson nailed him in a dangerous knee-to-knee collision. Resulting thigh ailments and major knee surgery limited Neely to just 22 games over the next two years.

Neely's comeback season of 1993-94 was nothing short of historic. Paired with centre Adam Oates, Neely went on to score 50 goals in his first 44 games from the start of the season, eclipsing benchmarks previously held by Rocket Richard and Mike Bossy, the first 50-in-50 players in NHL history. Neely was awarded the Bill Masterton Trophy at the end of the year.

A hip injury ended Neely's career at the end of the 1995-96 season. Setting a standard skill set for what is described as a "power forward," Neely was inducted into the Hockey Hall of Fame in 2005.

Pederson scored 76 points in his first full season in Vancouver, but his production declined in each subsequent year. He never reached the heights of the player that he was before his surgery. He was later traded again, in a six-player deal with Pittsburgh, in January 1990.

THE RESULT Boston general manager Harry Sinden pulled off one of the biggest heists in league history. To compound the imbalance of the trade in Boston's favour, Sinden selected Glen Wesley 3rd overall in 1987 with the 1st-round draft choice. Wesley, a dependable blueliner, played seven seasons in a Bruins uniform including a pair of Stanley Cup finals appearances in 1988 and 1990. In August 1994, Boston traded Wesley to Hartford for three 1st-round draft picks.

Had Vancouver not made the trade, the Canucks would have not only retained Neely but kept the draft choice to select the centre they coveted. After Pierre Turgeon was selected first overall in 1987, the second centre chosen in the draft – at 15th overall – was Joe Sakic.

This was a disastrous deal for the Canucks on many levels.

NOVEMBER 24, 1987

Coffey is First Piece of Oilers' Dynasty to Go

The Deal [PITTSBURGH PENGUINS trade **Craig Simpson, Dave Hannan, Moe Mantha,** and **Chris Joseph** to the EDMONTON OILERS for **Paul Coffey, Dave Hunter,** and **Wayne Van Dorp.**

"Over the seven years we had our bouts, but I have a lot of respect for [Sather]. He did what was right for the team in every argument that we had."
—Paul Coffey

///

THE DIRT The year 1987 was a monumental one for hockey fans, beginning with the February two-game Rendez-vous '87 series in Quebec City that matched the NHL All-Stars against the Soviet national team. In the spring, fans were treated to a classic Stanley Cup finals showdown as the Edmonton Oilers defeated the Philadelphia Flyers in a seven-game series. Three-and-a-half months later, Mario Lemieux – assisted by Wayne Gretzky – scored the winning goal in the deciding game of the Canada Cup.

Two of the defencemen on Canada's championship team were All-Stars Paul Coffey and Ray Bourque. Both were reportedly earning $320,000 per year, but Coffey's salary was in Canadian dollars and Bourque was paid in U.S. funds, the American greenback worth about 30% more than the loonie at the time. Coffey wished to renegotiate the last two years of his contract so that he could be paid equivalent to Bourque, the highest-earning defenceman in the league.

When Oilers general manager Glen Sather refused to budge, Coffey staged a holdout and did not report to the team. The stalemate continued past the 20-game mark of the 1986-87 season. Meanwhile the upstart Pittsburgh Penguins were showing keen interest in acquiring Coffey. They were in need of an offensive blueliner who could also boost their power-play. Just as importantly, they did not want Coffey to end up with their Patrick Division and Stanley Cup rivals, Philadelphia.

After the trade was finalized, Sather and Coffey parted ways on good terms. "I think Slats and myself were a bit stubborn," said Coffey. "Over the seven years we had our bouts, but I have a lot of respect for him. He did what was right for the team in every argument that we had."

Sather realized that he needed to maximize his return for the two-time Norris Trophy winner even though the Oilers had nothing to show for him over the first 23 games of the season. "I still had it in the back of my mind that Paul would return, but the more I kept thinking about it, I decided that he was at the point of no return," he said. "We weren't going to be blackmailed by anyone. But what's the point of a player sitting out a whole year?"

THE DEBATE Coffey made immediate contributions to the Penguins, registering 67 points in his abbreviated season. His late start to the year, plus a knee injury suffered in December, limited him to just 46 games. Pittsburgh's franchise star Lemieux, buoyed by his Canada Cup-winning performance, wrestled both the Art Ross and Hart Trophies from Gretzky, who had missed 16 games due to various injuries.

The Penguins finished above .500 for the first time in nine years with a 36-35-9 record, good for 12th overall in the NHL. However, they still finished in the basement of the strong six-team Patrick Division. Since the playoff criteria at the time provided for only the top four teams from each division to qualify, Pittsburgh's post-season drought extended another year.

An integral part of Pittsburgh's roster for five seasons, Coffey earned All-Star nods in 1988-89 and in 1989-90. He scored eleven points in 12 games during the

Well-travelled Hall of Famer

There is surely no great player of Coffey's ability who played for more teams and was traded or moved around as often as Coffey. A stud defenceman—indeed, one of the greatest of all time—Coffey played the first seven years of his career with the Oilers, but once he was traded to Pittsburgh, his travelling days began. He was with the Penguins for four and a half years and one Cup, which turned out to be the fourth and last of his career, and was traded to Los Anegeles. That stint lasted 60 games over a year and a half, and then it was on to Detroit for three and a half years. Hartford, Philadelphia, Chicago, Carolina, and Boston followed, nine teams in all.

1991 playoffs as the Penguins claimed their first Stanley Cup in team history. Coffey was traded to Los Angeles on February 19, 1992, for Brian Benning, Jeff Chychrun, and the Kings' 1992 1st-round draft choice.

The Oilers were disappointed in losing the veteran presence of Dave Hunter, who had been the team's longest-serving player at the time of the trade, dating back to the days of the WHA. He was re-acquired as compensation the next year after Pittsburgh picked Hannan from the Waiver Draft. Van Dorp played just 25 games for Pittsburgh before being moved to Buffalo.

In Craig Simpson, the Oilers received a promising young winger who had been a standout with the Michigan State Spartans in the NCAA. Simpson found instant chemistry playing on a line with veterans Mark Messier and Glenn Anderson. On March 15, 1988, in a game against Buffalo, Simpson scored his 50th goal of the season, reaching the milestone at age 21. The Oilers marched to the Stanley Cup, sweeping Boston in four games in the finals.

Simpson was a talented performer during his career in Edmonton, winning another championship in 1990. But as the assets from the dynasty years of the early 1980s left the team—including linemates Messier and Anderson—Simpson's production went from superb to average. He was traded to Buffalo for Josef Cierny and a 4th-round draft choice in 1994 (Jussi Tarvainen) on September 1, 1993.

In Chris Joseph, the Oilers obtained a stay-at-home defenceman who went back-and-forth between Edmonton and the team's farm team in Cape Breton before being traded to Tampa Bay in 1993. Moe Mantha didn't last the year in Edmonton. In January 1988 the Oilers traded him to the Minnesota North Stars for penalty-killing specialist Keith Acton. Dave Hannan's career with the Oilers lasted just 51 games before he was reclaimed by the Penguins in the Waiver Draft the following season.

THE RESULT The transaction benefited both teams. Coffey's talents weren't replaceable, but the Oilers had the depth to move him. With Gretzky and Messier up front, Kevin Lowe on defence, and Grant Fuhr in goal, their reign on the Stanley Cup was intact for another year, while they acquired a winger they coveted in Simpson.

The Penguins were willing to give in to Coffey's salary demands, as his first contract in Pittsburgh was for more than $400,000 U.S. a year. With a spark from the blue line bolstering a team already led by Lemieux, it was a worthwhile, Cup-producing investment.

Dorp's Dutch Debut

Wayne Van Dorp got to the NHL by strange means. Although he started in the WHL, with Seattle, he was never drafted and ended up in the ACHL with Erie in 1983-84. But then he played in Holland for two years, with the GIJS Bears of Groningen, a city with many more ties to Vincent Van Gogh than Wayne Van Dorp. Because of his heritage, Van Dorp managed to play for the Netherlands at the 1986 World Championship, B Pool. It was only then that he returned to North America and started in the AHL, in 1986-87, and getting in three games with the Oilers. A year later, he was with the Penguins, later moving on to Chicago and Quebec as a fighter more than a goalscorer, to be sure.

MARCH 7, 1988
Flames Get Cup; Blues Get Hull—Worth It?

The Deal [ST. LOUIS BLUES trade **Rob Ramage** and **Rick Wamsley** to the CALGARY FLAMES for **Brett Hull** and **Steve Bozek.**

> *"We needed an offensive threat, a guy who can pull the trigger. Hull is that man."*
> —Ron Caron

THE DIRT The landscape of the Smythe Division was changing as Flames general manager Cliff Fletcher was assembling a roster that aspired to challenge the Edmonton Oilers. In 1986-87, Calgary finished third overall in the NHL with 95 points, eleven points back of their provincial rivals. A much-anticipated second-round playoff matchup against the Oilers never materialized as the Flames were upset in the division semi-finals by the Winnipeg Jets in six games.

Calgary had more than its fair share of firepower with a roster that scored the second-most goals in the league. But the team's goals-against record was in the middle of the pack at eleventh overall. The team needed upgrades in both the net and on the blue line if it expected to contend for the Stanley Cup.

The Flames had a blue-chip prospect in 23-year-old Brett Hull, son of Hall-of-Famer Bobby, the "Golden Jet." Brett had been Calgary's 6th-round pick at the 1984 Entry Draft. Many pundits were projecting the right-winger to follow in his father's footsteps to one day become a 50-goal scorer. Fletcher never liked trading

/// Hull's Appetite was for More than Just Goals

Bobby Hull started his NHL career in 1957, and over the course of his career he revolutionized the game. His banana blade and ferocious slapshot were the bane of all goalies, and his streaking speed down the left wing was a sight to behold. He scored 50 goals in 1961-62, his first of five 50-goal seasons. In the summer of 1964, the Hawks were eliminated by Detroit in the semi-finals in seven games, and Bobby returned home to Belleville, Ontario, for the summer. That August, his wife gave birth to a baby boy they named Brett, but it wasn't long before the couple divorced. Brett grew up in British Columbia with his mother and later played at the University of Minnesota-Duluth, but although he was a great scorer he had one large problem—food. He was nicknamed Pickle because he ate anything and everything, and it wasn't until he became more disciplined that he turned a skill—scoring goals—into a career.

young players, but in this case he made an exception. Hull and Flames coach Terry Crisp didn't see eye-to-eye, and the player was a healthy scratch in 14 of the team's first 66 games in 1987-88. "Me and Terry were great together," said Hull on his way out of Calgary. "I don't know why I wasn't playing. I really don't. I'm sure you'll find out from him."

St. Louis general manager Ron Caron—whose Blues team was ranked 15th out of 21 teams in the points standings the the previous year—was more than happy with his acquisition. "We needed an offensive threat, a guy who can pull the trigger. Hull is that man," he said.

Meanwhile goalie Rick Wamsley welcomed the chance to escape the mediocre Norris Division in which the Blues finished first overall in 1986-87 despite having a losing record at 32-33-15. "I'm excited," he said. "I'm going to a contender and an organization with a reputation for the way it deals with its players."

THE DEBATE The Flames earned their first Presidents' Trophy at the end of the 1987-88 season, finishing with a record of 48-23-9. The newest edition of the "Battle of Alberta," against the Oilers, took place in the Smythe Division finals, but an overtime loss in game two deflated the team. The goal became another highlight in the career of Wayne Gretzky, who roared down the left wing to fire a slapshot past Mike Vernon and into the top corner of the Flames net. Calgary went down in an unexpected sweep in the series.

The shocking trade of Gretzky in the summer opened the window of opportunity even wider for the Flames to knock off their nemesis. Wamsley earned the job as backup to Vernon, replacing Doug Dadswell, whose chronic goals-against-average above 4.00 earned him a ticket out of Calgary and down to the minor leagues. On the blue line, Rob Ramage was an effective shutdown defenceman on a team with both potent offence and strong defence.

The Flames defended their Presidents' Trophy in 1988-89. Calgary's team goals-against-average dropped by nearly a goal a game, from 3.75 to 2.77, the second-lowest in the league. In the playoffs the Flames didn't even have to face the Oilers as Gretzky's new team, the Kings, rallied from a 3-1 series deficit to eliminate Edmonton in the opening round.

Calgary swept the Kings in the division finals, then cruised past the Chicago Blackhawks to face Montreal for the Stanley Cup. Led by Doug Gilmour's two goals and Lanny McDonald's famous shot past Patrick Roy in game six, the Flames capped off their dream season with a championship.

The Flames appeared to have cleared their playoff hurdles with the foundation of a team that could contend for the Stanley Cup over the next several years. Few would have predicted that their victory at the Montreal Forum would be their last post-season series win for 15 years.

Ramage and Wamsley were eventually dealt in separate deals to Toronto, in 1989 and 1992, respectively. Hull, of course, went on to have a Hall of Fame career in St. Louis. With Adam Oates at centre, the two men formed the deadliest tandem in the NHL. In 1989-90, Hull became just the sixth player in league history to score at least 70 goals in one season, topping the benchmark by two goals. The following year, Hull became a member of the exclusive 50-in-50 club, registering his 50th goal in just his 49th game, on January 25, 1991. For Hull it was merely a stepping stone on his way to an astonishing 86-goal campaign.

As well, "the Golden Brett" enjoyed team success as a member of the United States roster that won the 1996 World Cup of Hockey. A two-time Stanley Cup champion with Dallas (1999) and Detroit (2002), he was inducted into the Hockey Hall of Fame in 2009.

Bozek lasted just seven games with St. Louis before being dealt to Vancouver in a three-way deal prior to the start of the 1988-89 season.

THE RESULT There is always an inherent risk when trading away a future franchise player such as Hull. The strategy isn't recommended for teams which are rebuilding and developing prospects within their minor-league systems.

But for teams who may be one or two players away from winning a championship, the risk-reward proposition is enticing. In 1994, the New York Rangers traded youngsters Doug Weight and Tony Amonte in separate deals, obtaining veterans Esa Tikkanen, Brian Noonan, and Stephane Matteau in the process. The previous year, baseball's Toronto Blue Jays surrendered prospect Jeff Kent to get David Cone.

In both cases, the team trading for veteran leadership won a championship, as did the Flames, eventually, in 1989. Sometimes the long-term future must be sacrificed in order to get that single moment of triumph. Ask any fan in Calgary which he would have preferred—keeping Brett Hull and his hundreds of career goals and never winning the Cup, or trading Hull and winning one Stanley Cup— and any fan will agree the price is steep—but the reward well worth it!

MARCH 8, 1988
Contract Dispute Costs Oilers Moog

The Deal [EDMONTON OILERS trade **Andy Moog** to the BOSTON BRUINS for **Bill Ranford, Geoff Courtnall,** and **a 2nd-round draft choice in 1988 (Petro Koivunen).**

"They'd require me to play 40 or 45 games a season, but when the important games came up they'd call on the other guy, Grant Fuhr, regardless what I had contributed." —Andy Moog

THE DIRT Having a pair of elite goaltenders on the roster is a luxury that practically every NHL team would love to have. Such was the case for the Edmonton Oilers in 1983 with Andy Moog and backup Grant Fuhr sharing duties on a surging team that was on the verge of greatness. The dynamic offensive machine led by Wayne Gretzky and Mark Messier scored 424 goals in 80 regular season games in 1982-83, advancing to the Stanley Cup finals before being swept by the New York Islanders.

The following season saw a shift in responsibilities as Fuhr became the primary starter with 45 appearances compared to Moog's 38. Having learned many lessons from the painful playoff sweep the previous spring, the 1984 Oilers exacted revenge on the Islanders to claim the first Stanley Cup in franchise history and end New York's 'drive for five' straight titles. Fuhr had eleven of the team's playoff victories in goal.

Over the next three seasons, the Oilers earned two more championships, in 1985 and 1987. Moog and Fuhr shared the duties almost evenly during the regular seasons, Moog making two more appearances then his teammate in the

80-game 1986-87 campaign. But the big games were always reserved for Fuhr. As Edmonton earned its third Stanley Cup, in 1987, Fuhr started in 19 of the team's 21 playoff games.

Prior to the start of the 1987-88 season, Moog was offered a lowly one-year $150,000 contract from Oilers general manager Glen Sather. The goaltender declined, and instead played with the Canadian National Team while awaiting a trade. With no immediate end to the deadlock, Moog played for Team Canada at the 1988 Winter Olympics in Calgary, posting a 4-0 record as the host team finished fourth, just off the podium.

When the deal was finally completed, Moog was ecstatic. "I felt I was becoming stale and complacent in the Edmonton Oilers atmosphere," he said. "They'd require me to play 40 or 45 games a season, but when the important games came up they'd call on the other guy, Grant Fuhr, regardless what I had contributed."

Bill Ranford, meanwhile, was just as happy to leave Boston. Then 21 years old, he felt he was mishandled by incoming Bruins coach Terry O'Reilly, who had replaced Butch Goring behind the Boston bench. O'Reilly went with the duo of Reggie Lemelin and Doug Keans in goal in 1987-88, dispatching Ranford to

Two Number Ones Not Possible

It's near impossible to have two goalies capable of being number one on the same team, and that's what befell the Oilers in the mid-1980s. Grant Fuhr and Andy Moog were both too good to share the duties, and it was Moog who pressed matters by demanding a trade in 1987. Edmonton general manager Glen Sather refused to be bullied, so Moog joined the National Team and played for Canada at the Olympics in Calgary in February 1988. He posted a perfect 4-0-0 record but Canada finished in fourth place after losing to the Soviets, 5-0, in the medal round. Moog's partner Sean Burke was in goal for that game, but Moog's play, and his stubbornness, finally forced Sather's hand once the Games were over. Moog got his trade and never won the Cup after leaving Edmonton, but he was number one in Boston, which was his ambition all along.

Maine of the International Hockey League. "When I got to Maine, I knew there was something going on," said Ranford. "(Boston general manager) Harry Sinden was telling me all through the year how much he wanted me. Then all of a sudden I'm traded. I think I should have had the opportunity to play this year. Terry likes going with older players."

THE DEBATE While Ranford finally retained a full-time NHL job by going to Edmonton, he still saw scant ice time. Appearing in six regular season games following the trade, he watched every minute of the 1988 playoffs from the bench as Fuhr backstopped the Oilers to their fourth Stanley Cup in five years. Ranford was a clear number-two netminder to Fuhr in 1988-89, making 29 appearances and posting a 15-8-2 record, but gaining invaluable experience from a veteran team that knew how to win.

In 1989-90, Fuhr was sidelined with first appendicitis and then a shoulder injury. Ranford made the most of his opportunity as he was thrust into the leading role. Starting in the bulk of the Oilers' games, Ranford had a 24-16-9 record and, more importantly, finally earned a starting assignment in the playoffs. The 1990 Stanley Cup finals pitted the Oilers against the Bruins. Ranford played spectacularly in Edmonton's five-game triumph, earning Conn Smythe Trophy honours as the playoff MVP.

The accolades for Ranford continued at the 1991 Canada Cup where he was named the tournament's outstanding player as Canada brought a championship to home soil. Following the 1991-92 season, however, Ranford posted a winning record just once more in his career, returning to Boston in 1996, and also playing for Tampa Bay, Washington, and Detroit before hanging up the pads in 2000.

Geoff Courtnall played in 12 games to close out the 1987-88 regular season and had three assists in 19 playoff games as the Oilers won the Stanley Cup. He was traded to Washington for Greg Adams on July 24, 1988.

Moog was a solid performer for the Bruins as he and Reggie Lemelin formed a tandem as good as any in the league. In 1989-90, both netminders shared the William M. Jennings trophy for allowing the fewest goals against. While Moog earned the playoff ice time that he coveted for many years behind Fuhr, he had the misfortune of being crushed by his old team, the Oilers, twice in three years in the Stanley Cup finals and never won a Cup after he left Edmotnon.

THE RESULT With a Stanley Cup and Conn Smythe Trophy to show for his efforts, Ranford won the trade for the Oilers' Sather. Moog played extremely well for the Bruins, though, earning a career high 37 wins in 1992-93.

Boston may have earned more mileage out of Moog had it not dealt him to the Dallas Stars for Jon Casey in June of 1993. The transaction completed an earlier swap that saw Gord Murphy move to Dallas for future considerations.

Casey had a very good regular season in 1993-94, posting a 30-15-9 record, but his 5-6 record in the playoffs spelled his exit out of Boston. He signed with St. Louis in the summer while Moog played four years in Dallas before ending his career in Montreal.

Koivunen was no Kurri

The Oilers landed the first great Finnish player when they signed Jari Kurri to a contract after drafting him 69th overall in 1980, but they weren't so fortunate with Petro Koivunen, the player they selected with the 2nd-round draft choice in 1988 (39th overall) they acquired in the Moog trade. Koivunen played at the U20 World Championship in 1989 and 1990, but he never made it to North America. He played primarily for Espoo and KalPa in the Finnish league before finishing in France and Germany. The Oilers missed out on several great players still available by the time they chose Koivunen, namely Mark Recchi (67th overall), Tony Amonte (68th), Rob Blake (70th), and Joe Juneau (81st).

AUGUST 9, 1988
Unthinkable—99 Traded to LaLaLand

The Deal [EDMONTON OILERS trade **Wayne Gretzky, Mike Krushelnyski,** and **Marty McSorley** to the LOS ANGELES KINGS for **Jimmy Carson, Martin Gelinas, a 1st-round draft choice in 1989 (Jason Miller), 1991 (Martin Rucinsky),** and **1993 (Nick Stajduhar), and $15 million.**

"I appreciate Mr. Pocklington giving me the possibility to play for another club after ten years in Edmonton." —Wayne Gretzky

THE DIRT If you are old enough to remember the Wayne Gretzky trade, you can recall vividly where you were and what you were doing at the time that the shocking news of The Great One's departure to Los Angeles was announced. Fans across the country watched in disbelief as Gretzky—tears streaming down his face—tried to compose himself and said, "I promised 'Mess' I wouldn't do this." Gretzky was of course referring to Mark Messier with whom he was grinning gleefully just two-and-a-half months earlier as the Oilers paraded around Northlands Coliseum with their fourth Stanley Cup in five years.

It was a moment when hockey fans realized that the sport wasn't immune to the often cold-hearted business aspect of the game. Gretzky, the holder of eight Hart Trophies and seven scoring titles, and the man who was making the NHL record book his personal autobiography, was merely a commodity in the eyes of Oilers' owner Peter Pocklington. NHLPA Alan Eagleson referred to Pocklington's view of Gretzky as "a depreciating asset."

Gretzky said all the right things for the cameras. "I appreciate Mr. Pocklington giving me the possibility to play for another club after ten years in Edmonton. At this point I'm still young enough and still capable enough to help a new franchise win the Stanley Cup," said the recently married Gretzky, whose new bride, actress Janet Jones, lived in California. The Great One told a crowded group of reporters at Edmonton's Molson House that he asked to be traded because of family reasons.

But many were skeptical, including former teammate Paul Coffey, who had been dealt to Pittsburgh the previous season. "I think hockey was number one to Wayne," Coffey said. "There's no bloody way he wanted to go there (Los Angeles). I don't think the people in Edmonton who know Wayne should believe that. He's a small-town guy. I don't care if he married the Queen of England."

THE DEBATE Gretzky's impact in Hollywood was immediate, both on the ice and at the box office. L.A. Kings owner Bruce McNall excitedly watched as the Fabulous Forum played to sellout crowds with many celebrities among the attendees. In 1988-89, the Kings improved by 23 points in the standings from the previous season, finishing second in the Smythe Division with a 42-31-7 record. Incredibly, Gretzky added another Hart Trophy to his collection.

As fate would have it, Los Angeles and Edmonton faced each other in the opening round of the playoffs. The Oilers vaulted to an expected 3-1 series lead, but Number 99 rallied his troops and the Kings stormed back to win the next three games to eliminate Edmonton and end the Oilers' bid for a third straight Stanley Cup.

Gretzky added another pair of scoring titles in each of the next two seasons, but the Kings were ousted in the second round of the playoffs both times. The Kings had their greatest chance to win the Stanley Cup in 1993. Gretzky had 40 points in 24 playoff games, but Los Angeles lost to the Habs in a five-game finals series, three of the defeats coming in overtime.

The Great One won his last scoring title in 1993-94. He was traded to

St. Louis in February 1996, then signed as a free agent with the New York Rangers the following summer. On April 18, 1999, Gretzky played his last career game, entering the Hockey Hall of Fame seven months later.

Mike Krushelnyski posted 109 points in 156 games for Los Angeles. His finest moment in a Kings uniform came in game six of the Smythe Division semi-finals against Calgary when his overtime winner eliminated the Flames. He was dealt to Toronto for John McIntyre on November 9, 1990.

Tough guy Marty McSorley, Gretzky's personal bodyguard, provided insurance for number 99 in Los Angeles against potential headhunters, just as had been the case in Edmonton. He led the league in penalty minutes in 1992-93 with 399. In game two of the 1993 Cup finals, McSorley was infamously penalized for an illegal curve on his stick. Montreal scored on the resulting power-play, and scored again in overtime to turn the series in its favour.

The Oilers were able to get a 100-point season out of Carson, the only experienced player coming to Edmonton in the trade. But the pressure of playing in Gretzky's shadow was too great for the 20-year-old. Carson was shipped to Detroit in a six-player deal in November 1989. Three of the players that the Oilers received—Joe Murphy, Petr Klima and Adam Graves—were part of Edmonton's Stanley Cup championship team of 1990.

Martin Gelinas, a third-line left-winger, never evolved into the offensive star that he was as a junior playing for the Hull Olympiques, where he once scored 131 points in 65 games. He was traded to Quebec along with a draft pick on January 20, 1993.

The draft picks that Edmonton received turned out to be Jason Miller, Martin Rucinsky, and Nick Stadjuhar, none of whom had particularly memorable NHL careers or in any way helped offset the colossal loss of Gretzky.

THE RESULT Without Gretzky, the Oilers were still deep enough to win another Stanley Cup. But the franchise couldn't overcome the intangible loss of the game's greatest player. Eventually Messier, Jari Kurri, and Grant Fuhr all left the team on which they had created a championship dynasty. Looking back, it is devastating to the game not to know how many times the Oilers could have won the Cup had number 99 and his teammates remained as group for another decade.

Conversely, the trade had an enormous influence south of the border. While Los Angeles didn't win a Cup with The Great One, the growth hockey in the United States was evidenced by teams expanding to non-traditional places such Anaheim and San Jose, occurrences that would never have happened had Gretzky kept on playing in Edmonton.

The trade forever changed the landscape of hockey. Unfortunately for Edmonton, it cut the Oilers' dynasty short by several years.

The Most Unbreakable Records

While Gretzky set dozens of records during his magical NHL career, surely it is the most obvious that is also the most untouchable—2,857 points in the regular season. There are a few ways to describe its sheer size. Of course, a player would have to have 29 seasons of 100 points to get to the record. However, the player who has the most 100-point seasons is Gretzky himself, with "only" 15. That means, though, a player could have 15 seasons of 200 points to catch Gretzky, but 200 points has been achieved only four times, all by Gretzky! The other monumental stat is that Gretzky has more career assists—1,963—than the second place player has total points—1,887 by Mark Messier. In other words, had Gretzky not scored a single goal during his career, he still would have retired as the top scorer in the game's history. Those stats are unbeatable. Period.

NOVEMBER 2, 1989
Blockbuster Sees Klima, Carson Swap Teams

The Deal | DETROIT RED WINGS trade **Petr Klima, Joe Murphy, Adam Graves,** and **Jeff Sharples** to the EDMONTON OILERS for **Jimmy Carson, Kevin McClelland,** and **a 5th-round draft choice in 1991 (Brad Layzell).**

"This is a new start for hockey, a new start for life… [Carson]'s got a great shot, but I've got a lot of talent." —Petr Klima

THE DIRT Early in the 1988-89 season Edmonton was still rubbing salt in its wounds inflicted by the Gretzky trade made one year earlier. The Oilers' run of two straight Stanley Cups and four in five years was halted at the hands of Gretzky's Kings in a hard-fought, seven-game 1989 Smythe Division semi-finals series, a clear sign that the Cup was going to be much more difficult to win without number 99 than with him.

Jimmy Carson was the only player that came to Edmonton in the Gretzky deal who had NHL experience at the time of the trade. He scored 37 goals and 79 points for Los Angeles in 1986-87 and was named to the NHL's All-Rookie Team at centre. The next year, Carson exploded with 55 goals and 107 points. He was content living the Hollywood lifestyle before unexpectedly becoming part of the biggest trade in hockey history.

"I made up my mind I'd play a number of years in L.A. Then boom, the Gretzky deal," Carson said. "I went from being really wanted by the Kings to being brought to the Oilers in a set of circumstances. They'd lost the greatest player to ever play the game, and the fans weren't happy."

While Carson was also looking for a fresh start, so was his main counterpart in the swap, Petr Klima. At age 24, Klima had registered 124 goals in his first four seasons in the league with Detroit and was rated as one of the top talents in the league by Edmonton general manager Glen Sather. But Klima also had his share of off-ice issues. He battled alcoholism and had as many as three drinking-and-driving violations on his record.

Nevertheless, the Oilers were willing to take a risk, and the Czechoslovakian sniper was eager to make a change. "This is a new start for hockey, a new start for life," Klima said. When told by a Red Wings fan that he was a better player than Carson, Klima replied, "I think so, too. He's got a great shot, but I've got a lot of talent."

THE DEBATE Klima ended the season with 30 goals split between the two teams, and his Oilers advanced to the 1990 Stanley Cup finals. Game one was slated for Boston against the Bruins. With the score knotted 2-2, the game extended into a third overtime period. Fresh legs were needed, and Oilers coach John Muckler had used very little of Klima in the game. Coming off the bench, Klima fired a shot past Bruins goalie Andy Moog's glove to win the game.

Edmonton went on to win the series in five games. Kilma's overtime winner was one of five goals he registered in the post-season. The 1990 Oilers Cup-winning team saw the formation of the Kid Line with two of Klima's ex-Red Wings teammates Murphy and Graves teaming up with Martin Gelinas. Murphy, the first overall pick at the 1987 NHL Entry Draft, finished the post-season with 14 points in 22 games. Graves, a tenacious checking left-winger, collected eleven points in 22 appearances during the Stanley Cup run.

Klima scored a career-high 40 goals with Edmonton in 1990-91. He spent four seasons with the Oilers before being traded to Tampa Bay for 3rd-round draft pick on June 16, 1993.

Like Klima, Murphy was a consistent goal scorer. He posted his single-season best output in 1991-92 scoring 35 times and registering 82 points in 80 games. Murphy's production continued in the playoffs where, in just 16 post-season games, he had an amazing 24 points. The Oilers won a pair of series against the Kings and Canucks before losing to the Blackhawks in the Campbell Conference finals. A contract dispute caused Murphy to sit out the 1992-93 season. Sather finally traded Murphy to Chicago on February 24, 1993, for Igor Kravchuk and Dean McAmmond.

Adam Graves scored just 46 points in 139 games with Edmonton in a limited role as a defensive forward. Prior to the start of the 1991-92 season, he signed as a free agent with the New York Rangers, who took advantage of a controversial loophole that prevented a previous player's team from matching an offer sheet. The provision has since been removed for restricted free agents.

Jeff Sharples was traded to New Jersey for Reijo Ruotsalainen, a defenceman who was also part of Edmonton's 1987 Cup run.

In Detroit, Carson, a native of Southfield, Michigan, was given the opportunity to play in front of hometown fans, but with captain Steve Yzerman firmly entrenched as the number-one centre, Carson saw reduced ice time. He had productive seasons, but his output was well-short of the 100-point seasons that he

Graves Takes Manhattan

Adam Graves spent the best ten years of his 16-year NHL career with the New York Rangers. He signed with the Blueshirts in the summer of 1991 and was part of the team that developed into Stanley Cup champions in 1994, thanks largely to the efforts of Graves. While captain Mark Messier and goalie Mike Richter took most of the glory for that Cup team, 1993-94 was a career year for Graves. He had a career-best 52 goals in the regular season and was equally sensational in the playoffs, not only on offence but taking faceoffs, playing defence, and leading by example. One of the most popular Rangers' of all time, he later had his number 9 retired by the team and continues to do enormous amounts of charity work in New York.

posted in Los Angeles. Carson was shipped back to the Kings on January 29, 1993, in a six-player deal that saw veteran Paul Coffey land in the Motor City.

Kevin McClelland had nine points in 64 games for Detroit before signing as a free agent with Toronto in 1991.

THE RESULT The Oilers didn't get the dominant scorer that they expected to receive in Carson from the Gretzky trade, but the young players who replaced Carson in the lineup a year later helped them win their fifth championship in seven years. Edmonton would have received even more of a return had the Group 1 loophole in the Collective Bargaining Agreement that allowed the Rangers to sign Graves without compensation to the Oilers not existed.

While the Red Wings received little short-term gain in the deal, their ability to obtain Coffey was positive. Several years later, in 1996, Coffey and Keith Primeau were traded to Hartford for Brendan Shanahan. The power forward was instrumental in helping lead Detroit to back-to-back Stanley Cups in 1997 and 1998.

/// Carson's Career in Blockbusters

How many blockbusters can one player be involved in during his career? In the case of Jimmy Carson, the answer is three. Of course, the biggest was his first as he moved from Los Angeles to Edmonton in the Gretzky trade, but just 15 months later the Oilers traded him to Detroit along with Kevin McClelland, and a 1st-round draft choice in 1991 for Adam Graves, Joe Murphy, Petr Klima, and Jeff Sharples. Three years later, he was back in Los Angeles with Marc Potvin and Gary Shuchuk as the Kings sent Paul Coffey, Sylvain Couturier, and Jim Hiller to Detroit. Less than a year later, though, Carson was little more than a spare part and was sent to Vancouver for nothing more than Dixon Ward and a 1995 draft choice. In just five and a half years, he went from being the centrepiece of the biggest trade of all time to a mere shuffling of extra players.

JUNE 16, 1990

Jets Trade All-Time Scorer in Package Deal

The Deal
WINNIPEG JETS trade **Dale Hawerchuk, a 1st-round draft choice in 1990 (Brad May),** and **future considerations** to the BUFFALO SABRES for **Phil Housley, Scott Arniel, Jeff Parker,** and **a 1st-round draft choice in 1990 (Keith Tkachuk).**

"In my era, there were two Winnipegs. There was the John Ferguson era, which was positive, upbeat… and then the Mike Smith era, which was negative and pessimistic." —Dale Hawerchuk

THE DIRT As a second-year team in the NHL in 1980-81, the Winnipeg Jets were the laughingstock of the league, posting an embarrassing 9-57-14 record. However, their poor showing secured the team the first overall pick in the 1981 NHL Entry Draft. Their selection was very easy. Winnipeg chose Hawerchuk, the Canadian Major Junior Player of the Year and Memorial Cup most valuable player with the Cornwall Royals.

Hawerchuk quickly evolved into the Jets' franchise player. In his rookie year, 1981-82, he scored 45 goals and 103 points on the way to winning the Calder Trophy. Over his first seven seasons in the NHL, Hawerchuk topped the 100-point mark six times. His career-best output was during the 1984-85 campaign when he netted 53 goals and collected 130 points, earning a berth as a Second Team All-Star. Hawerchuk earned his greatest international achievement in 1987 by playing on the Canada Cup championship team that defeated the Soviet Union on Mario Lemieux's famous goal.

But when Mike Smith replaced John Ferguson as Jets general manger during the 1988-89 season, Hawerchuk was not enthused. "In my era, there were two Winnipegs," Hawerchuk told the *Toronto Sun* several years later. "There was the John Ferguson era, which was positive, upbeat, a really community driven team. And then the Mike Smith era, which was negative and pessimistic. That ran through the media. I thought I'd be a Winnipeg Jet forever, but at the end Mike pretty much made it impossible for me to really push forward with my career there."

Hawerchuk officially asked for a trade on May 16, 1990, and Smith granted his wish at the draft, one month later. Hawerchuk's only regret was that he would not be playing with his good friend Scott Arniel, who was a late inclusion in the trade talks between Smith and Sabres general manager Gerry Meehan. Hawerchuk and Arniel were Jets teammates years earlier, and also linemates on the Memorial Cup-winning Royals, once co-owning a minority share in the Cornwall team. "I'm a little disappointed that my buddy Scotty is coming back to Winnipeg," said Hawerchuk. "I know how much he liked Buffalo, and I know he had talked to Gerry about getting me. But I'm happy to go to Buffalo. I'm glad it's done. "

THE DEBATE The Sabres needed depth at centre. The deficiency became evident during the 1990 playoffs when Buffalo was eliminated in six games by the Montreal Canadiens in large part because their top-line centre, Pierre Turgeon, was stifled throughout the series by Guy Carbonneau.

Hawerchuk led the team in scoring in 1990-91 with 89 points. The following year, the Sabres traded Turgeon as part of a blockbuster trade with the Islanders to get Pat LaFontaine. As LaFontaine formed a lethal combination with Alex Mogilny, Hawerchuk was slotted as the team's number-two centre, but he still produced at over a point-per-game clip.

Hawerchuk never cracked the 100-point mark in any season after leaving Winnipeg, but in his five seasons in Buffalo he compiled 385 points in 342 regular season games. He signed as a free agent with St. Louis on September 8, 1995.

The Sabres selected Brad May with their 14th overall pick obtained from the Jets at the 1990 draft. Cast in an enforcer's role, May spent six-and-a-half seasons with Buffalo collecting 1,323 penalty minutes in 425 games. Throughout all of the fisticuffs, May's shining moment with the team was his overtime, series-winning goal in the 1993 Adams Division semi-finals. The Sabres completed a sweep of the Bruins with broadcaster Rick Jeanneret screaming "May Day!" into the homes of Sabres fans everywhere. May was dealt, along with a draft pick, to Vancouver on February 4, 1998, for Geoff Sanderson.

From the Jets' perspective, their acquisition of Housley complemented a fast-skating team that already had players such as Dave Ellett, Randy Carlyle, and Teppo Numminen on the blue line. "I don't think people realize how good a player Phil Housley is," said Hawerchuk after the trade. "The Winnipeg system suits him so well."

Housley posted excellent numbers over three seasons in Winnipeg being utilized as a power-play specialist. He earned 64 goals and 259 points in 232 games while playing for the Jets. Prior to the 1993-94 season, he was traded to St. Louis for Nelson Emerson and Stephane Quintal.

Arniel's second tour of duty in Winnipeg lasted just one season, 1990-91, in which he registered 22 points in 75 games. Parker never played for the Jets, signing as a free agent with Hartford in February 1991.

The prize for the Jets in the trade was selecting Keith Tkachuk at 19th overall

/// The Decisive Faceoff

Dale Hawerchuk won three medals at the World Championship (a silver and two bronze), but his most famous moment came in game three of the 1987 Canada Cup finals. He had a goal and two assists in the decisive 6-5 win for Canada, but more important he was the player who won the faceoff deep in Canada's end to start the winning rush. Not only did he win the draw, as he moved up ice he checked his man, allowing Mario Lemieux to spring free and take a pass from Wayne Gretzky for the winning goal with less than two minutes remaining.

in 1990 with the pick previously belonging to Buffalo. A power forward from Boston University, Tkachuk was a force at left wing, scoring 50 goals in 1995-96, the Jets' final season win Winnipeg, and then following up with a 52-goal campaign in the team's first season following their transfer to Phoenix. By the time he was traded to St. Louis in 2001, Tkachuk had posted 623 points and 1,508 penalty minutes in 640 games with the Winnipeg/Phoenix franchise.

THE RESULT While both teams were able to fill their immediate needs, neither was able to garner much—if any—post-season success. The 1993 Sabres' win, sealed by May's goal, was the only playoff victory for Buffalo during either Hawerchuk's or May's tenure.

At the other end, the trade couldn't stop Winnipeg's run of post-season futility. Despite the later arrival of superstar Teemu Selanne, the Jets franchise didn't win a playoff round until 2012 when Phoenix defeated Chicago, ending a drought of 25 years.

Drafting Tkachuk earned the Jets a slight victory, but it was a trade that could have or should have done more for both teams.

Coach Phil

Although Phil Housley was a natural to play for Team USA at the top international events, his was a far less likely success story as a coach. But after playing in six World Championships and two Canada Cups among his many appearances, he coached the Americans to a stunning gold medal at the 2013 U20 World Championship in Ufa, Russia. Later that year he was an assistant when the U.S. won an even more shocking bronze at the senior Worlds.

JUNE 29, 1990
Savard for Chelios a Win-Win Deal

The Deal [CHICAGO BLACKHAWKS trade **Denis Savard**
to the MONTREAL CANADIENS for **Chris Chelios** and
a 2nd-round draft choice in 1991 (Mike Pomichter).

"Mike [Keenan] has told me a lot of things. He has always told me he loved me and would never trade me." —Denis Savard

THE DIRT The Blackhawks drafted one of the most dynamic players in franchise history in Savard in 1980 with the 3rd overall selection. For an entire decade in the Windy City, Savard dazzled spectators at the Stadium, carrying the puck and faking the defenceman with a 360-degree spin. The move was nicknamed the "Savardian Spinerama" even though the term was originally coined for a similar play crafted by legendary Habs defenceman Serge Savard, years earlier.

In ten years playing for Chicago, Savard topped the 100-point mark five times, finishing in the top ten in NHL scoring on each occasion. He earned a Second Team All-Star in selection in 1982-83, a year in which he registered 121 points. It was his only All-Star selection in his career, although he might have earned more such honours had he not played in an era when the centre-ice position was dominated by Wayne Gretzky and Mario Lemieux.

Mike Keenan was named coach of the Blackhawks in 1988. Over the next two years, Keenan and Savard endured a relationship described as 'stormy.' Keenan added the role of general manager to his portfolio prior to the start of the 1990-91 season and was responsible for Savard's trade out of Chicago. Savard denied ever asking to be moved.

"Mike has told me a lot of things," he said. "He has always told me he loved me and would never trade me." When asked about the prospect of playing in his home province, Savard said. "I feel very good about it. It's been a dream, now a dream come true for me, quite honestly. I'm very excited. I'm looking forward to being there."

But Chelios, a Norris Trophy winner and First Team All-Star in 1988-89, was less than thrilled about switching teams. "It just sucks, but that's life," said Chelios bluntly. "I kind of expected it, but I didn't. I knew they were after Savard. I just had a strange feeling. I didn't really expect it. I wanted to finish my career in Montreal."

THE DEBATE In Chelios the Blackhawks received a defenceman with an unbridled passion for the game that was second to none. Before Chelios even suited up for his first game in his native Chicago, his résumé had already included noteworthy achievements. After playing for the United States in the 1984 Olympics, in Sarajevo, Chelios played his first full season for the Habs in 1984-85, scoring 64 points in 74 games.

The following year, Chelios was part of a Montreal team that unexpectedly

///The Gordie Howe of the Blue Line

Chris Chelios just kept playing and playing until he was 48 years old. He didn't start in the NHL until after the 1984 Olympics in Sarajevo and then began a seven-year career with Montreal. After eight and a half seasons with the Hawks, he was traded to Detroit, and it was there he stayed for more than nine years. Chelios, now in his forties, simply refused to retire. He ended the 2008-09 season with Grand Rapids in the AHL and played almost all of the next season in the AHL as well, with the Chicago Wolves, farm team of Atlanta. The Thrashers rewarded him with a seven-game callup, but at season's end he finally called it quits.

won the Stanley Cup. He had eleven points in 20 games during the championship run. Chelios had also participated in two Canada Cup tournaments, two All-Star games, and one other Stanley Cup finals series (1989) at the time of the trade.

As popular as Savard had been, the Chicago Stadium fans quickly took a liking to Chelios, who earned a Second Team All-Star selection after his first year as a Blackhawk in 1990-91. Chicago won the Presidents' Trophy, finishing atop the NHL standings with a 49-23-8 record. But the team's hopes for a Stanley Cup were dashed at the hands of the Minnesota North Stars—a team that finished 38 points below them—in the first round of the playoffs.

The next year Chicago acquired defenceman Steve Smith from Edmonton. Smith and Chelios formed a solid defensive pairing that patrolled the Blackhawks zone for years. In the 1992 playoffs the team recovered from the humiliating defeat a year earlier by winning 12 of their first 14 post-season games en route to the Stanley Cup finals. However, Mario Lemieux, Jaromir Jagr, and the Penguins swept the Blackhawks aside in winning Pittsburgh's second straight title. Playing in his third career Cup finals series, Chelios earned 19 points in 21 games.

Chelios was named an All-Star in four of the next five seasons, and he earned another Norris Trophy in 1992-93. When the 1995-96 campaign rolled around, Chelios took over the captaincy from Dirk Graham. The season ended with Chelios being named the NHL's best defenceman for a third time.

But the Hawks deteriorated from Cup finalists in 1992 to a non-playoff team in 1997-98. Unable to come to terms with the team on a contract extension, Chelios was traded on March 23, 1999, for Anders Eriksson and two 1st-round draft picks to Detroit, where he had the opportunity to win two more Stanley Cups, in 2002 and 2008.

The Canadiens had been looking for a playmaking centre at the time of the trade. Their top two centres in 1989-90 were Guy Carbonneau and Brian Skrudland, who were primarily defensive specialists. Although Savard's three seasons in Montreal resulted in perfectly respectable totals—179 points in 210 games—he was a shadow of the player who never had less than 75 points in ten seasons with Chicago.

But Savard's crowning moment was winning a Stanley Cup with Montreal in 1993. He scored five points in 14 playoff games. Savard didn't dress for the Cup-clinching game but joined the post-game celebration on the Forum ice with his arms raised in triumph. He signed as a free agent with Tampa Bay that summer.

THE RESULT Measured by on-ice achievements, Chicago came out on top because Chelios became a franchise defenceman with the Blackhawks. With Ed Belfour in goal and Chelios on the blue line, Chicago's goals-against never finished lower than fifth-best in the nine seasons immediately following the trade.

However, the Habs, and especially Savard, didn't lose in the exchange, either. It was a fitting career highlight for Savard to win his only Stanley Cup while playing in his home province of Quebec. He was inducted into the Hockey Hall of Fame in 2000.

The Three Denis

Denis Savard is one of an incredible troika of players. Known as the "three Denis," the players were Denis Savard, Denis Cyr, and Denis Tremblay. All were born on February 4, 1961, within a few miles of each other, and all three grew up together and played together with the Montreal Juniors. All were later drafted into the NHL, but it was then that their careers diverged. Tremblay never made it to the NHL; Cyr made it, but didn't have a sensational career; Savard went on to a Hall of Fame career.

SEPTEMBER 19, 1991

Fletcher Begins Rebuild with Fuhr to Leafs

The Deal [EDMONTON OILERS trade **Grant Fuhr, Glenn Anderson,** and **Craig Berube** to the TORONTO MAPLE LEAFS for **Vincent Damphousse, Peter Ing, Scott Thornton, Luke Richardson,** and **future considerations.**

"In a way it's a relief that it's done, but on the other hand, it's hard to say goodbye. We had a lot of fun." —Grant Fuhr

THE DIRT   On June 4, 1991, Cliff Fletcher was introduced as the new president and general manager of the Toronto Maple Leafs. After 19 years of running the Atlanta/Calgary Flames franchise, Fletcher—whose club won a Stanley Cup in 1989—was hired to salvage a sinking team. The Leafs had finished the previous season with the second-worst record in the 21-team league and had not won a play-off round in the previous four years, missing the post-season twice over that stretch.

The Leafs needed a vast upgrade over the goaltending tandem of Peter Ing and Jeff Reese. Toronto's goals-against was 20th overall in 1990-91. In Edmonton, Fletcher found a willing trade partner in Oilers' general manager Glen Sather. Fuhr, a one-time Vezina Trophy winner who had five Stanley Cups to his name, was suspended for one year by NHL president John Ziegler after the goaltender confessed to substance abuse in the summer of 1990. Fuhr was reinstated in February 1991 after missing 59 games. That left Edmonton with a tandem of Fuhr and Bill Ranford, who had led the Oilers to a championship the previous year, winning the Conn Smythe Trophy as playoff MVP.

With Ranford on the Edmonton roster, Fuhr became expendable. "In a way it's a relief that it's done, but on the other hand, it's hard to say goodbye. We had a lot of fun," said Fuhr regarding the trade. "A fresh start never hurt anyone, I don't think," he added.

In Damphousse the Leafs were giving up the highest scorer on their roster by a wide margin. The sharpshooting left-winger had 94-points in 1989-90. His 73 points in 1990-91 were almost double the output of his next closest teammate, Mike Krushelnyski, who had all of 39 points. "I feel like I'm starting all over again, like I'm a rookie again," said Damphousse, who was initially disappointed to be heading west. "But I know from day one that a priority of Cliff's was a proven goalie, and from the start Grant Fuhr was the number-one choice."

THE DEBATE Damphousse quickly became the leading scorer on his new team much like he had been on his old one. His 38 goals and 89 points were tops among all Oilers in 1991-92 as he earned an invitation to play in the All-Star Game for a second straight year. Despite his fine performance, though, the Montreal native eventually got the chance to play in his home town. On August 27, 1992, the Oilers traded Damphousse to the Canadiens for Shayne Corson, Brent Gilchrist, and Vladimir Vujtek. The timing was perfect as Damphousse ended up hoisting the Stanley Cup the next year.

In Luke Richardson the Oilers received a steady, durable defenceman who was coming off a season in which he collected a career-high 238 penalty minutes.

/// All-Star MVP

One of Vincent Damphousse's finest moments came at the 1991 All-Star Game. Representing the Maple Leafs and playing on a line with Steve Yzerman and Adam Oates, Damphousse scored four goals and won MVP honours. He scored midway through the first period to give the Campbell Conference a 2-1 lead, and then he added three goals in the middle ten minutes of the third period, the last three goals for the team to make it an 11-5 win over the Wales Conference.

Richardson played in all 82 games for three of his five seasons in Edmonton and went on to play 1,417 career games over 20 NHL seasons, among the all-time leaders in games played. He was signed as a free agent by Philadelphia on July 23, 1997.

Thornton split his first two seasons as an Oiler between Edmonton and the AHL farm team in Cape Breton. A third- or fourth-line forward, Thornton was traded on September 6, 1996, to Montreal for Andrei Kovalenko.

Ing played only one season in Edmonton, posting a 4.28 goals-against-average in a dozen games in 1991-92. He spent the following years in the minors and was traded to Detroit along with a late-round draft pick for future considerations in August 1993.

On the Leafs' side of the deal, they also received Glenn Anderson, who, like Fuhr, was a member of the Oilers' Stanley Cup dynasty of the 1980s. Anderson, a two-time 50-goal scorer, had found his way into Sather's doghouse after the two men couldn't come to terms on a new contract. While past his prime, Anderson was still a productive contributor in Toronto, scoring 65 points in the 1992-93 season and proving his worth as a clutch playoff performer by netting the overtime winner in game five of the Campbell Conference finals versus Los Angeles that year. At the trade deadline in 1994, he was dealt to the New York Rangers for Mike Gartner.

Craig Berube, a 6'1" enforcer, played a season-and-a-half for the Leafs, collecting 373 penalty minutes in 116 games before being traded to Calgary in a ten-player blockbuster deal involving Doug Gilmour and Gary Leeman in January 1992.

As expected, Fuhr helped the Leafs improve to 14th overall in goals-against, posting a 25-33-5 record in 1991-92. But, as in Edmonton, the emergence of a younger goalie on the roster made Fuhr expendable. While the Leafs evolved into a playoff contender in 1992-93, Felix Potvin was given the starting nod in the Toronto goal. In February 1993, the Leafs traded Fuhr for scorer Dave Andreychuk, goalie Darren Puppa, and a first-round draft choice.

Iron Man of the Blue Ice

Grant Fuhr distinguished himself in many ways. Adopted as a small boy, he went on to become one of the greatest goalies of the modern era. He handled the puck as well as any goalie and holds the record of 14 assists in a season (1983-84), although he never scored a goal. Later in his career, with St. Louis, he set an astonishing record by playing in 79 of the team's 82 games, most games by a goalie in one season. Further, 76 of those appearances were consecutive, a long way from Glenn Hall's record of 502, to be sure, but pretty amazing in the modern era. In all, Fuhr played in 868 regular-season games and won 403, both among the all-time leaders.

THE RESULT Neither of the primary principals of the trade—Fuhr or Damphousse—stayed with their new teams for very long. Interestingly, the returns of the deal are measured by the players for which the two men were dealt in subsequent transactions.

By that measuring stick, Fletcher easily won the swap. Andreychuk and Anderson were key figures during the Leafs' surprise run to the conference finals in 1993, and Andreychuk scored 52 goals the next year as Toronto made another run to the final four.

On the other hand, Corson and Gilchrist were checking forwards who were effective in their roles but couldn't compensate for the loss of Damphousse's scoring. The trade marked one of the last links to the Oilers' glory years as the team transitioned into rebuilding during the 1990s.

OCTOBER 4, 1991
"Mess" on His Way to Broadway Miracle

The Deal [EDMONTON OILERS trade **Mark Messier** and **future considerations** to the NEW YORK RANGERS for **Bernie Nicholls, Steven Rice,** and **Louie DeBrusk.**

"I'm starting a second career, and I'm every bit as confident about my second career as I was my first." —Mark Messier

THE DIRT Despite the shocking trade of Wayne Gretzky in 1988, the powerhouse Oilers were still able to claim a Stanley Cup two years later. But because the team was based in a small-market such as Edmonton and struggled to compete against teams south of the border that paid contracts in U.S. dollars, keeping the core of the team was not sustainable.

One-by-one the superstars and future Hall of Famers were traded to greener pastures. Jari Kurri was moved to Los Angeles in a three-way trade. Glenn Anderson and Grant Fuhr found their way to Toronto. Then, the final exclamation point on the end to the Edmonton dynasty was punctuated with Messier's trade to New York.

"I'm starting a second career, and I'm every bit as confident about my second career as I was my first," said Messier. "New York is the media mecca for sports. They want to win, but I don't worry about pressure." The Rangers were unfazed about Messier's injuries which had limited him to just 53 games and 12 goals in 1990-91. "This guy is in his prime," said Roger Neilson, coach of the Blueshirts.

///Longevity Means Nothing

This is the kind of superstar Mark Messier was. He made his NHL debut in 1979 with Edmonton and then played 25 years in the league. He retired with 1,887 career points, second all-time to Wayne Gretzky, but perhaps no player paid a greater price for the two lockouts, in 1994-95 and 2004-05, than "Mess." He retired having played 1,756 regular-season games, only eleven games behind Gordie Howe's record which many thought was untouchable. Yet had there been a full season in either lockout year, Messier would have easily surpassed Howe. And, the Rangers wanted him back in 2005-06, at which time he also would have hit 1,756. But he was 44 years old and didn't want to play simply for the sake of a record.

Messier, all of 30 years old, was coming from an Edmonton team with which he had won five Stanley Cups in seven years. He had won the Conn Smythe Trophy after their first championship, in 1984. A four-time All-Star in Edmonton who succeeded Gretzky as team captain, Messier was named the Hart Trophy winner in 1990 as the league's most valuable player.

The trade was not welcomed by Nicholls, whose wife was expecting twins in four weeks. He threatened not to report to the Oilers despite being offered a flight to Edmonton in owner Peter Pocklington's private jet. "I know it's awfully cold there," Nicholls said. "Getting traded to a team that's rebuilding doesn't make me feel really good."

THE DEBATE Upon Messier's arrival he was named team captain, his leadership reputation from Edmonton preceding him. The Rangers improved by 20 points and soared to the top of the NHL standings with a 50-25-5 record, claiming their first Presidents' Trophy. Messier finished fifth in NHL scoring with 107 points and was named a First Team All-Star while earning the second Hart Trophy of his career. In the playoffs, New York lost in the division finals to the Pittsburgh Penguins, who were on their way to a second consecutive Stanley Cup.

The following year revealed much turmoil between Messier and Neilson.

"This year, he just didn't lead us," Neilson said regarding the captain. "Last year, Mark was on top of all the little things. He was leading meetings and noticing things. This year, he didn't get it done." Then at the midway point of the 1992-93 season, the Rangers posting an average 19-17-4 record, Neilson was fired.

Neilson also revealed that he had summoned Messier's teammates Adam Graves, Kevin Lowe, and Mike Gartner to a meeting, telling them they had to assume the leadership role on the team. Messier countered, "I'm the captain until someone takes it from me." The Rangers limped to a 34-39-11 finish, alarmingly ending up out of the playoffs after finishing first overall the previous year.

The 1993-94 season saw a new regime in Manhattan with the hiring of Mike Keenan as coach. The Rangers responded by claiming their second Presidents' Trophy in three years. In the 1994 Eastern Conference finals against New Jersey, Messier famously guaranteed a victory and then scored a hat trick in game six to help the Rangers stave off elimination. Stephane Matteau's overtime winner in the seventh game sent New York to the Stanley Cup finals against Vancouver. The two teams battled ferociously, playing a game seven at Madison Square Garden. Messier had a goal and an assist—including the game-winner—as the Rangers won 3-2, ending a 54-year Stanley Cup drought.

Messier went on to play three more seasons in New York. By the time his career in the Big Apple had ended, he had collected 691 points in 698 regular season games in a Rangers uniform, and 80 points in 70 playoff games. He signed as a free agent with Vancouver on July 30, 1997.

Nicholls never reached the output that he did during his peak years as a member of the Kings. While in Los Angeles, he reached the 100-point plateau three times including a 70-goal, 150-point campaign in 1988-89 playing on a line with Wayne Gretzky. "I would have been a better player if I played with more offensive-oriented players," Nicholls said upon leaving New York. After parts of two seasons in Edmonton where he scored 89 points in 95 games, Nicholls was traded to New Jersey on January 13, 1993, for Zdeno Ciger and Kevin Todd.

DeBrusk, an enforcer, collected 797 penalty minutes in 228 career games with Edmonton over six seasons. He signed as a free agent with Tampa Bay in September 1997. Rice, who had an excellent junior career with Kitchener that included two appearances for Team Canada at the U20 World Championships, had 31 points in 94 career games for the Oilers before signing with Hartford in August 1994 as a free agent.

THE RESULT The cash-strapped Oilers were in too poor of a bargaining position to get fair return for Messier, who transformed the Rangers from playoff under-achievers into Stanley Cup champions. Unfortunately for Edmonton, the team's elimination in the conference finals against Chicago in 1992 preceded a stretch of missing the playoffs in each of the next four years.

Following a three-year stint in Vancouver, Messier returned to finish his career as a Ranger. He retired in 2004 and was inducted into the Hockey Hall of Fame in his first year of eligibility three years later.

The Gretzky Effect

Bernie Nicolls was a fine player, but like everyone else who played with Wayne Gretzky he became a sensational player alongside number 99. To wit, Nicholls had seasons of 41 and 46 goals with Los Angeles in the pre-Gretzky era, but in 1988-89, the two played on a line together and Nicholls pumped in 70 goals and had 150 points, astronomical numbers he never came close to achieving with any other team in any other year and any other linemate. He was famous for doing the "Pumper Nicholl" after scoring a goal, his unique celebration consisting of a fist pump which he performed so frequently during his one season with Gretzky he must surely have had a sore arm.

OCTOBER 25, 1991

LaFontaine Centrepiece of Eight-Player Swap

The Deal [NEW YORK ISLANDERS trade **Pat LaFontaine, Randy Hillier, Randy Wood,** and **a 4th-round draft choice in 1992 (Dean Melanson)** to the BUFFALO SABRES for **Pierre Turgeon, Uwe Krupp, Benoit Hogue,** and **Dave McIlwain.**

"I took a stand for my principles, for being honest, for being treated the way you deserved to be treated. Promises were made that were broken by this ownership." —Pat LaFontaine

THE DIRT In 1990-91 the New York Islanders finished 19th overall out of 21 teams in the NHL. Their dismal output of 60 points was their lowest total since they were a second-year expansion team in the early 1970s. The team hadn't won a playoff round since 1987, the year that star forward Pat LaFontaine ended a marathon seventh game of the playoffs in quadruple overtime against Washington.

LaFontaine, the Islanders' first-round, 3rd-overall draft choice in 1983, made the team after playing in the Winter Olympics in Sarajevo the following year. He scored 13 goals in just 15 regular season games and was a consistent part of the lineup that lost in the Stanley Cup finals to the Edmonton Oilers, ending the team's bid for a fifth straight championship.

The team declined through the mid-1980s, but LaFontaine emerged as a top-line centre, eventually taking over from the aging Bryan Trottier as the cornerstone of the Islanders' offence. In a bleak 1988-89 season, the Islanders finished tied for the fewest points in the league.

Then, in 1989-90, LaFontaine had his best year as an Islander, registering 54 goals and 105 points. But a rift began to surface at the end of the season when the team, owned by John Pickett, offered to renegotiate LaFontaine's contact and then reneged on the offer. LaFontaine requested a trade in January 1991 while still continuing to produce impressively on Long Island. Indeed, he threatened to sit out the entire 1991-92 season before his wish to be dealt was finally granted. "I took a stand for my principles, for being honest, for being treated the way you deserved to be treated," said LaFontaine. "Promises were made that were broken by this ownership, where money was no longer the issue with me, and mistrust was."

THE DEBATE In Turgeon, the Islanders were receiving a dynamic forward four years younger than LaFontaine and who would easily be cast into the number-one centre role. The case was polar opposite to Buffalo where Turgeon had to compete for ice time with the recently acquired Dale Hawerchuk. Turgeon had 106 points in the 1989-90 season, one ahead of LaFontaine and good for seventh place in scoring that year.

"You can't compare Pierre Turgeon to Pat LaFontaine," said Islanders general manager Bill Torrey at the time of the deal. "Pierre is more of a playmaker and Pat is more of a pure goalscorer. But I had to get quality. We owed it to the rest of our players to get moving, get the furor over with."

Turgeon didn't look out of place in an Islanders uniform, collecting 87 points in 67 games in his first season. In 1992-93, he had a breakout season. Playing on a line with Derek King and Steve Thomas, Turgeon exploded for 58 goals and 132 points to place him fifth for Art Ross Trophy contention. In the playoffs, however, he was on the receiving end of an infamous blindside hit from the nefarious Dale Hunter after celebrating a goal that effectively eliminated the Washington Capitals.

For his transgression, Hunter received a 21-game suspension, the longest ban imposed in league history at the time for an act of on-ice violence. Turgeon missed

American Junior

Pat LaFontaine was one of the first top American stars to come to Canada to play junior hockey rather than play NCAA hockey at home. In his case, he chose the high-scoring Quebec league and promptly re-wrote the record book in the process. In his only season, 1982-83, he had 104 goals and 234 points in only 70 games, beating out Mario Lemieux for the scoring championship and being named top junior in all of Canada. He was drafted third overall in the summer of 1983 behind Brian Lawton and Sylvain Turgeon, and then joined the U.S. National Team. LaFontaine played at the Sarajevo Olympics before starting an NHL career later in the 1983-84 season.

six games with a separated shoulder. At the end of the year he was named the winner of the Lady Byng Trophy.

In three-and-a-half seasons with the Islanders, Turgeon collected 343 points in 255 regular-season games. On April 5, 1995, he was dealt, along with Vladimir Malakhov, to Montreal for Kirk Muller, Mathieu Schneider, and Greg Darby.

Uwe Krupp, a towering 6'6" defenceman, became an anchor on the Islanders' blue line for three years while also displaying some offensive upside. He collected 94 points in 180 games for New York. At the 1994 draft, Krupp was traded to the Quebec Nordiques for Ron Sutter, and the two teams also exchanged first-round draft picks.

Benoit Hogue had three consecutive 30-goal seasons for the Islanders and produced at nearly a point per game before his production cooled during the lockout-shortened season of 1994-95. He was dealt along with two draft picks to Toronto on April 6, 1995. McLlwain played 54 games for the Islanders before going to the Leafs along with Ken Baumgartner in a swap that sent Daniel Marois and Claude Loiselle to New York.

In Buffalo, the Sabres received in LaFontaine the perfect centre to complement right-winger Alexander Mogilny. The tandem was at their peak in the 1992-93 season when Mogilny scored 76 goals and LaFontaine finished second in NHL scoring with 148 points on the way to being named a Second Team All-Star.

Injuries derailed LaFontaine's career. The superstar forward missed all but 16 games in 1993-94 due to knee problems. In 1996-97, he suffered a concussion after a hit from Pittsburgh's François Leroux, limiting him to 13 games. He was dealt to the Rangers on September 29, 1997, for a 2nd-round draft pick. A freak collision with teammate Mike Keane resulted in another concussion, forcing him into retirement.

Wood played three seasons for the Sabres, registering 117 points in 236 games. He was claimed by Toronto in the 1995 Waiver Draft. Defenceman Hillier played just 28 games in Buffalo before leaving the NHL to finish his career in Austria.

THE RESULT Both teams received an offensively-gifted centres in the transaction. However, the Islanders received more mileage out of the trade because of the greater production of the complementary players in Hogue and Krupp, and also the opportunity to parlay Turgeon with Malakhov to get Muller and Schneider.

LaFontaine, an eventual Hall of Famer, was clearly the best player in the deal. However, because of injuries, his trade value diminished in hindsight.

German History

Uwe Krupp was part of the LaFontaine trade and ended up having perhaps the best career ever for a German national in the NHL. In the spring of 1996, he scored the Stanley Cup-winning goal for Colorado, the first German to do so, and he achieved that feat after having missed most of the season with a serious knee injury. Incredibly, Krupp rehabbed the knee in large part by pursuing his hobby of dogsledding, something that got him in hot water a couple of years later after signing with the Wings. He was out of the lineup with a herniated disc, and again used sledding to train, something that made the Wings none too happy.

JANUARY 2, 1992

Dougie Comes to Leafs in Biggest Trade Ever

The Deal [CALGARY FLAMES trade **Doug Gilmour, Jamie Macoun, Ric Nattress, Kent Manderville,** and **Rick Wamsley** to the TORONTO MAPLE LEAFS for **Gary Leeman, Alexander Godynyuk, Jeff Reese, Michel Petit,** and **Craig Berube.**

"I'm very happy to be a Maple Leaf. I had to walk out more for peace of mind than anything else. It's the biggest move I've ever made in my career." —Doug Gilmour

THE DIRT Maple Leafs general manager Cliff Fletcher had already begun to place his mark on the team in 1991-92, his first season on the job in Toronto, by trading Vincent Damphousse for Grant Fuhr. Heading into the new year, however, the club was just 10-25-5 and struggling offensively. Meanwhile in Calgary, where Fletcher had managed the franchise for 19 seasons including a 1989 Stanley Cup win, one of the key players on that championship roster was dissatisfied.

Doug Gilmour left the Flames on New Year's Day to express his displeasure at an arbitration ruling on a new contract. A consistent 80-point producer in each of his first three years in Calgary, Gilmour was awarded a deal worth $750,000 annually, which was about a half million dollars below his expectations.

Talks of a Gilmour-for-Gary Leeman trade were initiated during the previous season when Fletcher was still managing the Flames. Now at the helm of the Leafs, Fletcher finalized the trade with the man whom he had groomed to be his successor, Flames general manager and coach Doug Risebrough. "No one can say

I was just relaxing down in Florida over New Year's," Fletcher quipped. "I guess you could call this a deal of significant magnitude. Not many ten-player deals are made, especially one that can help both teams now and in the future."

Gilmour was understandably pleased with the move. "I'm very happy to be a Maple Leaf," he said. "I had to walk out more for peace of mind than anything else. It's the biggest move I've ever made in my career."

THE DEBATE   From the moment he put on a Maple Leafs sweater, Gilmour displayed an offensive prowess few in Toronto could have anticipated. He collected 15 goals and 49 points in 40 games over the last half of the 1991-92 season. Despite a ten-point improvement in the standings from the previous year, the Leafs still finished out of the playoffs, barely, in the basement of the Norris Division, three points behind Chicago.

In the summer Fletcher made his next bold move, hiring Pat Burns as the Leafs coach. The former bench boss with the Montreal Canadiens, Burns instituted a system of defensive responsibility from which the team would benefit. The 1992-93 season produced an epic turnaround for the Leafs, who had missed the playoffs the last two years. Among the highlights was the emergence of rookie goaltender Felix Potvin and also a trade with Buffalo for winger Dave Andreychuk.

But the offence was run by Gilmour, who erupted for 95 assists and 127 points, both totals eclipsing club records previously held by Darryl Sittler. Gilmour's tenacity also brought another dimension to the team, and he was named the winner of the Frank J. Selke Award as the league's best defensive forward. The Leafs finished with 44 wins and 99 points and made a surprise run to the Campbell Conference finals. Gilmour was runner-up to Mario Lemieux for the Hart Trophy at season's end.

In an encore performance, Gilmour posted a 111-point season in 1993-94. With Andreychuk on board for a full season in a Leafs uniform, the former Sabre scored 53 goals playing with Gilmour. Once again the Leafs were one of the last

Frank Mahovlich was part of two huge deals, one that sent him from Toronto to Detroit, and another that sent him on to Montreal to play with his brother, Peter.

When Boston acquired Phil Esposito from Chicago, it marked one of the most lop-sided trades in NHL history and helped take the Bruins to two Stanley Cup wins, in 1970 and 1972.

Bernie Parent could have played his career with the Maple Leafs had circumstances been different, but they weren't, and the Philadelphia Flyers were the beneficiaries.

One of the most shocking trades in all of sport, Wayne Gretzky's departure from Edmonton to Los Angeles marked the start of the modern era when no player could be called untouchable any longer.

It's hard to imagine that Dominik Hasek was so little used in Chicago or that the Hawks traded him to Buffalo for so little, but the Dominator became one of the greats when the Sabres gave him a chance.

Eddie Shore (right) shares a private moment with Red Dutton. Shore was the only player to skate in the NHL and AHL at the same time, thanks to his owning the Springfield Americans and still wanting to play in the NHL.

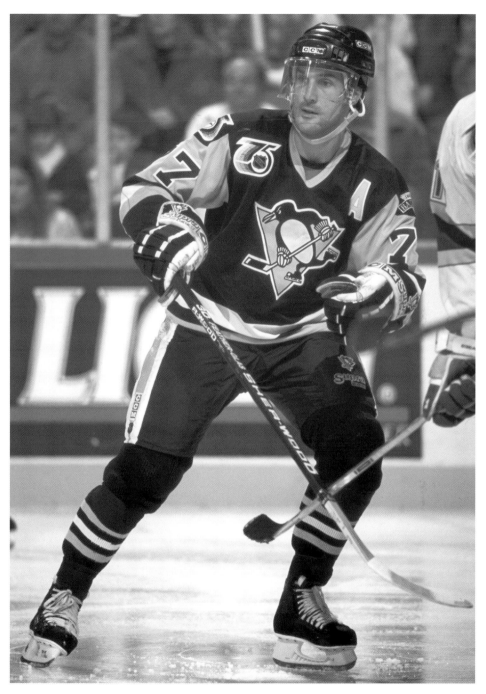

*Paul Coffey was cut from the same cloth as Bobby Orr, but after he left Edmonton,
Coffey played for Pittsburgh and seven other teams before retiring.*

Brian Engblom was a solid defenceman in Montreal but didn't truly shine until the Habs traded him to Washington.

four teams remaining in the playoffs, eventually bowing to the Vancouver Canucks.

Gilmour assumed the role of team captain when popular mainstay Wendel Clark was traded in the summer in a deal to acquire Mats Sundin. The Leafs regressed through the mid-1990s, eventually costing Burns his job in March 1996. After a five-year career in Toronto in which he registered 452 points in 393 regular season games, Gilmour was traded to New Jersey on February 25, 1997, for Jason Smith, Steve Sullivan, and Alyn McCauley. Gilmour's career playoff marks of 60 assists and 77 points, established in 52 post-season games, remain franchise records.

In contrast, Leeman, whose 51-goal output for Toronto in 1989-90 made him a briefly viable commodity, was a complete bust in Calgary. In 59 games with the Flames, Leeman scored just eleven goals and added but 12 assists. He was traded to Montreal for Brian Skrudland on January 28, 1993, hoisting the Stanley Cup five months later but still producing little.

Jamie Macoun was a serviceable defenceman who was part of Burns' six-man unit that made life easier for Potvin. He played 466 games for Toronto over six-and-a-half seasons. The impact of Nattress and Wamsley was negligible for the Leafs; both players saw limited action for Toronto, and both retired after 1992-93. Manderville lasted four seasons as a fourth-line forward before being traded to Edmonton in December 1995.

From the Flames' perspective, enforcer Berube had 364 penalty minutes in

/// One-Game Wonder

Goalie Jeff Reese was hardly an integral piece of the puzzle, but while in Calgary he set a record for goalies that almost surely will never be beaten. In a 13-1 victory over then lowly San Jose on February 10, 1993, Reese earned three assists on the night. In fact, he had an assist in each period of a game in which the Sharks lost for the 16th straight game, one shy of the record set by Washington in 1974-75. The Sharks were in only their second season and actually had a 1-0 lead for the first half of the first period. Robert Reichel and Theo Fleury each had six points. The top goalie point getters of all time are Tom Barasso (48 assists) and Grant Fuhr (46).

The Phantom High-stick

Gilmour was the centre of one of the great officiating controversies of all time. Playing for the Leafs against Wayne Gretzky and the L.A. Kings in the 1993 Conference finals, he was high-sticked by number 99 in overtime of game six. Rules at the time called for an automatic four-minute penalty for accidental high-sticking, but referee Kerry Fraser missed the incident and didn't make a call. Moments later, Gretzky scored the game winner and then starred in game seven at Maple Leaf Gardens to eliminate the Leafs. Most heart-breaking was the fact that the Montreal Canadiens had advanced to the Cup finals, so Fraser's miss wasn't so much about costing the team a game as it was about denying fans the first Toronto-Montreal Cup finals since 1967.

113 games for Calgary before being shipped to Washington for a 5th-round selection at the 1993 Entry Draft. Godynyuk produced little and was claimed by Florida in the 1993 Expansion Draft. Petit played for three seasons, eventually signing with Los Angeles as a free agent. Reese was only in Calgary for one full year, moving to Hartford for Dan Keczmer in November 1993.

THE RESULT Gilmour became one of the most popular Leafs in team history and has his number 93 honoured by the team despite playing for just five seasons in Toronto. His presence was the catalyst in turning around the fortunes of a Leafs franchise that wallowed in misery during the 1980s.

After dealing the player who scored the 1989 Stanley Cup-winning goal, Risebrough and the Flames embarked on a run of playoff futility. The franchise didn't win another playoff series until 2004, making clear how badly he lost in the biggest deal in league history.

JUNE 30, 1992

Lindros Sent to Flyers as Nords Acquire Cup Pieces

The Deal [QUEBEC NORDIQUES trade **Eric Lindros** to the PHILADELPHIA FLYERS for **Peter Forsberg, Steve Duchesne, Kerry Huffman, Mike Ricci, Ron Hextall,** a 1st-round draft choice in 1993 (Jocelyn Thibault) and 1994 (Nolan Baumgartner), future considerations (Chris Simon), and $15 million.

> *"Eric is a young player who can change the face of the game."*
> —Russ Farwell

THE DIRT With an intimidating combination of size and skill, Eric Lindros was by far the highest ranked prospect heading into the 1991 NHL Entry Draft. The 6'4" native of London, Ontario, proclaimed in many hockey circles to be "The Next One," had a Memorial Cup and World Junior Championship on his résumé, and collected 149 points in 57 games with the Oshawa Generals in his final full year of junior hockey.

But to Lindros's disappointment, he was selected 1st overall by the Quebec Nordiques. Lindros, through his agent Rick Curran, and his parents, had made several pleas in advance to Nordiques general manager Pierre Page not to draft him. Lindros's wishes were based on several factors such as Quebec's political environment, lack of sponsorship opportunities in a small NHL city, and the state of the lowly Nordiques franchise that had finished last overall for a third straight year.

Lindros infamously refused to wear the Nordiques sweater when his name was called at the draft. The controversy continued when Lindros refused to report to Quebec's training camp in the fall even though it was obvious the 18-year-old was ready to play in the NHL. After earning a spot on the Team Canada roster that won the 1991 Canada Cup, he briefly returned to Oshawa, then joined the Canadian Olympic team, winning a silver medal at the 1992 Games in Albertville, France.

The stalemate finally ended at the 1992 draft in Montreal. In a bizarre twist, Page inadvertently traded Lindros to two teams, the New York Rangers and the Philadelphia Flyers. The Rangers were certain they had a deal in place that would send goaltender John Vanbiesbrouck, forwards Doug Weight, Tony Amonte, and Alexei Kovalev, New York's 1st-round draft choices in 1993, 1994, and 1995, and $12 million for Lindros. After five days of deliberation, however, arbitrator Larry Bertuzzi ruled in favour of the Flyers.

"I don't think we gutted ourselves to get Eric," said Flyers general manager Russ Farwell. "We drew a line in the sand. It consisted of two young forwards, Mark Recchi and Rod Brind'Amour. We didn't let Quebec cross it." He added, "Eric is a young player who can change the face of the game."

THE DEBATE Lindros collected 75 points in 61 games in 1992-93 and was named to the NHL's All-Rookie Team. He evolved into the franchise player that the Flyers had projected him to be, winning both the Hart Trophy and the Art Ross Trophy in the lockout-shortened campaign of 1994-95.

/// Team Canada's Big E

Eric Lindros doesn't get nearly the credit he deserves for his international career with Team Canada. As a junior he led his country to two gold medals at the U20 World Championship. He was only 18 when he was on Canada's winning team at the 1991 Canada Cup and also played at the 1996 World Cup. He played at only one World Championship (a 4th-place finish in 1993), but represented Canada at three Olympics, winning a gold medal in 2002 and a silver in 1992. He was named the Best Forward by the IIHF at both the 1991 World Juniors and the senior Worlds in 1993, and over the balance of his career he averaged more than a point a game.

That season saw the creation of the "Legion of Doom" line that grouped Lindros, the team's new captain, between wingers John LeClair and Mikael Renberg after LeClair was acquired from Montreal in February. The Flyers ended a five-year playoff drought, advancing to the conference finals before losing to New Jersey.

Two years later, Lindros led Philadelphia to the Stanley Cup finals only to see the Flyers get swept by Detroit. In eight seasons with the team, Lindros registered 659 points and 946 penalty minutes in 486 games, but he endured a fair share of adversity during his time in Philadelphia.

In 1999, Lindros suffered a collapsed lung that was misdiagnosed as a rib injury. When he openly criticized the team's medical staff, he was stripped of the captaincy by general manager Bobby Clarke. Lindros suffered a devastating concussion in the 2000 playoffs after a crushing hit from New Jersey's Scott Stevens, then sat out the following season in a contract dispute with Clarke. On August 20, 2001, Lindros was traded to the Rangers for Kim Johnsson, Jan Hlavac, Pavel Brendl, and a 3rd-round draft pick.

As much as the Flyers reaped the benefits of the 1992 transaction, the magnitude of Quebec's return on the deal was even greater. Forsberg, fresh off his gold-medal winning shootout goal for Sweden at the 1994 Olympics, burst onto the NHL scene in 1994-95, winning the Calder Trophy. The next year the Nordiques moved to Colorado and were renamed the Avalanche.

Patrick Roy was acquired in a mid-season trade, and the once basement-dwelling franchise was instantly a Stanley Cup contender. The top two centres, Joe Sakic and Forsberg, were as good as any in the league, with Ricci providing grit and tenacity on a checking line. The team improved by 39 points in the standings, then capped off the 1995-96 season by winning the first Stanley Cup in franchise history.

Forsberg continued to be a dominant force in the league, earning First Team All-Star selections in 1997-98 and 1998-99. Another Stanley Cup followed in 2001, although Forsberg missed the final two series due to a ruptured spleen, an ailment that forced him to sit out the entire 2001-02 regular season as well. His greatest personal achievements with Colorado came the next year when he compiled 106 points and won both the Hart and Art Ross Trophies. Ironically, Forsberg signed with Philadelphia as a free agent when the 2004-05 lockout ended.

THE RESULT Both Lindros and Forsberg had magnificent careers that were shortened due to various injuries, posting remarkably similar regular season totals: Lindros 760 games played, 865 points; Forsberg 708 games played, 885 points.

While the two superstars compare fairly evenly, the Nordiques/Avalanche franchise comes out clearly winning the trade based on the performance of the many additional players Quebec acquired. Ricci was a very effective defensive forward for six seasons. He was dealt in a package to San Jose for a draft pick that turned out to be Alex Tanguay, a key component of Colorado's 2001 Stanley Cup win. Duchesne and Huffman spent limited time with the club, while Hextall and a first-round pick (Todd Bertuzzi) were traded to the Islanders for Mark Fitzpatrick and a first-round pick used to take Adam Deadmarsh, an important contributor in the Avalanche's first Stanley Cup.

/// Triple Gold Foppa

Peter Forsberg's membership into the Triple Gold Club is nothing short of unique and spectacular. He won World Championship gold in 1992 at age 18, won Olympic gold two years later at age 20, and then won the Stanley Cup, with Colorado, in 1996. And then he did it all over again. "Foppa" won another Worlds gold in 1998, another Cup in 2001, and a second Olympic gold in 2006 to cap his extraordinary career.

AUGUST 7, 1992

Dominator Becomes a Legend
After Trade from Hawks

The Deal [CHICAGO BLACKHAWKS trade **Dominik Hasek** to the BUFFALO SABRES for **Stephane Beauregard** and a **4th-round draft choice in 1993 (Eric Daze).**

"Hasek will be given the opportunity to be the number-one goalie. We've liked Hasek for a long time. We've been trying to get the trade done since February or March." —Gerry Meehan

THE DIRT Dominik Hasek played in his native Czechoslovakia for nine seasons before joining the Blackhawks as a 25-year-old in 1990. Studying under goaltending coach and renowned Hall of Famer Vladislav Tretiak, Hasek backed up Ed Belfour in the 1991 playoffs. Belfour, a rookie netminder, was establishing himself as a bona fide starter, winning both the Calder and Vezina Trophies that year.

The following season, Hasek saw an increase in ice time, appearing in 20 games and posting a 10-4-1 regular-season record. Chicago advanced to the Stanley Cup finals in 1992 but was swept by Pittsburgh. The decisive fourth game saw Hasek produce a superb effort in a losing cause, coming off the bench in relief of Belfour as the Blackhawks lost, 6-5.

Chicago had an outstanding goalie in Belfour and excellent defensive corps led by Chris Chelios. But the team was lacking in offensive punch, finishing just 15th out of 22 teams in league scoring and collecting just ten goals in four games in the Stanley Cup finals. The Blackhawks coveted Christian Ruuttu, a consistent

20-goal scorer for the Buffalo Sabres. But Winnipeg made a prior trade with the Sabres for Ruuttu, giving up goalie Beauregard, whom the Jets didn't want to lose in the Expansion Draft.

Because the Blackhawks decided to go with Belfour and Jimmy Waite as their tandem in goal, they made the swap with Buffalo and sent Hasek to the Sabres. "Hasek will be given the opportunity to be the number-one goalie," Buffalo general manager Gerry Meehan told the *Chicago Tribune*." We've liked Hasek for a long time. We've been trying to get the trade done since February or March."

Three days later, Chicago flipped Beauregard to Winnipeg for Ruuttu, making the roundabout three-way transaction complete.

THE DEBATE Hasek spent his first two seasons competing with Daren Puppa and Grant Fuhr for ice time. By 1993-94, he had established himself as the starter, leading the NHL with seven shutouts. That year he captured an NHL First Team All Star selection while also winning the Vezina Trophy. Hasek posted a .930 save percentage in what would be the first of six consecutive years leading the league in that category.

Hasek had an unorthodox style. He would often flop on the ice, contort, kick out a pad from on his back or slide an arm along the ice to make a spectacular save. Hasek vaulted into the upper echelon of elite NHL goalies, winning another Vezina Trophy and All-Star selection in 1994-95.

Two years later, Hasek posted a 37-20-10 record and became the first goalie in 35 years to win the Hart Trophy as the league's most valuable player. His third Vezina Trophy and All-Star election also followed, and the Sabres won their first playoff series in four years thanks to an overtime goal by Derek Plante in game seven against Ottawa.

The 1997-98 season saw Hasek produce one of the finest single seasons in hockey history by a goalie. Hasek's 13 shutouts were the most in a season since Tony Esposito earned 15 shutouts some 28 years earlier. And, at the 1998 Winter

A Great Career

"The Dominator" is the only goalie in IIHF history to be named Best Goalie at all levels of play. He received the Directorate honour at the U20 in 1983, the World Championship honour in 1987 and 1989 while playing for Czechoslovakia, and then was named top goalie at the 1998 Olympics in Nagano, his crowning glory. In 2002, he won the Stanley Cup with Detroit, but he never won gold at the Worlds and so never became the first goalie to join the Triple Gold Club. His last appearance for the Czechs came at the 2006 Olympics, and he retired in 2011 at age 46.

Olympics in Nagano, Hasek broke the hearts of Canadian fans in the semi-finals, stopping all five skaters in the shootout in an upset win by the Czech Republic. His shutout in a 1-0 win over Russia propelled the Czechs to an historic first gold medal in Olympics history. Hasek then repeated as Hart Trophy winner, becoming the first goalie in NHL history to be named the league's most valuable player in consecutive years.

The following season, 1998-99, Hasek and the Sabres advanced to the 1999 Stanley Cup finals against the Dallas Stars. The series was decided in game six when Brett Hull scored a controversial goal in triple overtime with his foot clearly in the crease. The stringent enforcement of crease violations at the time demanded the goal be disallowed, but the call stood and the Stars won the Cup.

Not all of Hasek's memories in Buffalo were fond ones. The netminder had a public rift with Buffalo coach Ted Nolan, telling the press that he didn't respect the Sabres' bench boss. Hasek also missed half of the 1999-2000 season with a groin injury. His final year with Buffalo was an excellent one, however. In 2000-01, Hasek once again led the league in shutouts, with eleven, and earned both his sixth Vezina Trophy and All-Star selections. On July 1, 2001, he was traded to Detroit for Vyacheslav Kozlov and a 1st-round draft pick.

For the Blackhawks, Ruuttu never achieved the production that he did as a member of the Sabres. He collected 90 points in 183 games, well short of his first four years in the league when he averaged 64 points a season. Meanwhile, in

Winnipeg, the Jets decided to go with Bob Essensa and Rick Tabaracci in goal, sending Beauregard to Philadelphia for future considerations before the start of the 1992-93 season.

THE RESULT Chicago received more mileage out of the deal by using the 4th-round pick they acquired to select Eric Daze. A 6'6" right-winger, Daze scored 20 or more goals in eight consecutive seasons for the Blackhawks, netting a career-high 38 goals in 2001-02 in a season that saw his only All-Star appearance. He was named to the All-Rookie Team in 1995-96 and represented Canada at the World Championships in 1998 and 1999.

While the deal was certainly lopsided in Buffalo's favour, few could blame Chicago general manager Mike Keenan for counting on Ed Belfour to be the number-one goalie at the time of the trade. Ruuttu's potential was overestimated, but Daze's production compensated nicely for the Blackhawks.

The only item missing from Hasek's Buffalo résumé was a Stanley Cup, which he won with Detroit in both 2002 and 2008.

A Solid Draft Choice

Eric Daze was a great player for Chicago. He came to the Hawks when they traded Hasek to Buffalo and was drafted 90th overall in 1993. Two years later, at the end of his junior career, he led Canada to gold at the U20 and then joined Chicago. After finishing second to Daniel Alfredsson in voting for the Calder Trophy, Daze became a model of consistency, scoring 20 goals or more every full season with the Hawks and reaching a career best 38 in 2001-02. But as time passed, he developed serious back problems. He played only 19 games in 2003-04 because of a herniated disc, rehabbed during the lockout, and returned for the start of the 2005-06 season. But after playing just briefly in the home opener that year he left the team and retired soon after.

JUNE 28, 1994

Heart and Soul Wendel the Price for Mats

The Deal TORONTO MAPLE LEAFS trade **Wendel Clark, Sylvain Lefebvre, Landon Wilson,** and **a 1st-round draft choice in 1994 (Jeff Kealty)** to the QUEBEC NORDIQUES for **Mats Sundin, Garth Butcher, Todd Warriner,** and **a 1st-round draft choice in 1994 (Nolan Baumgartner).**

"I'm looking forward very much to playing in Toronto. I think it's a good team with the possibility to win a Stanley Cup." —Mats Sundin

//

THE DIRT From the time Wendel Clark was drafted 1st overall in the 1985 Entry Draft, he was an instant fan favourite in Toronto. The once-proud Maple Leafs were the doormats of the NHL, enduring tumultuous years under the reign of eccentric Leafs owner Harold Ballard. Clark sparked the team with a combination of skill and brawn, possessing a lethal wrist shot while also delivering thundering body checks. His 34-goal rookie season in 1985-86 earned him consideration for the Calder Trophy, ending up as a finalist to Gary Suter.

But Clark's physical style of play took its toll on his body. After he posted a 37-goal campaign in 80 games in his sophomore year of 1986-87, back spasms limited Clark to just 81 games over the next three seasons. On the ice, the Leafs were slowly beginning a transition from pretenders to contenders, starting with the hiring of Cliff Fletcher as general manager in the summer of 1991. Clark was named team captain. Future hall of famer Doug Gilmour arrived in a trade from Calgary in January 1992, and Pat Burns was brought in a few months later to

The Big Hitter

On December 29, 1984, Wendel Clark delivered likely the most devastating check in the history of the U20 World Championship. Canada was playing the Soviet Union in Turku, Finland, midway through the round robin event. Defenceman Mikhail Tatarinov was carrying the puck around his net with his head down, and boom! Clark leveled him with a ferocious but clean check that knocked the Soviet unconscious and out of the game. Canada won, 5-0, and Clark scored the tying goal later in the tournament against the Czechs which assured the country of gold. That was the level of intensity he brought to the Leafs, but with checks like that came injuries, and over time they took their toll on a player who was inspirational in spirit but not large in body.

coach the team. The Leafs made consecutive appearances in the conference finals in 1993 and 1994, the furthest that the club had advanced in the playoffs in a decade-and-a-half. The 1993-94 regular season saw Clark explode for career highs in goals (46) and points (76).

In spite of the relative post-season success of the past two seasons Fletcher decided that the team was in a need of a makeover. At the 1994 draft in June, the popular captain was traded to the Quebec Nordiques for Sundin, the two players the key figures of a multi-player deal.

Sundin at age 23 was five years younger than Clark and already had a 103-pont season to his credit. The first European to be selected first overall at the NHL draft (in 1989), Sundin was a target of criticism of Quebec coach Pierre Page for the Nordiques' underachievement in the playoffs, most notably in 1993 when a visibly upset Page accosted Sundin on the bench as the team blew a 2-0 series lead to Montreal.

"I'm looking forward very much to playing in Toronto," said Sundin upon his arrival. "I think it's a good team with the possibility to win a Stanley Cup. I liked Quebec a lot, but this is what happens in the NHL. You must take the circumstances that happen."

THE DEBATE Sundin became expendable in Quebec because of the abundance of centres, notably Joe Sakic, Peter Forsberg, and Mike Ricci. Conversely, the only other measurable talent that the Leafs had in the centre position was Doug Gilmour, who was eight years older than Sundin. In February 1997, Gilmour was traded to New Jersey, Sundin inheriting the captaincy.

The Leafs missed the playoffs in consecutive years in 1996-97 and 1997-98, but the arrival of Pat Quinn as coach, and subsequently as general manager, saw a reversal in the team's fortunes. With Sundin firmly entrenched as Toronto's star forward, the Leafs made return appearances to the conference finals in 1999 and 2002. The 2001-02 regular season finished with Sundin earning a Second Team All-Star selection as he finished with 41 goals, tied with Glen Murray and Bill Guerin and second only to Rocket Richard Trophy winner Jarome Iginla.

Sundin was a model of consistency over his 13 seasons in Toronto. Excluding the lockout-shortened campaign of 1994-95, he never scored fewer than 27 goals or 74 points in any season, and he led the Leafs in scoring in 12 of those 13 years. By the time he signed with Vancouver as a free agent in September 2008, Sundin had become the franchise's all-time leader in goals (420) and points (987). His production would almost certainly have been even greater had he played with a winger who could complement his tremendous skill. At the time of his retirement in 2009, Sundin had 1,349 career points, making him the NHL's all-time leading scorer among Swedish-born players. He was inducted into the Hockey Hall of Fame in 2012.

Clark played just one season with the Nordiques, appearing in 37 out of a possible 48 games in 1994-95 and scoring 30 goals. Prior to the team's first game as the newly-minted Colorado Avalanche after the franchise was relocated, Clark was sent to the New York Islanders in a three-way trade in which Claude Lemieux arrived to the Avs from New Jersey. Clark had two additional stints with the Leafs before retiring on June 29, 2000.

As beloved as Clark was, the bigger loss to the Leafs was defenceman Sylvain Lefebvre. Acquired by Toronto from Montreal in August 1992 for a 3rd-round draft pick, Lefebvre paired with blueliner Bob Rouse to form an effective shutdown unit. Following the move to Colorado, Lefebvre continued in his stay-at-home role, forming a tandem with Uwe Krupp as the Avalanche won the Stanley Cup in 1996.

THE RESULT Sundin's evolution as a franchise player in Toronto won the deal easily for Fletcher. Although he couldn't play on a Stanley Cup winner with the Leafs, Sundin enjoyed success at the international level, winning a gold medal with Sweden at the 2006 Winter Olympics in Torino.

The transaction paid moderate short-term return for Quebec/Colorado. In addition to receiving Lefebvre's defensive prowess, the team was able to parlay Clark into Lemieux, a controversial player yet a proven playoff performer. He had 12 points in 19 playoff games in the Avalanche's 1996 playoff run.

Salming Over to Sundin

When Mats Sundin heard he was traded, he did what any young and impressionable Swede would have done at the time—he phoned Borje Salming. Salming was a hero to every player in Sweden, the man who went to the NHL in 1973 and proved Swedes could play tough hockey over a long season full of travel and physical demands. He had left the NHL in 1990 and returned home to play for three years, including the 1992 Olympics in Lillehammer. Salming gave Sundin his blessings, telling him he was going to the greatest hockey city in the world. Relieved, Sundin arrived knowing he was capable on ice but unsure how he would replace Clark off ice as one of the most popular players of all time. Sundin, ever graceful, did just that during his stellar career with the Leafs.

JULY 4, 1994

Flames Trade Slapshot for Skater

The Deal [CALGARY FLAMES trade **Al MacInnis** and **a 4th-round draft choice in 1997 (Didier Tremblay)** to the ST. LOUIS BLUES for **Phil Housley** and **a 2nd-round draft choice in 1996 (Steve Begin) and 1997 (John Tripp)**.

"Housley's going to help in the transition game. We're going to play a little bit differently. I hope we can play at the same level." —Dave King

THE DIRT Owner of the hardest shot in the NHL, Al MacInnis struck fear into the hearts of opposing goalies. A first-round draft choice of the Flames in 1981, MacInnis was a mainstay on Calgary's blue line as the team evolved into a Stanley Cup contender during the 1980s. The Flames finally reached the pinnacle of hockey supremacy in 1989, winning their first championship in team history. MacInnis recorded a point in each of the Flames' final 17 post-season games and was named winner of the Conn Smythe Trophy as playoff MVP.

Calgary failed to live up to the playoff expectations in the wake of their Stanley Cup win, however, suffering first round losses in 1990 and 1991. MacInnis, though, achieved great success on a personal level, finishing with 90 and 103 points in those years, respectively, while being named a First Team All-Star on both occasions.

By the time the Flames endured yet another opening round playoff loss in 1994, this at the hands of Pavel Bure and the Vancouver Canucks, the financial landscape of the NHL was changing dramatically at the expense of smaller teams.

Wooden Behemoth

No matter how good a defenceman he was or how many Halls of Fame he has been inducted into, Al MacInnis is first and foremost famous for his shot. He won the hardest shot contest at the NHL skills competition seven times and was feared by puck-blocking defencemen and fully-masked goalies for his "cannonading blast," as Danny Gallivan would have described. But what was truly amazing was that in an era of sophisticated equipment, MacInnis never changed his stick to a composite or one-piece. He always used a wood stick. So for any player who swore he got a harder or faster shot using a laminate, there was always the supreme example, MacInnis, to prove that the new sticks were as much a mental as physical advantage. If MacInnis can blast with wood, so can anyone.

The Canadian dollar was valued approximately 40 per cent lower than its U.S. counterpart, hindering Canadian teams from signing players.

When Blues general manager Ron Caron offered MacInnis a contract worth $13.7 million in U.S. funds (some $19 million Canadian) over four years, the price was simply too steep for the Flames. Calgary general manager Doug Risebrough, forced into making a trade, held out for Housley when Caron offered the less-talented but lower-priced Steve Duchesne. "The organization was determined to get back value for Al MacInnis," said Risebrough. "The organization was determined to be fiscally responsible."

Calgary coach Dave King was left with a lineup drastically different from the one he had in place four months earlier. Defenceman Gary Suter and goalie Mike Vernon were previously packaged in separate trades in which Zarley Zalapski, James Patrick, Michael Nylander, and Steve Chaisson joined the Flames. "I know we're no weaker," said King. "We're in about the same area, but we're going to have a different look. Housley's going to help in the transition game. We're going to play a little bit differently. I hope we can play at the same level."

THE DEBATE MacInnis continued his sharpshooting ways in St. Louis, showing no signs of slowing down even as he approached his mid-thirties. When the Blues acquired Chris Pronger in July 1995, the stage was set for the duo to develop into one of the top defensive pairings in the league. Both men were selected to represent Canada at the 1998 Winter Olympics in Nagano, the first Games that featured participation of NHL players.

In 1998-99, MacInnis led all defencemen with 62 points. For his efforts, he was awarded the Norris Trophy and the sixth All-Star Team recognition of his career, his third on the First Team. The following year the Blues earned their first Presidents' Trophy in franchise history, posting a 51-19-11-1 record. However, regular season success didn't translate into playoff success as St. Louis was upset in the conference quarter-finals by San Jose.

MacInnis and Pronger received Olympic redemption in 2002 when they were part of the Team Canada roster that brought home the country's first gold medal in hockey in 50 years. The next season, 2002-03, was the final year of MacInnis's career. Proving that he was still effective at age 39, he finished tenth in the NHL with 52 assists, once again making his way to the NHL First All-Star Team. An eye injury suffered in a game against Nashville on October 16, 2003, effectively ended MacInnis's career. His marks of 352 assists and 452 points are both career franchise records for a defenceman, which MacInnis accomplished in 613 games with St. Louis.

Although Housley lasted just two seasons in Calgary, he made the most of his opportunity wearing the Flames' sweater. Like MacInnis, Housley posted offensive numbers that were respectable if not impressive. As a Winnipeg Jet, Housley had his best single-season output in 1992-93 with 18 goals and 79 assists. Between 1994 and 1996, he compiled 95 points in 102 games for Calgary. He was traded along with Dan Keczmer to New Jersey on February 26, 1996, for Tommy Albelin, Cale Hulse, and Jocelyn Lemieux.

THE RESULT Given that Risebrough had been backed into a corner, he was unlikely to receive comparable return for an All-Star defenceman of MacInnis's calibre. In fact, MacInnis's salary in his first full season with the Blues nearly equaled the payroll of the entire 1989 Calgary team that won the Stanley Cup. Following the departure of MacInnis, along with Suter and Vernon, very few players remained on the Flames roster from the championship squad—Theo Fleury, Joe Nieuwendyk, Gary Roberts, Jim Peplinski, and Joel Otto. The small-market Flames had difficulty attracting star players in the late 1990s and into the 21st century, and the 1997-98 season marked the beginning of a stretch of seven straight years in which the Flames failed to qualify for the playoffs.

MacInnis established himself as one of the greatest defencemen in Blues' history in nine years with the team. However, the teams on which he played had only moderate playoff success. Following the devastating loss to San Jose in 2000, St. Louis advanced to the conference finals the next year, losing to the eventual Stanley Cup champions, Colorado. It was the only time during MacInnis's St. Louis tenure that the Blues advance to the third round.

In 2007, MacInnis was inducted into the Hockey Hall of Fame in his first year of eligibility.

/// Tripp to Germany

John Tripp was selected by Calgary with a 2nd-round draft choice in 1997 acquired in the trade for Al MacInnis. He had been drafted two years earlier by Colorado but never signed with the team and was eligible once again. Tripp played only briefly in the NHL before embarking on a career in Germany that eventually saw him become a national in 2007. Since then he has played for Germany at every World Championship except 2009, including the 2010 Olympics.

FEBRUARY 9, 1995
LeClair Haunts Habs 'Til End of Time

The Deal | MONTREAL CANADIENS trade **John LeClair, Eric Desjardins,** and **Gilbert Dionne** to the PHILADELPHIA FLYERS for **Mark Recchi** and **a 3rd-round draft choice in 1995 (Martin Hohenberger).**

"The more power-forward kind of guys you can have in this league today, the more it's going to allow you to have success." —Terry Murray

THE DIRT Coming out of the 103-day NHL lockout that canceled the first half of the 1994-95 season, Montreal general manager Serge Savard was searching for an offensive spark for his team. The Habs had finished in the middle of the pack the previous year in goals scored (283, tenth-best out of 26 teams) and had tallied just 13 goals in six games to start the lockout-shortened campaign.

Savard's solution was Mark Recchi, an explosive right-winger who had just turned 27. Four years earlier, in 1990-91, Recchi collected 40 goals and 113 points, winning a Stanley Cup with the Pittsburgh Penguins. He continued to produce at an elite level in Philadelphia, to where he was traded in February 1992 in a deal that sent Rick Tocchet to Pittsburgh, earning a nod as a Second Team All-Star. In his first two full seasons as a Flyer, Recchi compiled totals of 123 and 107 points, respectively, finishing fifth in NHL scoring in 1993-94.

To obtain Recchi, the Canadiens traded three members of their 1993 Stanley Cup-winning team. In LeClair, the club's 2nd-round draft choice in 1987, the

Habs surrendered a 6'3" winger who never lived up to his full potential in Montreal. His greatest moments in a Canadiens uniform came in the third and fourth games of the 1993 finals when he scored both overtime goals in Los Angeles en route to the Stanley Cup.

Eric Desjardins was a solid defenceman who didn't miss any of the team's 166 games in the previous two seasons. He was the first blueliner in NHL history to score a hat trick in the Cup finals, capitalizing on Marty McSorley's famous illegal stick penalty in game two to turn the series in Montreal's favour. Gilbert Dionne, the little brother of Hall of Famer Marcel, was an underachiever who fizzled after his 1991-92 rookie season when he had a decent 34 points in 39 games.

"I'm a little surprised, but I had a feeling that a trade was a possibility," said LeClair. "As you get older you kind of expect more ice time, but there were times when we ran into trouble with ice time. I think every player runs that course." LeClair's new coach in Philadelphia, Terry Murray, was eager to get more size into his team's lineup. "The more power-forward kind of guys you can have in this league today, the more it's going to allow you to have success," he said.

THE DEBATE LeClair cited the Habs' coaching staff's decision to move him to centre instead of his natural wing position as the reason for his lack of productivity

Learning to Skate

Scoring always came easily to John LeClair but skating not so much. As a kid, he could put the puck in the net from everywhere but he labored to make his way across the ice. These problems persisted even in high school when he was at Bellows Free Academy. He failed to make the school team because of his weak skating, but he was dogged enough that by the time he was ready for university he was drafted by Montreal in 1987 and attended the University of Vermont in the fall. He stayed four years and didn't make his NHL debut with the Canadiens until he was nearly 22 years old, but he went on to score 50 goals in a season three straight years with the "Legion of Doom."

in Montreal. He scored in the 1994-95 season opener, then had an eight-game goal drought prior to the trade. When he arrived in Philadelphia, Murray reinserted him on the wing, playing on a line with Eric Lindros and Mikael Renberg. The forward trio became known as the "Legion of Doom," and the unit paid huge dividends for the Flyers. The season ended with Philadelphia finishing first in the Atlantic Division and Lindros winning the Hart Trophy. LeClair finished with 25 goals in 37 games with his new team, and he was named an All-Star for the first time in his career. The Flyers advanced to the conference finals before losing to New Jersey, the eventual Stanley Cup champions.

In 1995-96, LeClair exploded for what would be the first of three consecutive 50-goal seasons. Philadelphia lost to Florida in the conference semi-finals, but LeClair received a measure of success at the international level. He was chosen to represent Team USA at the inaugural World Cup of Hockey and scored six goals and ten points in seven games as the Americans upset Canada to claim the championship. The 1996-97 season saw the Flyers advance to the Stanley Cup finals, LeClair getting the opportunity to earn his second championship ring. But Philadelphia was swept by Steve Yzerman and the Detroit Red Wings.

LeClair played for ten seasons in Philadelphia, registering 333 goals and 643 points in 649 games. He was named an end-of-season All-Star for five straight seasons ending in 1998-99 and twice played for the United States at the Olympics, winning a silver medal in 2002. On August 15, 2005, he signed with Pittsburgh as a free agent.

Desjardins was a durable force on the Flyers blue line for eleven years. He played for Team Canada's entry at the 1996 World Cup and also at the 1998 Olympics in Nagano. His career high in points was set in 1999-2000 when he had 14 goals and 41 assists in 81 games. He retired in the summer of 2006. Dionne played just 22 games for Philadelphia before leaving as a free agent.

THE RESULT Savard's plan to bolster the Canadiens offence backfired. Even with the arrival of Recchi, the Habs finished 22nd out of 26 teams in goals scored in 1994-95. More importantly the Habs finished five games under .500 and missed the playoffs for the first time in 25 years. Recchi was a consistent, solid contributor in the five seasons that he played in Montreal, recording 322 points in 346 regular season games and another 24 points in 21 playoff games. But without a superstar centre like he had in Pittsburgh in Mario Lemieux, or in Philadelphia in Eric Lindros, Recchi didn't post the same offensive totals. Perhaps most frustrating for Habs fans, LeClair played his best against his old team, time and again recording the winning goal or multi-point games which frustrated Montrealers to no end.

Even when Recchi was traded back to Philadelphia late in the 1998-99 season, his 47 points in 61 games played with Montreal still led the Habs in scoring at season's end. The transaction was a clear win for the Flyers.

Austrian Goes to Canada's Junior League

The Flyers selected Austrian Martin Hohenberger with their 3rd-round draft choice in 1995 that they acquired with LeClair. Hohenberger has been noticed by Montreal because he was playing in the WHL, with three teams between 1993 and '97, clearly dedicating himself to being seen by NHL scouts. He went on to the ECHL and played a handful of games in the AHL, but that's as far as he went. Soon after, he returned home to Austria where he played in two Olympics and several more World Championships over the next decade. After retiring early in the 2010-11 season, he became head coach of Graz, a second division team in the Austrian league.

APRIL 3, 1995

Bowman Builds Russian Wings with Fetisov

The Deal [NEW JERSEY DEVILS trade **Slava Fetisov** to the DETROIT RED WINGS for **a 3rd-round draft choice in 1995 (David Gosselin).**

"I'm very happy to go to Detroit. I talked with Scotty Bowman today, and he told me that they traded for me because they want me to play." —Slava Fetisov

THE DIRT The Detroit Red Wings of the early 1990s were evolving into Stanley Cup contenders but had difficulty transferring their regular season success into the post-season. After Detroit was upset by Toronto in the 1993 division semi-finals, Bryan Murray relinquished his dual role as general manager and coach, focusing on the front office, while Scotty Bowman took over behind the bench. When Detroit suffered an opening round upset the following year at the hands of the eighth-seeded San Jose Sharks, Murray was gone altogether.

With defending Hart Trophy winner Sergei Fedorov on the roster and Vyacheslav Kozlov and Vladimir Konstantinov also entrenched in the lineup, Bowman set forth a plan to assemble a five-man unit consisting of players born in the former Soviet Union. A master of his craft who coached a Canadian squad that was thumped by the USSR in the 1981 Canada Cup finals, Bowman had an appreciation for the Russian strategy of employing a cohesive unit in which the three-man forward line and two-man defence pairing were synchronized.

Something for Almost Nothing

David Gosselin was all that the Devils received when they traded Fetisov to Detroit. A 1995 draft choice, Gosselin had been playing in the QMJHL with Sherbrooke, but after four years of junior he was not much closer to making the NHL. He ended up in the IHL and eventually played a few games with the Nashville Predators, but he spent most of his career in the minors until 2003 when he moved to Germany to continue his career. He returned home a few years later to play in the LNAH, a mostly goon league in Quebec which is virtually the lowest rung of pro hockey in North America.

Fetisov's credentials were impeccable. He had captained both the Soviet national team and Central Red Army team in Soviet league play, forming a sound defence pairing with Alexei Kasatonov. A two-time Olympic gold medalist and a seven-time World Championship gold medalist, Fetisov was named the best defenceman at the Worlds on five occasions.

Originally drafted by Montreal in 1978, Fetisov re-entered the draft in 1983 when he was selected by the Devils. But he didn't arrive in the NHL for fully six years. After being stripped of his captaincy early in the 1988-89 season by Red Army coach Viktor Tikhonov, Fetisov declared his intention to play in New Jersey following a Super Series exhibition game between the Devils and the touring Red Army in January 1989.

Fetisov left the team, then returned in April as the squad was preparing for the World Championships. When Tikhonov surprisingly left Fetisov off the roster, teammates Kasatonov, Igor Larionov, Sergei Makarov, and Vladimir Krutov all threatened to boycott the tournament. Tikhonov relented, and the Soviets cruised to the gold medal, winning all ten games by a combined score of 47-16. Three weeks later Fetisov, Larionov, and Makarov were allowed to pursue opportunities in the NHL.

THE DEBATE Towards the end of the 1994-95 season Detroit traded for Fetisov after blueliner Mark Howe suffered a separated shoulder. "I'm very happy to go to

Detroit," said Fetisov when he learned that he would be going to the Motor City. "I talked with Scotty Bowman today, and he told me that they traded for me because they want me to play."

The Red Wings advanced to the Stanley Cup finals but were swept aside by the Devils. Early into the 1995-96 campaign, Detroit traded for Larionov to make the five-man Russian unit complete.

Detroit steamrolled through the regular season, setting an NHL record with 62 wins, two more than the Montreal Canadiens achieved in 1976-77 under Bowman. The Presidents' Trophy winners finished the year 27 points ahead of their closest rival in the standings, Colorado, and were clear favourites to win the Stanley Cup. But after being pushed to seven games in the conference semi-finals against St. Louis, the Red Wings found themselves in a viciously competitive series against the Avalanche. The third-round matchup was marred by a dirty hit from behind by Colorado's Claude Lemieux on Detroit's Kris Draper. The Avalanche prevailed, extending Detroit's championship drought to 41 years.

At the beginning of the 1996-97 season the Red Wings made a major change to their lineup, sending Paul Coffey and Keith Primeau to Hartford for Brendan Shanahan. With extra grit on their roster, Detroit exacted revenge on Colorado in a fight-filled regular season game in March. Wings forward Darren McCarty pummeled Lemieux as retribution for the Draper hit, while Shanahan body-checked Avalanche netminder Patrick Roy who was about to engage Mike Vernon in a goaltender's duel.

Detroit's 6-5 overtime win that night was the catalyst in reinforcing the team's mindset that they could defeat Colorado in a playoff series. As expected, the teams dueled once again in the conference finals in 1997. Detroit won the series in six games, then swept Philadelphia to earn the franchise's first Stanley Cup since 1955. With the victory, Fetisov and Larionov became the seventh and eighth members of the Triple Gold Club which consists of players who have won a Stanley Cup, World Championship and Olympic gold medal.

The celebrations in Detroit were short-lived as Konstantinov and team masseur Sergei Mnatsakanov were seriously injured in a limousine accident six days later. Sustaining serious head injuries and paralysis, Konstantinov was no longer able to play hockey. The Red Wings rallied around their fallen members to repeat as Stanley Cup winners in 1998, wearing a patch with the word "Believe" (in English and Russian) on their sweaters. Yzerman passed the Stanley Cup trophy to a wheelchair-bound Konstantinov to cap the Red Wings' triumph.

The game marked the last of Fetisov's NHL career.

THE RESULT Throughout his three-year career with Detroit, Fetisov, arguably the greatest defenceman in Russian hockey history, proved that he could be a force on the blue line into his late thirties. Upon his retirement, he returned to the Devils as an assistant coach, and the team won another Stanley Cup in 2000. The following year, Fetisov was inducted into the Hockey Hall of Fame.

New Jersey used the draft pick received in the trade to select David Gosselin, who never played a game for the Devils. He signed with Nashville as a free agent on July 1, 1998, eventually playing 13 career games for the Predators.

Fetisov Lucky Under Terrible Circumstances

Although Slava Fetisov was known as a tough-as-nails defenceman who endured the Soviet regime, played across the globe into his forties, and was as physically strong as any player, he suffered three serious traumas during his career that luckily did not hinder his ability to play the game at which he excelled. During the 1978-79 season in the Soviet Union, Fetisov suffered a serious back injury and missed most of the year after being carried off the ice on a stretcher. When he was 26 and the clear star of the Soviet national team, he was involved in a car accident in which his 18-year-old brother, Anatoli, was killed. Even later, after winning the Cup with Detroit in 1997, he was involved in a car accident which ended the career of team-mate Vladimir Konstantinov and team masseur Sergei Mnatsakanov.

APRIL 5, 1995

Captain Kirk Beamed to Island

The Deal [MONTREAL CANADIENS trade **Kirk Muller, Mathieu Schneider,** and **Craig Darby** to the NEW YORK ISLANDERS for **Pierre Turgeon** and **Vladimir Malakhov.**

"I bought a house, and I loved the city. I had no desire to play anywhere else. I'm shocked. But it's a business. I enjoyed it here, but life goes on."
—Kirk Muller

THE DIRT With 15 games remaining in the lockout-shortened 1994-95 season, the Montreal Canadiens had a record of 12-16-5 and were in danger of missing the playoffs for the first time in 25 years. A 5-4 win in Ottawa on April 3 was just the Habs' third victory in 19 road games. Only three teams in the Eastern Conference—Tampa Bay, Ottawa, and the New York Islanders—had fewer goals than Montreal's total of 85.

General manager Serge Savard had traded for Mark Recchi earlier in the season but felt that even more of an offensive boost was necessary to avoid failing to qualify for the post-season for the first time since Jean Béliveau was the captain. Turgeon, a native of Rouyn, Quebec, was just two years removed from a 1992-93 campaign during which he scored 58 goals and 132 points for the Islanders. He immediately became the team's top-line centre, inserted between Recchi and Vincent Damphousse. "Making the playoffs is always a priority," said Savard. "There's no way this team is going to throw in the towel. We're not going to lose games so we can get a better draft pick."

Kirk Muller was devastated to leave Montreal. Eight months earlier, he had been named the 13th captain in Habs history after Guy Carbonneau was traded to St. Louis. "I loved to play here," said Muller. "I bought a house, and I loved the city. I had no desire to play anywhere else. I'm shocked. But it's a business. I enjoyed it here, but life goes on."

On the other hand, Schneider, who had started the season in a contract dispute with the team, welcomed the opportunity to play in his native state of New York. "I'm nervous, and I'm excited," he said. "I'm excited about going back to the U.S. but sad to be leaving friends. I have mixed emotions, but I look at it as a new start."

THE DEBATE Turgeon's impact on the Montreal lineup was immediate as he collected eleven goals and 20 points in 15 games to close out the year. But the team finished just 6-7-2 over that stretch, and Savard's immediate goal of making the playoffs was unsuccessful.

The following season a major shakeup occurred when Patrick Roy was traded to Colorado. Mike Keane, who had replaced Muller as captain, accompanied Roy to the Avalanche in the deal, Turgeon inheriting the "C." Turgeon received an invitation to play in the 1996 NHL All-Star game in Boston. Two months later at the closing ceremonies of the Montreal Forum, he symbolically carried the torch that was passed to him by a generation of Canadiens' captains. The ritual was symbolic of the Habs' motto which is posted in their dressing room: "To you from failing hands we throw the torch, be yours to hold it high," taken from the poem "In Flanders Fields" by John McRae. Turgeon finished the season with 38 goals and 96 points. His 17 power-play goals ranked eighth in the NHL.

But as Montreal returned to the playoffs, only to lose to the New York Rangers in six games, Turgeon was made the scapegoat. Fans and media accused him of coasting through the series, despite the fact that he had six points in as many games. Critics said that Turgeon didn't deserve the captaincy and inherited the role only because team president Ronald Corey wanted the honour to be held by a

French-Canadian. On October 29, 1996, Turgeon was traded to St. Louis with Rory Fitzpatrick and Craig Conroy for Shayne Corson, Murray Baron, and a draft pick.

Vladimir Malakhov, a native of the former Soviet Union, was a skilled defenceman who had already won a World Championship (1990) and Olympic gold medal (1992) prior to joining the NHL with the Islanders. For just over four seasons he was a steady presence on the Montreal blue line, collecting 141 points and 287 penalty minutes in 283 games for the Canadiens. On March 1, 2000, Malakhov was traded to New Jersey in a deal that saw Sheldon Souray end up in Montreal. The Devils won the Stanley Cup that summer, completing Malakhov's membership in the Triple Gold Club.

Muller's time on Long Island was short-lived. After playing for the Islanders for just 27 games in parts of two seasons, he was involved in a three-way transaction with Toronto and Ottawa on January 23, 1996. The end result saw Muller end up with the Leafs; forwards Martin Straka and Ken Belanger went to the Islanders; and, Ottawa and the Islanders swapped the first two defencemen taken in the 1995 draft, Bryan Berard and Wade Redden.

Two months later Schneider, who had played a total of 78 games for the Islanders, was packaged in a trade with Toronto that returned former Leafs captain Wendel Clark to the team that originally drafted him. In return, the Islanders received defenceman prospect Kenny Jonsson and also Toronto's first-round draft pick in 1997.

/// Triple Gold Malakhov

Vladimir Malakhov was one of the players Montreal acquired for Muller. Malakhov is a member of the Triple Gold Club. In all, he played for five NHL teams before retiring in 2006 at age 37, but it was his four full seasons (and parts of two others) in Montreal that were his best. Drafted by the Islanders in 1989, he was later traded four times during his career. With the Soviet Union/Russia, he also won a bronze medal at the 2002 Olympics and at the 1991 World Championship. He played at the 1991 Canada Cup and 1996 World Cup of Hockey as well.

THE RESULT The trade didn't satisfy Montreal's immediate goals of advancing far in the playoffs, and the Habs ran Turgeon out of town after only one full season. But the Canadiens reaped bigger rewards in the long-term by trading Malakhov for Souray. With one of the hardest shots in the NHL, Souray became a power-play specialist on the Habs' blue line for five years, netting 19 goals with the man advantage in 2006-07.

For the Islanders, the return on the transaction can be measured by the acquisition of Jonsson and the Leafs first-round pick in the deal for Schneider and Clark. Jonsson played 597 games over nine solid years on Long Island before joining the Swedish Elite League, while the Islanders selected Roberto Luongo with the draft choice.

Captain to Coach Kirk

Kirk Muller started an interest in coaching once his playing days were over. He began as head coach for Queen's University in Kingston, his birthplace, and after one year he was named assistant coach of the Canadiens. After five seasons in this capacity, he took the next step by becoming the head coach of Nashville's farm team, the Milwaukee Admirals, but early in the 2011-12 season, when Carolina got off to a rough start, the Hurricanes fired Paul Maurice and hired Captain Kirk, who has now coached the 'Canes for nearly two years. The team, though, has missed the playoffs both years.

JULY 27, 1995
One for One, Pronger for Shanny

The Deal [HARTFORD WHALERS trade **Chris Pronger**
to the ST. LOUIS BLUES for **Brendan Shanahan.**

"I don't understand what happened between Brendan and Mike, and I don't really care. Whatever happened made a very, very good player available." —Jim Rutherford

THE DIRT Coming out of the 1994-95 lockout-shortened season, the Hartford Whalers had not made the playoffs in three seasons and had not won a post-season series in nine years. General manager Jim Rutherford was eager to obtain a top-line forward who would make his team competitive on ice and could drive ticket sales off it. The top scorer on the team was Andrew Cassels who had just 37 points in 46 games played and was clearly not the man for the job.

After unsuccessfully pursuing Winnipeg Jets superstar Teemu Selanne, Rutherford landed Brendan Shanahan from the Blues. The transaction surprised many people in hockey circles, not only because of the star magnitude of the players involved, but because Hartford, a franchise that lost $11.5 million the previous year, was responsible for all but $1 million of the remainder of Shanahan's contract, valued at $10.8 million over three years.

"What we needed to do to improve our team was add an impact player," Rutherford told *The Courant* newspaper. "Shanahan is an impact player, a proven star, in exchange for a guy we're still waiting to be a star." Shanahan's highest single-season production had come in 1993-94 when he scored 52 goals and 102 points, good for eighth in NHL scoring and a selection as a First Team All-Star.

But the right-winger had entered Blues coach and general manager Mike Keenan's doghouse, by virtue of Keenan criticizing Shanahan's work ethic. The relationship soured when Shanahan's linemate Craig Janney was traded to San Jose in March 1995. "I don't understand what happened between Brendan and Mike, and I don't really care," Rutherford said. "Whatever happened made a very, very good player available. Their personalities collided."

In Pronger, Rutherford dealt the player for whom the Whalers traded up in the 1993 Entry Draft to be able to select him 2nd overall in a series of manoeuvres made by Brian Burke, the general manager at the time. Then 20 years old, Pronger had fallen out of favour with both Hartford management and fans. "It feels good they've got me at that same level as Shanahan," Pronger said. "Obviously, Shanahan was an important thing missing from our team last year. It hurt. A power forward who could score. We lost games 3-2, 2-1. A goal a game makes a difference."

THE DEBATE Shanahan's 1995 playoffs came to an abrupt end when he suffered an ankle injury in the fifth game of St. Louis' opening round series against Vancouver. He recovered to score 44 goals and 78 points in the 1995-96 season, although his performance alone wasn't enough to get the Whalers into the playoffs. In September, Shanahan scored six points in seven games for Team Canada at the World Cup of Hockey.

The NHL's 1996-97 campaign was just five days old when Shanahan was moved to Detroit in a trade that brought Paul Coffey and Keith Primeau to Hartford. At age 35, Coffey was well past his prime and played only 20 games in a Whalers uniform before being shipped to Philadelphia for Kevin Haller. Primeau, a powerful 6'5" centre, stayed with the franchise for three seasons, including the club's first two years in Carolina when the team relocated to become the Hurricanes.

Primeau was dealt in January 2000 to Philadelphia in a swap in which Carolina obtained Rod Brind'Amour. A consistent scoring threat with a reputation for being among the most fit players in the game, Brind'Amour went on to have a nine-and-a-half year career in Carolina. He inherited the captaincy in 2005-06 upon the retirement of Ron Francis. That season ended with Brind'Amour hoisting the Stanley Cup as the Hurricanes outlasted Edmonton in a seven-game series. Brind'Amour also won the first of two consecutive Frank J. Selke Trophies that year as the league's best defensive forward. He announced his retirement from the league on June 30, 2010, after playing in 1,484 career games.

In St. Louis, Pronger developed into the elite-level defenceman that he was projected to be when he was chosen as the 2nd overall draft pick behind Alexandre Daigle in 1993. He also garnered the attention of Team Canada management, earning an invitation to play at the 1997 World Championship where he helped the team win a gold medal. Pronger also earned a spot on the 1998 Olympic team, as did his counterpart in the trade, Shanahan.

The 1999-2000 season represented a career year for Pronger as he won both the Norris Trophy as league's best defenceman and the Hart Trophy as the NHL's most valuable player. The accomplishment marked the first time since 1972 that

/// The End of the Line?

Where Chris Pronger goes, so goes victory. Few players have had an impact on their team at every level the way the giant defenceman had during his career, a career that seems to have ended like so many in the modern era—because of post-concussion syndrome. On October 24, 2011, he was hit in the eye by the errant stick of Mikhail Grabovski. Although he returned to action, he took a hit from Martin Hanzal on November 19, and that was the last time he played. Doctors told him his eye was vulnerable, and he felt he lost that sense of "seeing in the back of his head," as it were. But even if the eye weren't an issue, he can't even do light workouts without suffering headaches. Destined for the Hockey Hall of Fame, Pronger has had to leave the game before his time.

The Great Decider

While Brendan Shanahan was both a great scorer and tough hombre on ice, he has proved since retiring that his passion for the game extends to its very core. "Shanny" was named the NHL's new director of player discipline on June 1, 2011, taking over for Colin Campbell, and since then he has both tried to decrease the violence in the game as well as experienced firsthand the difficulty of a job in which he can never make everyone happy. But perhaps his greatest innovation was to create videos for many of his supplemental discipline decisions to explain his rationale behind suspending a player and trying to come up with a consistent interpretation of plays and incidents to at least make the process transparent and, hopefully, clearer to players, teams, and the general public.

a blueliner won the Hart Trophy. Bobby Orr took the honours that season. Pronger's Blues had won 51 regular season games, earning 114 points en route to the Presidents' Trophy, but the team was upset by the San Jose Sharks in a seven-game opening round playoff series.

Pronger played eight full seasons in St. Louis. Coming out of the lockout that wiped out the 2004-05 campaign, the Blues had salary cap concerns after tendering qualifying offers to Pronger, Keith Tkachuk, and Doug Weight. In a cost-cutting move, St. Louis traded Pronger to Edmonton for Eric Brewer, Jeff Woywitka, and Doug Lynch on August 2, 2005.

THE RESULT As expected when two players of such high quality are exchanged, the deal benefited both teams. Pronger enjoyed the greater success on an individual level, winning two trophies in 2000 and earning four All-Star selections during his tenure in St. Louis. However, the Blues had only moderate playoff success, never advancing past the third round.

On Hartford/Carolina's side, the ability to eventually parlay Shanahan into Brind'Amour paid off in the long run as Brind'Amour's grit and leadership paved the way for a Stanley Cup win.

OCTOBER 24, 1995
Wings Get Professor of Cup Knowledge

The Deal [SAN JOSE SHARKS trade **Igor Larionov** and **future considerations** to the DETROIT RED WINGS for **Ray Sheppard**.

"Igor's a complete, all-around player we can use in all situations, including the power play and penalty-killing. He was also a big part in the Sharks' success in the playoffs the past two years." —Scotty Bowman

THE DIRT The Detroit Red Wings entered the 1995-96 season in a period of unrest and uncertainty. After consecutive first-round playoff exits in 1993 and 1994, the Wings advanced to the Stanley Cup finals in 1995 where they were promptly swept by the New Jersey Devils. Long-serving captain Steve Yzerman was the subject of trade rumours, his hometown Ottawa Senators at the top of the list of potential suitors.

The Red Wings, already deep down the middle, fueled the Yzerman trade speculation by acquiring another centre in Larionov. Detroit coach Scotty Bowman was influential in trading for Larionov as the Wings' bench boss completed the assembly of his five-man Russian unit. Larionov joined Sergei Fedorov and Vyacheslav Kozlov on a forward line with Vladimir Konstantinov and Vyacheslav Fetisov as a defensive pairing.

"Igor's a complete, all-around player we can use in all situations, including the power play and penalty-killing," Bowman noted. "He was also a big part in the Sharks' success in the playoffs the past two years." A huge part of San Jose's success had been a monumental upset win in 1994 when the eighth-seeded Sharks toppled the Red Wings in seven games in the conference quarter-finals. Larionov had led San Jose in scoring during that playoff run with 18 points in 14 games.

Larionov harboured some resentment towards the Sharks organization after they dropped his good friend and long-time Russian teammate Sergei Makarov from the roster. "The chemistry was gone," said Larionov. "For the last year and a half, I have not been happy with the way the team is going. The last thing was Sergei Makarov being released. He was part of the team; he was a veteran player."

Sheppard, a one-time 50-goal scorer, was brought in to San Jose's lineup to try to ignite the team's offence. The Red Wings deemed him expendable because his contract was set to expire and right-winger Dino Ciccarelli had already signed a long-term deal. "It was a shock," said Sheppard. "I knew I would be traded. I didn't think it would be this early in the season. I hope I can bring some experience and hopefully add some scoring punch."

THE DEBATE Larionov was certainly no stranger to his fellow countrymen in Detroit's lineup, especially Fetisov. The two veterans were teammates on the 1981 Soviet team that crushed Canada—a squad coached by Bowman—by a score of 8-1 in the final game of the Canada Cup. Together Larionov and Fetisov won two Olympic gold medals (1984 and 1988) and four World Championships (1982, 1983, 1986, and 1989). But more importantly, the two men, along with Makarov, Alexei Kasatonov, and Vladimir Krutov, were instrumental in beginning the exodus of players out of the Soviet Union and into the NHL. The long-time Central Red Army teammates joined their respective NHL clubs shortly after the 1989 World Championship.

Detroit racked up victories at an incredible pace during the 1995-96 campaign, quelling the Yzerman trade talk once and for all. The five-man Russian unit was instrumental in leading the Red Wings to a 62-win season, setting an NHL record in the process. Larionov registered 21 goals and 71 points in 69 games for his new club, but the Wings were unceremoniously bounced by Colorado in the conference finals.

The Red Wings exacted a measure of revenge on their nemesis the Avalanche with a six-game victory in the third round of the playoffs in 1997. Larionov's best outing of the series came in game four when he scored twice in a 6-0 rout. Late in the regular season, Larionov had shown a rare pugilistic side to his game when he fought Peter Forsberg in a brawl-filled encounter.

For Detroit, the confidence boost in toppling Colorado gave the team all the momentum they needed to sweep Philadelphia in the finals. As the Stanley Cup celebrations kicked off at Joe Louis Arena, Larionov was the first player to accept the coveted trophy from Yzerman, the captain. In August, Larionov, Fetisov, and Kozlov brought the Stanley Cup to Russia for the first time in the 104-year history of the hallowed silverware.

Detroit repeated as champions the following year, sweeping the Washington Capitals in the finals. The Red Wings spent the 1997-98 rallying around their teammate Konstantinov, whose career had been ended as a result of injuries suffered in a limousine accident. Larionov played an additional two years in Detroit before signing with Florida as a free agent in July 2000, joining countryman Pavel Bure in the lineup. But Larionov's time with the Panthers lasted just 26 games

A Man of Principles

"It's a wonder our wives manage to give birth," might well be the most pithy quote from a hockey player. Spoken by Igor Larionov at the height of the Cold War, he was referring to the near cruel treatment the Soviet hockey team was subjected to at the hands of their dictatorial coach, Viktor Tikhonov, who forced players to live in army barracks eleven months of the year while they trained full-time for the World Championships and Olympics. Larionov was a brave and rare outspoken critic of Soviet tactics, and he could do so only because he was such a great player. Any lesser and he would have been exiled, but he stood for what he believed in, and those principles eventually got him to the NHL.

before he was traded back to the Red Wings, before the New Year, for Yan Golubovsky. Larionov earned one final Stanley Cup with Detroit, in 2002.

Sheppard had a productive output of 46 points in 51 games with San Jose after the trade. But with a glut of right-wingers, Sharks general manager Dean Lombardi traded Sheppard to Florida in a deal for draft picks. The trade benefited Sheppard as he went from a non-playoff team to a Panthers squad that advanced to the 1996 Stanley Cup finals.

THE RESULT Bowman's masterful assembly of the Russian quintet paved the way to consecutive championships for the Red Wings in 1997 and 1998, while Larionov and Fedorov also enjoyed a third Stanley Cup in 2002. Despite being six years older than Sheppard, Larionov had the longer career. He was inducted into the Hockey Hall of Fame in 2008.

After leaving San Jose, Sheppard was a consistent goal scorer in Florida, but not at the 30- or 50-goal pace that Detroit fans had been accustomed to seeing. The transaction was a clear win for the Red Wings.

Wine List

An oenophile as well as Hall of Famer, Larionov boasted of his nightly ritual of two glasses of red wine before bed. In retirement, he has kept in contact with the grape, as it were, establishing his own winery and producing labels such as Slapshot and Triple Overtime, the latter a self-referential nod to his game-winning goal in the third extra period of game three of the 2002 Stanley Cup finals to give Detroit a 2-1 series lead over Carolina. The Wings won the Cup in five games.

DECEMBER 6, 1995

Bad Game Puts Roy on Plane to Denver

The Deal [MONTREAL CANADIENS trade **Patrick Roy** and **Mike Keane** to the COLORADO AVALANCHE for **Jocelyn Thibault, Martin Rucinsky,** and **Andrei Kovalenko.**

"I didn't put any team first. It was important to be ready to go anywhere. Now that it's done, I've got to admit Colorado was my first choice. I'm happy to be part of the Avalanche." —Patrick Roy

THE DIRT The contributions that Patrick Roy made over the course of a decade with the Montreal Canadiens cannot be overstated. As a 20-year-old rookie in 1986, he took the hockey world by storm with a Conn Smythe Trophy performance in the playoffs, all but single-handedly leading a team loaded with young players to the Stanley Cup. Roy repeated those heroics seven years later, backstopping the Habs in 1993 to their 24th Cup title in a miraculous post-season run that included ten consecutive overtime victories.

But harder times fell on the Canadiens franchise soon after. In the 48-game schedule of 1994-95—shortened because of a lockout—the team missed the playoffs for the first time in a quarter century. The situation was compounded at the start of the following season as Montreal lost each of its first four games. President Ronald Corey made swift changes at the general manager and coaching positions, appointing Rejean Houle and Mario Tremblay, respectively.

With Tremblay behind the bench, the crisis appeared to have been averted.

The team surged to a 12-7-0 record before hitting a late November slump. Heading into a home game against the Western Conference-leading Detroit Red Wings on December 2, 1995, the time was right for the Habs to show their mettle. The game, however, proved to be an unmitigated disaster for Montreal. As Detroit pounded the Canadiens with goal after goal, Tremblay refused to replace Roy. The two had never seen eye to eye, and for the coach to humiliate Roy, who was clearly having a bad night, was both insulting and provoking. The high-flying Wings led 7-1 nearly midway through the second period when Roy made a routine save off Sergei Fedorov.

A merciless Forum crowd gave Roy sarcastic applause, to which the goaltender retaliated by raising his arms in equally-mocking triumph. When Roy was finally replaced with backup Pat Jablonski, he angrily walked over to Corey—who was sitting in his usual place behind the Canadiens' bench—to say that he'd played his last game in Montreal. Then he glared at Tremblay before storming to the dressing room.

Following the game, which ended in an 11-1 embarrassment, Roy was suspended by the team. The two-time playoff MVP asked to be traded to a contender, and his wish was granted four days later. "I didn't put any team first," said Roy on his way to Denver. "It was important to be ready to go anywhere. Now that it's done, I've got to admit Colorado was my first choice. I'm happy to be part of the Avalanche."

//// Only One Team Canada Sweater

Incredibly, Roy played only one event internationally for Canada. He never went to a U20 tournament, never attended an end-of-season World Championship, never played in a Canada Cup or World Cup. He did play at the 1998 Olympics, though, losing the final two games which counted the most, the first in a shootout to the Czechs, the next in the bronze-medal game.

THE DEBATE Roy had faced his new Colorado teammates several times previously as provincial rivals during the franchise's days as the Quebec Nordiques up to the 1994-95 season. Now an ally of superstars such as Joe Sakic and Peter Forsberg, Roy only added greater depth to a team poised to win a championship.

The Avalanche cruised to a Pacific Division title with 104 points, 25 points better than their next closest team, the Calgary Flames. Colorado was runner-up to Detroit for the Presidents' Trophy, but the Red Wings' phenomenal 62-win season had the Avalanche beaten in a wide margin.

In the 1996 playoffs, however, Roy flashed the same brand of cockiness that he did during his Cup-winning years in Montreal. Case in point, when he winked at Los Angeles's Tomas Sandstrom in 1993 after making a save. The conference semi-finals pitted the Avalanche against the Blackhawks where Roy engaged in a trash-talk war with Chicago forward Jeremy Roenick.

Responding to media questions about taunting from Roenick, Roy famously responded: "I can't really hear what Jeremy says because I have my two Stanley Cup rings plugging my ears." After eliminating the Blackhawks, Colorado went on to outlast the first-place Red Wings in the next round. In the finals against the Florida Panthers, Roy completed his first season in Denver with a 1-0 triple-over-time shutout as Uwe Krupp scored the Stanley Cup-winning goal to complete a four-game sweep.

Throughout his time in Colorado, Roy continued to play at an elite level. On October 17, 2000, he recorded his 448th career regular season victory, breaking a long-standing mark that had been held by Terry Sawchuk (since broken by Martin Brodeur). The Avalanche faced the defending Stanley Cup champion New Jersey Devils in the 2001 finals. Trailing 3-2 in the series, Colorado staved off elimination with a 4-0 shutout performance by Roy in game six. After the Avalanche's win in the seventh game, Roy—coming off a 16-7 playoff run with four shutouts—was named the Conn Smythe Trophy winner for an unprecedented third time in his career.

Roy retired two years later, finishing with 551 career victories and 66 shutouts.

Improbable Roy

Roy's rise to the top of the NHL heap was meteoric, to say the least. After being drafted in 1984 while playing with the lowly Granby Bisons of the QMJHL, he was called up to play one game with Montreal in 1984-85 and ended up leading Sherbrooke to an unlikely Calder Cup victory in the AHL. The next year, he played his way into the starter's role in Montreal and took the team to an even more unlikely Stanley Cup. He was named Conn Smythe Trophy winner and was soon nicknamed "Saint Patrick" for his incredible playoffs. After his retirement, he turned to coaching and led the Quebec Remparts, the team he owned, to a Memorial Cup in 2006, and in the summer of 2013 he was named head coach of the Colorado Avalanche, the team he led to two Stanley Cup wins. Incroyable.

He was inducted into the Hockey Hall of Fame in his first year of eligibility, in 2006.

In Mike Keane, the Avalanche picked up a tenacious, penalty-killing forward with strong leadership attributes. A member of the 1996 Cup-winning team, he played 136 games in Colorado before signing with the New York Rangers as a free agent.

THE RESULT A mistake by Tremblay, a rookie coach, ultimately led to the departure of a Canadiens legend. With the circumstances of the fateful Wings-Habs 1995 game occurring so rapidly, and with every team knowing that Roy was looking to be traded, it was all but impossible for Montreal to receive fair return.

Thibault, just shy of 21 when the trade was made, was in the unenviable position of playing in Roy's shadow. Three years later, he was sent to Chicago in a deal involving goalie Jeff Hackett.

Rucinsky became a mainstay on the forward lines, compiling 297 points in 432 career games with Montreal. On the other hand, Kovalenko was traded to Edmonton before the start of the 1996-97 season.

Roy, with another pair of Cup rings earned in Colorado, probably can't hear Tremblay either, but the message was clear. Montreal lost this trade as it had never done before in nearly one hundred years of the franchise's existence.

DECEMBER 19, 1995

Flames Get Franchise Face with Iggy

The Deal [CALGARY FLAMES trade **Joe Nieuwendyk** to the DALLAS STARS for **Jarome Iginla** and **Corey Millen**.

"While we feel Jarome would have been a major part of our future, he was not likely to participate for us for at least the next two years." —Jim Lites

THE DIRT The Flames entered the 1995 playoffs amidst great optimism, having finished third in the Western Conference some 13 points in the standings above their first-round opponents, the San Jose Sharks. But Calgary couldn't hold a 3-2 series lead and lost a heartbreaking seventh game in overtime thanks to a goal by the Sharks' Ulf Dahlen.

General manager Doug Risebrough was in the hot seat. Still reeling from the effects of the disastrous Doug Gilmour trade three years earlier, Risebrough was under pressure not only to end the Flames playoff series winless drought—extended into six seasons—but also to sign captain Joe Nieuwendyk and star forward Theo Fleury. The two fan favourites were among the small number of the few remaining players from the 1989 Stanley Cup-winning team.

As the 1995-96 season started, Fleury signed a contract after initially refusing to report to training camp. But Nieuwendyk decided to sit out when he and Risebrough were unable to come to terms on a new deal. With new coach Pierre

/// "Iggy! Iggy!"

Not only has Jarome Iginla had a Hall of Fame career in the NHL, he has figured prominently in two Olympic gold medal victories for Canada. As a young star in 2002, he produced a break-out performance at Salt Lake, scoring two goals in the decisive 5-2 win over the U.S. in the final game. Then, in Vancouver in 2010, he made the pass from the corner to Sidney Crosby for the golden goal in overtime, again against the Americans, for a 3-2 victory.

Page behind the bench, the Flames stumbled at first, winning just one of their first 12 games of the new season. Newly-appointed vice president Al Coates fired Risebrough and assumed the general manager's role himself.

Coates eventually found a trading partner in Dallas, making the transaction for Iginla just over a week after new Stars owner Thomas Hicks replaced Norm Green. Hicks was eager to obtain more marquee players—and more fans—by spending additional money on the team, in stark contrast to Green's cost-conscious habits. "The biggest thing is, Dallas is making a commitment to me," said Nieuwendyk after learning of the deal. "I've come to terms on a new five-year deal. That's a big positive for me—to show that commitment. Modano's there, the Hatchers, Dave Gagner's there. Hopefully we can make some moves."

THE DEBATE Coming to Calgary in the deal was Iginla, a junior star with the Kamloops Blazers who won rare back-to-back Memorial Cups, in 1994 and 1995. In the latter year, Iginla was named the winner of the George Parsons Trophy as the tournament's most sportsmanlike player. "While we feel Jarome would have been a major part of our future, he was not likely to participate for us for at least the next two years," Stars president Jim Lites explained. "This trade serves to make our club better immediately."

The trade took place just one week prior to the start of the World Junior Championship in Boston. Iginla went on to have a phenomenal tournament, leading all players with 12 points in six games and getting the nod as the top forward. Canada went a perfect 6-0-0 on the way to its fourth consecutive gold medal. Iginla made his NHL debut during the 1996 playoffs, suiting up in two of Calgary's games as they were swept in the first round by Chicago.

Iginla played in all 82 games in his rookie season of 1996-97. He scored 21 goals and 50 points and was a finalist for the Calder Trophy, being out-voted by Islanders defenceman Bryan Berard. Iginla was also named to the NHL All-Rookie Team. Over the next several years, the Flames struggled on the ice. Facing the hardships of a small-market Canadian team, Calgary consistently finished out of the playoffs.

But Iginla—with a combination of hockey skills and congenial personality—became the face of the franchise. In 2001-02, he won the both the Rocket Richard Trophy and Art Ross Trophy by virtue of his league-leading totals in goals (52) and points (96). In the closest Hart Trophy voting in the history of the award for most valuable player, Iginla and Jose Theodore finished tied in voting points, but Theodore earned the award based on having more first-place votes.

In the 2004 playoffs, Calgary not only won its first post-season series in 15 years but embarked on an unexpected run to the Stanley Cup finals. The Flames battled the Tampa Bay Lightning for hockey supremacy. Iginla registered a goal, an assist, and a fight—a Gordie Howe Hat Trick—in game three. The scrap came against Lightning superstar Vincent Lecavalier in a heralded moment of emotion. Ultimately the Flames had their Cup dreams dashed in the decisive seventh game in Tampa. Iginla's 13 goals in 24 games led all playoff scorers.

By the time Iginla was traded to Pittsburgh in 2013, he left as the franchise's all-time leader in seasons played, games played, goals, and points.

In Dallas, the Stars' new owner Hicks held his promise of icing a competitive team, beginning with Nieuwendyk. Pat Verbeek soon joined the lineup, followed by Darryl Sydor. The team evolved into Stanley Cup contenders with the acquisitions of goalie Ed Belfour, and the prize of the 1998 free agent market, Brett Hull.

The Stars marched to their first Stanley Cup victory in team history in 1999. Nieuwendyk scored eleven playoff goals, six of them game-winners, leading all players in both categories. For his efforts, he was awarded the Conn Smythe Trophy.

THE RESULT Few players in the history of team sports have become as instrumental to a single franchise as Iginla was to Calgary. For many years, he was arguably the only reason fans bought tickets to Flames games at the Saddledome. Coates' first major trade was clearly his best one.

The Stars, on the other hand, had no regrets about giving up a prospect who turned out to be a superstar. They acquired a proven Cup-winner in Nieuwendyk, a veteran who eventually led them to a championship and later became the team's general manager.

When a trade benefits both teams, it's difficult to say that either side lost.

// Winning, Winning Everywhere

Joe Nieuwendyk is one of only seven players to win the Stanley Cup with three teams (and Jack Marshall did it with four), but he is one of only three to win in three decades (along with Claude Lemieux and Mark Recchi). Nieuwendyk won first with Calgary in 1989, then with Dallas in 1999, and then again with New Jersey in 2003. Incredibly, he was overlooked entirely at the 1984 draft and was chosen by Calgary a year later only because he had a fine season with Cornell University in 1984-85. He was a prolific scorer with the Big Red, scoring nearly a goal a game and two points a game during his three years. He shares with Ken Dryden the distinction of being the first players to have their numbers retired by the school, Nieuwendyk's 25 hanging beside Dryden's number 1 in the rafters.

FEBRUARY 7, 1996

Finnish Flash to Ducks Forever

The Deal WINNIPEG JETS trade **Teemu Selanne, Marc Chouinard,** and **a 4th-round draft choice in 1996 (Kim Staal)** to the MIGHTY DUCKS OF ANAHEIM for **Oleg Tverdovsky, Chad Kilger,** and **a 3rd-round draft choice in 1996 (Per-Anton Lundstrom).**

"Teemu is a tremendous person with a lot of character. But what we're getting back is two future stars who are playing in the NHL now and contributing." —John Paddock

THE DIRT As the Winnipeg Jets bled financial red, team owner and president Barry Shenkarow was left with no option but to sell the team. Businessmen Richard Burke and Steven Gluckstern bought the Jets early in the 1995-96 season, announcing in December that the franchise would be relocated to Phoenix for the start of the next season.

Less than two months later, the Jets decided to shape the future of the Arizona-bound team by trading for a pair of blue-chip prospects in Tverdovsky and Kilger. But the price in giving up their marquee player, Selanne, was astronomically high. Angry Winnipeg fans, already feeling jilted that their hockey team was moving south of the border, were even more livid that their leading scorer would no longer be on the Jets' roster for the final 31 games of the year.

"Teemu is a tremendous person with a lot of character," said Winnipeg general manager John Paddock. "But what we're getting back is two future stars who are playing in the NHL now and contributing. I knew I was going to make a very big move and I lost some sleep over it."

Selanne endeared himself to Winnipeg fans during his rookie campaign of 1992-93 when he shattered the records for goals (76) and points (132) by a first-year player, unanimously winning the Calder Trophy by earning all 50 first-place votes. He was not only named to the NHL All-Rookie Team but also to the NHL First All-Star team. An Achilles tendon injury limited him to just 51 games in his sophomore season, although he still registered 54 points. Throughout the lockout-shortened 1994-95 campaign as well as the first four months of the following year, he continued his better than point-per-game pace. Selanne was eighth in the league in scoring with 72 points in 51 games at the time he was dealt.

Defenceman Tverdovsky, the second-overall pick in the 1994 draft, was stunned by the move. "We were a little in shock," he admitted. "We were called into the coach's office, and when he told us, we thought he was kidding, but he wasn't." Kilger, a 6'4" centre, was projected to bring some muscle into the Jets' lineup. "Chad is a big, strong centre with enormous potential," said Paddock. "He is a quality player and a quality individual who will be a great addition to our club."

THE DEBATE Upon arriving in Anaheim, Selanne was placed on a line with Paul Kariya at left wing and Steve Rucchin at centre. The pairing of Selanne and Kariya was instantly one of the most dangerous combinations in the league, and both players ended the year eclipsing 100 points.

/// Not that Staal

The draft choice that went to Anaheim in the deal first belonged to Toronto, then the Jets, Anaheim, and finally Montreal. The Habs selected a Danish player named Kim Staal. To NHL fans, that name means nothing, really, but to international fans, it is a name encountered annually at the World Championship. Since the Danes returned to the top pool in 2003, Staal has participated in every World tournament except 2012, and while they have never come close to winning a medal, they have managed to stay in the top division.

Wise Man Plays On

If one is to believe Teemu Selanne, he has been on borrowed time since 2007 after winning the Cup with Anaheim and scoring 48 goals in the regular season and becoming, at 37, the oldest player in league history to reach the 45-goal mark. That summer, he decided he was not going to play again. But before retiring, he decided to come back, in January 2008, and he averaged a point a game down the stretch. Every year since, a year older, he has waited until the summer to decide if he would play another year, and every year he has returned to play as well if not better than previous years. In 2011-12, when he had 26 goals, he became, at age 41, the oldest player to reach even the 20-goal plateau.

In 1996-97, Selanne's first full season in Anaheim, the man nicknamed "The Finnish Flash" scored 51 goals and 109 points to finish runner-up to Mario Lemieux for the scoring championship. Selanne's linemate Kariya finished in third place. At season's end, Selanne earned the first of what would be three consecutive All-Star selections at right wing.

The following year saw Selanne's point production drop, largely due to the absence of his left-winger. Kariya missed the first two months of the year because of a contract dispute, then suffered a season-ending concussion in January 1998 after taking a cross-check from Gary Suter. Selanne, however, who replaced Kariya as captain on an interim basis, still led the NHL with 52 goals. He also won a bronze medal with Finland at the Winter Olympics in Nagano, despite not playing in the bronze-medal game against Canada.

The 1998-99 season saw both Selanne and Kariya finish over the 100-point mark again. Selanne's 47 goals, tops in the league, earned him the inaugural Maurice "Rocket" Richard Trophy. Selanne's first stint with Anaheim ended in March 2001 when he was dealt to San Jose for Jeff Friesen, Steve Shields, and a second-round draft choice. After playing just over two years with the Sharks, plus one season in Colorado, Selanne returned to the Ducks, signing as a free agent on August 22, 2005. Coming out of the lockout, new Anaheim general manager Brian Burke was aggressively building a Cup contender, having signed defenceman Scott Niedermayer earlier in the month.

In 2007, Selanne reached the pinnacle of his career. Playing on a line with Andy McDonald and Chris Kunitz, Selanne won his first Stanley Cup just days before his 37th birthday. The Ducks' all-time franchise leader in almost every offensive category, Selanne continued to play with the Ducks, but as he got older he waited until the summer to decide his fate for the following year. But every year he played incredibly well, motivating himself to return for another season. Such is the fate he considered again at the end of the 2012-13 season when he played in 46 of the team's 48 games and had 12 goals and 24 points.

Oleg Tverdovsky was a solid defenceman who played three-and-a-half seasons in Winnipeg/Phoenix, earning invitations to play for Russia twice in 1996, first at the World Championship and later at the World Cup of Hockey. Phoenix traded Tverdovsky back to the Ducks in June 1999 for Travis Green and a first-round draft choice. The Russian rearguard won a bronze medal with at the 2002 Olympics then found greener pastures with Stanley Cup wins in New Jersey (2003) and Carolina (2006).

Chad Kilger, once a linemate of Kariya's in Anaheim, never lived up to the potential of being a fourth-overall draft choice. He spent most of his time in the Jets/Coyotes organization between the NHL and the farm team in Springfield. On March 3, 1998, Kilger was traded to Chicago for Jim Cummins and Keith Carney.

THE RESULT The transaction was the ultimate insult that added to Winnipeg's injury of losing its hockey team. While the franchise received a talented defencemen in Tverdovsky as well as serviceable players Green and Carney in future deals, the return was nowhere close to compensating for the loss of a future Hall-of-Famer in Selanne.

The Ducks definitely flew higher than the Jets in this deal.

MARCH 20, 1996

Canucks Acquire Naslund, Almost for Free

The Deal [PITTSBURGH PENGUINS trade **Markus Naslund** to the VANCOUVER CANUCKS for **Alek Stojanov.**

"We think we improved our skill level with a little more depth and scoring on our third line."
—Pat Quinn

THE DIRT At the trade deadline in 1996, Canucks general manager Pat Quinn was looking to add some depth to his team's blue line. But instead of a veteran defenceman, he acquired three forwards in deals with separate teams: Joey Kocur from the New York Rangers; Jesse Belanger from the Florida Panthers; and, Naslund from the Pittsburgh Penguins.

Quinn's initial plan was to use Naslund to bolster the third line. Vancouver's production up front was coming almost exclusively from its top six forwards: Cliff Ronning centering Esa Tikkanen and Alex Mogilny; Trevor Linden centering Martin Gelinas and Russ Courtnall.

"We think we improved our skill level with a little more depth and scoring on our third line," said Quinn. "Belanger is a nifty player at centre, and Naslund has played behind great scorers in Pittsburgh and already has put some good numbers on the board."

Naslund, a left-winger, had the good fortune of playing with superb talent early in his hockey career. As a 19-year-old with MoDo of the Swedish Elite League, he was a linemate of Peter Forsberg. The duo led Sweden to a silver medal at the 1993 World Junior Championship on home ice, Naslund registering 24 points in just seven games. Originally a first-round draft pick of the Penguins in 1991, Naslund found himself playing on a line with Mario Lemieux early in the 1995-96 season. After being dropped from the Penguins' top forward unit in late December, Naslund demanded a trade.

"I really wanted out of here, and I'm happy to be in Vancouver," Naslund said upon leaving Pittsburgh. "I've been asking for a trade now over two months. I'm looking forward to getting more chance to play, and a new start." He had collected 19 goals and 52 points in 66 games at the time of the transaction.

Stojanov, selected nine spots ahead of Naslund in the 1991 draft, had trouble hiding his disappointment with the move. "Some of the best times in my life were here," he said. "I love Vancouver. I didn't want to leave. It's a great bunch of guys, and I'll miss them all."

THE DEBATE The Canucks were ousted in the first round of the 1996 playoffs by Colorado, the eventual Stanley Cup champions. Naslund accepted invitations to play for Sweden at both the World Championship and later the inaugural World Cup of Hockey.

Following a pair of average full seasons in Vancouver, Naslund started to emerge as an offensive threat during the 1998-99 season, earning 36 goals and 66 points and becoming the Canucks' scoring leader on a team ranked fifth-worst in goals scored (192). He also played in his first career NHL All-Star Game, joining countryman and teammate Mattias Ohlund on Team World.

Two years later, Naslund topped the 40-goal plateau for the first time. He registered 41 goals in 72 games before his season came to an end because of a knee injury. In 2001-02, Naslund represented Sweden on the international stage once again as the best NHL players competed at the Winter Olympics in Salt Lake City.

However the Swedes suffered a colossal upset at the hands of Belarus in the quarter-finals.

Returning to Vancouver, Naslund capped off the regular season with 40 goals and 90 points, finishing second to Jarome Iginla in the race for the Art Ross Trophy. In the playoffs, Naslund had the misfortune of watching his netminder give up a weak goal from centre ice for the second time in two months.

The loss at the Olympics in February came after Tommy Salo had a long shot from Belarus's Vladimir Kopat bounce off his mask and into the net for the winning goal. In April, it was Canucks' goalie Dan Cloutier who surrendered a 90-foot shot off the stick of Nicklas Lidstrom to turn the series in favour of the Detroit Red Wings, who went on to win the series and the Stanley Cup.

The following season, 2002-03, was the best year of Naslund's career. On a forward line with Todd Bertuzzi and Brendan Morrison, Naslund was part of one of the most dangerous trios in the NHL. He produced a 104-point campaign and finished just two points behind his junior teammate Forsberg for the scoring championship. Naslund was recognized by his peers by winning the Lester B. Pearson Award.

Throughout his career, Naslund was a consistently productive player, never scoring fewer than 24 goals or 55 points in nine straight years in Vancouver. He missed only five games over his final six years in a Canucks uniform. By the time Naslund signed as a free agent with the New York Rangers in July 2008, he was the Canucks'

/// Polar Opposite

No two players could be more dissimilar than Markus Naslund and Alek Stojanov. The former was a skilled scorer and excellent skater; the latter was known for his ability to fight. But Stojanov had major shoulder surgery in 1993, missed a full season, and was never the same. He earned some measure of respect for a decent AHL season in 1994-95, but in 1995-96, before the trade, he scored not a single goal in 58 games with the Vancouver Canucks. Stojanov got his first NHL goal in his first game with the Penguins, scored one again the year after, and was a minor leaguer thereafter.

all-time leader in goals (346) and points (756). The milestone for points was broken by both Henrik and Daniel Sedin during the 2012-13 season.

Stojanov had more grit and size than Naslund but didn't surpass his trade counterpart in any other category. After collecting 84 penalty minutes in just 45 games with Pittsburgh, Stojanov played for several minor league teams in four different leagues.

THE RESULT Quinn's search for a third line player turned into the acquisition of a cornerstone for the franchise. On December 11, 2010—one year after his retirement—Naslund had his number 19 raised to the rafters of Vancouver's Rogers Arena.

Stojanov suffered a shoulder injury early in his career that forced him to miss a full year of hockey. In Quinn's opinion, Stojanov's skating development was hampered as a result. Whatever the reason, the result was a clear mismatch in one of hockey's most lop-sided trades of all time.

/// Slow Start

Looking back, it's easy to see Markus Naslund having been a superstar in the NHL, but day by day after being drafted by Pittsburgh in 1991, such was not the case. He stayed in Sweden and played two more years for MoDo and then attended Penguins' training camp in 1993 at age 20. The Penguins wanted him to be an NHLer, but in 71 games during his rookie season he scored only four goals and hardly looked like a first-round prospect. He was a healthy scratch in the playoffs, and the next year, shortened by lockout, he was equally unimpressive, spent time in the minors, and again watched the playoffs from the press box. Unhappy, he played the final year of his three-year contract with the Penguins and started to show promise, scoring 19 goals and 52 points in the first 66 games. Nevertheless, he was traded at the deadline for a player who was selected 7th overall at the same 1991 draft.

OCTOBER 9, 1996

Shanahan and His Goals Go to the Joe

The Deal [HARTFORD WHALERS trade **Brendan Shanahan** and **Brian Glynn** to the DETROIT RED WINGS for **Paul Coffey, Keith Primeau,** and **a 1st-round draft choice in 1997 (Nikos Tselios).**

"I don't know how many players there are like him in the league. He's a winger, a power winger who can score. Obviously that's what we're expecting."
—Scotty Bowman

THE DIRT The end of the 1996 playoffs prolonged a streak of futility for the Detroit Red Wings, a team which continued to underachieve amidst optimistic Stanley Cup expectations. Twelve months after being swept by the New Jersey Devils in the finals, Scotty Bowman's squad fell in six games to the Colorado Avalanche in the third round. The defeat was especially bitter in the wake of Detroit's record-setting 62-win regular season that had the Wings earmarked as Cup favourites.

The following season opened under a cloud of controversy in Motown. Coffey, a three-time Norris Trophy winner, was looking to leave Detroit and was feuding with Bowman. Primeau was relegated to the role of third line centre, having to play behind Steve Yzerman and Sergei Fedorov.

The trigger on the deal was pulled on the day of the Red Wings' home opener. In fact, the team's charter plane placed on standby so that Shanahan could play in the game. Shanahan, who earned a major penalty in a first-period fight, was a good

/// A Bit of Everything

Brendan Shanahan holds the unofficial record with 17 career "Gordie Howe Hat Tricks." The term was first coined by Bob Probert after a game in which he scored a goal, earned an assist, and got into a fight. Probert's turn of phrase was a brilliant way to highlight the reputation of Howe, the game's greatest offensive player until Wayne Gretzky came along and also the player with a reputation for being the strongest and most intimidating. In truth, Howe didn't fight much after he fell hard into the boards, fractured his skull, and nearly died in a game early in his career, but by that time he had won enough battles that his reputation carried him another two decades. Shanahan was the modern day Howe. He had a sensational shot and was hard on the puck to create more than his fair share of goals and assists, but he was tough as nails when he had to be.

fit for Detroit. He had been unhappy in Hartford because of the instability of the Whalers' franchise. Shanahan replaced the power-forward grittiness that was lost when Detroit traded Dino Ciccarelli to Tampa Bay in the summer. "Hockey-wise, I think everybody knows he's hard-nosed," said Bowman. "I don't know how many players there are like him in the league. He's a winger, a power winger who can score. Obviously that's what we're expecting."

Coffey complicated matters by threatening not to report to Hartford. Like Shanahan, Coffey was reluctant to play for a team with an uncertain future. "I'll sit here for a couple of days, put my feet on the ground, and see what is going on," said Coffey. "It's a good team, and an exciting team, but I do not want to have to get up and move in two years. We'll see what happens."

THE DEBATE Shanahan picked up from where he left off in his first Red Wings season, winning the hearts of Detroit fans by leading the team with 46 goals and 85 points. His 20 power-play goals were the best total in the league. Shanahan also showed a nasty, scrappier side to his game by picking up 131 penalty minutes. His willingness to drop the gloves was most evident during a brawl on March 26,

1997, when the Red Wings faced their hated rivals, the Avalanche.

While Darren McCarty was exacting revenge by pummeling Claude Lemieux for knocking Kris Draper out of the previous year's playoffs, goalies Mike Vernon and Patrick Roy skated from their nets to engage in a fight at centre ice. But Roy was briefly intercepted by a Shanahan bodycheck. Roy recovered to tussle with Vernon while Shanahan fought Colorado defenceman Adam Foote. Amidst all the fighting, Detroit won the game in overtime. The momentum carried over into the 1997 playoffs when the Red Wings defeated the Avalanche in the semi-finals.

Detroit swept Philadelphia in the Stanley Cup finals at the end of that 1996-97 season, ending a 42-year championship drought for the franchise. Shanahan's nine goals led all Detroit players, and his 17 points were second only to Sergei Fedorov.

The next year Shanahan was selected to play on Team Canada as NHL players participated in the Winter Olympics for the first time. Shanahan had the unfortunate distinction of being the last player to shoot—and miss—against Dominik Hasek in the semi-finals shootout in which the Czechs won, 2-1, ousting Canada from gold-medal contention in the process. Despite the disappointment on the international stage, Shanahan returned to smiles later in the season as Detroit captured its second consecutive Stanley Cup.

Shanahan continued to be a productive force on the left wing, earning a First Team All-Star selection in 1999-2000 and a nod to the Second Team two years later. The 2001-02 season saw him complete his membership in the Triple Gold Club as he played on the Canadian team that ended a 50-year gold medal drought at the Olympics. By winning his third Stanley Cup with the Red Wings in June, Shanahan and Yzerman became the first players to win an Olympic gold medal and Stanley Cup in the same year since Ken Morrow became the first player to do same, in 1980 with the United States and New York Islanders.

Shanahan's career in Detroit lasted nine seasons during which time he played 716 games, scoring 309 goals and 633 points. He signed as a free agent with the New York Rangers in July 2006.

On Hartford's end, Primeau filled the role of a top-line centre that the Whalers had been lacking. He played for three years with the franchise, and the team relocated to Carolina at the beginning of the 1997-98 season. He played in 234 games, collecting 186 points, before being dealt to the Flyers in a multi-player deal in which Rod Brind'Amour went to Carolina.

As expected, a disgruntled Coffey spent very little time in Hartford, playing just 20 games. In December 1996, he was packaged in a trade with Philadelphia that saw defenceman Kevin Haller end up as a Whaler.

THE RESULT Shanahan had by far the more illustrious career as a result of this deal. When he was not inducted into the Hockey Hall of Fame in 2012 in his first year of eligibility, critics called the snub a glaring omission, but by the same token he was working with the NHL and some felt it would have been a nepotistic honour at this point in his career.

Primeau was a centre-ice force during his brief time in Hartford and Carolina, but the Hurricanes received an even greater benefit by trading for Brind'Amour. After coming over from the Flyers, Brind'Amour became a mainstay in the lineup for ten years, captaining the club to its first Stanley Cup in 2006.

Tselios or Chelios

Nikos Tselios (Greek spelling) is cousins with Chris Chelios (American spelling), who played in the NHL until age 48. But while Chris is a future Hall of Famer, Nikos didn't reach anywhere near such lofty heights. He was drafted 22nd overall by Carolina in 1997 after playing one season with Belleville in the OHL, but after two subsequent years in the IHL following his junior career he showed little promise. Tselios played two games with the Hurricanes in 2001-02, his only NHL appearances, as it turned out. He played in the minors and in Sweden until retiring in 2007 to open his own hockey camp.

JUNE 26, 1999
Burke's Pollock Imitation Nets Swedish Twins

The Deal [VANCOUVER CANUCKS trade **1st overall draft choice in 1999** to the ATLANTA THRASHERS **(Patrik Stefan)** for **2nd overall choice (Danel Sedin), a conditional 3rd-round draft choice,** and **the promise by Atlanta not to draft either Daniel or Henrik Sedin.**

"I think this is not only great for the franchise, but great for Canadian teams in general. It's a big deal to land two players of this calibre." —Brian Burke

THE DEAL (DETAILS) Vancouver traded defenceman Bryan McCabe and a 1st round draft choice in 2000 (11th—Pavel Vorobiev) to the Chicago Blackhawks for a 1st round draft choice (4th—later traded to NY Rangers—Pavel Brendl), in 1999. Vancouver traded the 4th overall selection and two, 3rd-round draft choices in 1999 (75th—Brett Scheffelmaier & 88th—Jimmie Olvestad) to the Tampa Bay Lightning for the 1st overall draft choice in 1999. Vancouver traded 1st overall draft choice to the Atlanta Thrashers (Patrik Stefan) for 2nd overall choice (Danel Sedin) and a conditional 3rd-round draft choice and the promise by Atlanta not to draft either Daniel or Henrik Sedin.

THE DIRT The 1998-99 season ended miserably for the Vancouver Canucks. The team won just one of its final eight games, and Vancouver's final outing of the season was decided by Cory Stillman of Calgary, who scored the game-winning goal with just four seconds remaining in regulation time. The defeat was a blessing in disguise because Vancouver, with fewer wins, finished lower in the standings than the New York Islanders, thus earning a higher draft position.

Heading into draft day at Boston's Fleet Center in 1999, the top four picks were held by Tampa Bay, which finished last in the standings; Atlanta, the new expansion team; Vancouver, which finished second-last; and Chicago, which won the draft lottery to move up four spots and knock the Islanders down to fifth.

Shrewd Canucks general manager Brian Burke had his sights set on Daniel and Henrik Sedin, twins from Ornskoldsvik, Sweden who played for MoDo in the Swedish Elite League. The coveted 18-year-olds, born six minutes apart, had garnered the attention of hockey world. If there was anyone who could work the phones to secure the rights to both players—whom everyone knew would play better as a pair than individually—it was Burke. As general manager of the Hartford Whalers in 1993, Burke made two draft-day deals to obtain the second-overall pick which he used to select Chris Pronger. Six years later, history repeated itself.

Burke reluctantly surrendered Bryan McCabe, an emerging young defenceman, to obtain Chicago's fourth-overall pick. The price was high, but the leverage that Vancouver had was invaluable. Burke was able to make the deal for the first-overall pick with Lightning general manager Rick Dudley because Tampa Bay wanted to deal with the New York Rangers for goalie Dan Cloutier.

/// Sedin Sedin

The Sedins do everything together. To wit, their international hockey careers are identical. They both played at three U20 tournaments together—1998, 1999, 2000. They both played at four World Championships early in their careers—1999, 2000, 2001, 2005. They both played at the 2006 and 2010 Olympics, and in the spring of 2013, they both played for Tre Kronor again after the Canucks were eliminated in the opening round of the playoffs. The Sedins flew to Stockholm and helped Sweden win gold, the first time in 27 years the host nation had won World Championship gold. They played only four games at the 2013 event, but these included all playoff-round games when it's win or go home. The Sedins were sensational and were the toast of the town.

The pieces fit nicely since the Lightning-Rangers deal was contingent on either Patrick Stefan or Pavel Brendl being available to New York in the fourth spot. Burke's interest in the Sedins guaranteed the desired scenario for the Blueshirts. After the Tampa Bay deals were consummated, a call from Burke to Atlanta general manager Don Waddell completed Burke's masterpiece. The only further challenge for Burke at the podium was to determine how to tell the twins apart, when he handed over the pair of Canucks sweaters.

"I think this is not only great for the franchise, but great for Canadian teams in general," said Burke. "It's a big deal to land two players of this calibre." Both brothers remained calm and comfortable upon learning they were both headed to an NHL career in Vancouver, together. Daniel called the twins' selection at number two and three in the draft "fun," while Henrik, when asked if he were looking forward to playing with hometown native Markus Naslund, simply said "Yes, he's a great guy."

THE DEBATE The Sedins returned to MoDo for another year of development, and both were chosen to represent their country at the World Junior Championship for a second straight year. As Sweden was hosting the tournament in Skelleftea, there was much excitement around a team that also included Henrik Zetterberg and Niklas Kronwall. But the Swedes lost in the quarter-finals to the United States and finished fifth. Henrik led the tournament in scoring with 13 points in seven games, with Daniel finished in third place just two points behind, although both brothers collected the majority of their points against weaker teams.

The 2000-01 season marked the NHL debut of the Sedins. As Daniel patrolled the left wing and Henrik played centre, they formed an effective third line with right winger Trent Klatt. Vancouver ended a four-year playoff drought but was promptly swept by Colorado. The following year saw the Canucks suffer a first-round exit at the hands of the Red Wings. Burke showed his frustration at the treatment his star twins were subject to during the tougher playoffs when referees allowed more infractions to go unpunished, angrily proclaiming that,

"Sedin is not Swedish for punch me, or headlock me in a scrum."

Playing over the next few seasons alongside linemates such as Klatt, Trevor Linden, and Anson Carter, the Sedins developed into top-line forwards. Their natural chemistry—evident since they were youngsters—created no-look passes and give-and-go rushes that delighted Vancouver fans. The twins enjoyed a gold-medal victory with Team Sweden at the 2006 Winter Olympics, defeating Scandinavian rivals Finland, 3-2, in the final game. The following season, 2006-07, marked the first time that both players topped the 80-point mark as their fellow Ornskoldsvik native Naslund played the right wing on the line.

Henrik was the first of the brothers to win an NHL award, capturing both the Art Ross Trophy and Hart Trophy in 2009-10. His 83 assists and 112 points led all players in both categories. He accomplished the feat despite a foot injury to brother Daniel that sidelined the sibling for six weeks earlier in the year.

Not to be outdone, Daniel won the scoring championship in 2010-11, also taking home the Ted Lindsay Award as the best player as voted by NHLPA members. The Canucks advanced to the Stanley Cup finals, only to be crushed 4-0 by Boston in the decisive seventh game.

THE RESULT　Burke's brilliant manoeuvres landed a pair of dynamic franchise players for the Canucks. Henrik and Daniel finished the 2012-13 season as Vancouver's top two all-time leading scorers with 792 and 758 points, respectively.

The total sacrifice was McCabe and three draft choices. McCabe lasted one season in Chicago before being traded to the Maple Leafs on October 2, 2000, for Alexander Karpovtsev and a fourth-round pick.

It was clear that the Sedins wanted to play together. In the end, it was Burke winning a staring match with the other general managers to make the scenario happen for his team. It was one of the most complex and shrewdest series of trades in the game's history.

FEBRUARY 22, 2001

Blake a D-Man for Avs' Cup Run

The Deal

LOS ANGELES KINGS trade **Rob Blake** and **Steve Reinprecht** to the COLORADO AVALANCHE for **Adam Deadmarsh, Aaron Miller, a 1st-round draft choice in 2001 (David Steckel) and 2003 (Brian Boyle),** and **future considerations (Jared Aulin).**

"L.A.'s been great for me. They gave me my start in the league. But I don't think a new deal was ever going to come together…It was a business decision."
—Rob Blake

THE DIRT Rob Blake anchored the blue line of the Los Angeles Kings for nine seasons, excelling as an offensive defenceman with a hard, accurate shot to complement an ability to dish out a solid bodycheck. He made an immediate impression in the NHL, earning a spot on the All-Rookie team in 1990-91. Two years later, Blake was on a Los Angeles squad led by Wayne Gretzky that made it to the Stanley Cup finals versus Montreal. When the Great One was traded to St. Louis in 1996, Blake succeeded him as team captain.

In a career year of 1997-98, Blake earned a spot on Team Canada's entry at the 1998 Winter Olympics in Nagano, Japan. Canada finished a disappointing fourth, but Blake was named the best defenceman at the tournament. Finishing that NHL season with 23 goals and 50 points, he won the Norris Trophy and was named an NHL First Team All-Star.

As the 2001 trade deadline approached and Blake playing in his ninth full season, it became evident that the Kings would no longer be able to afford his salary demand of $9.6 million per season. Los Angeles general manager Dave Taylor had no choice but to make Blake, a pending unrestricted free agent, available to the highest bidder.

The deal was finalized at 1:30am and came as a surprise to countless hockey fans who were asleep at the time the deal was finalized. "We're all a little bit shocked," said long-time teammate Luc Robitaille. "Somehow, I don't think I believed it was going to happen."

Blake's departure from the team that drafted him in 1988 was emotional, but he also expressed joy at leaving a borderline playoff roster for a Stanley Cup contender. "There's no animosity," he began. "L.A.'s been great for me. They gave me my start in the league. But I don't think a new deal was ever going to come together. I knew from the beginning we were too far apart. It was a business decision."

THE DEBATE The Avalanche were on a mission to win a Stanley Cup for Ray Bourque, the long-time Boston defenceman who was acquired by Colorado the previous year. A 40-year-old veteran who had played in the league for more than half his lifetime, Bourque was heading into retirement having accomplished pretty much everything except having won a Stanley Cup.

Blake and Bourque, who were teammates in Nagano three years earlier, formed a sturdy defensive pairing over the final six weeks of the regular season. The Avalanche won the Presidents' Trophy, and Blake was named to the NHL's Second All-Star team. In the Stanley Cup finals, Colorado was heavily challenged by New Jersey, the defending champions.

The Avalanche, however, overcame a 3-2 series deficit to win the final two games. A jubilant Bourque eagerly accepted the Stanley Cup from captain Joe Sakic as the 22-year veteran ended his career on a high. Somewhat lost in Bourque's well-deserved accolades was the accomplishment of Blake winning his first championship as well.

Blake went on to play four full seasons in Colorado. He returned to the

Deadmarsh or Deadmarch?

When Adam Deadmarsh helped Colorado win the Stanley Cup in 1996, he was elated to have his name stamped on the hallowed trophy. But when he saw the Cup later that year, he noticed his name had been spelled "Deadmarch." Displeased, he insisted the error be corrected, which it was, but in so doing he removed a small bit of Cup trivia. Many names have been misspelled over the years, adding to the trophy's charm and intimacy. But instead of leaving fate to decide how his name appeared, he wanted accuracy above all else. Understandable, to be sure, but not nearly as special as an unintentional misspelling.

Canadian Olympic team in 2002 when the Games were played in Salt Lake City. Canada's 5-2 win over the United States in the final game earned Blake an Olympic gold medal. With two world championships (1994, 1997) and a Stanley Cup already in tow, Blake became a member of the Triple Gold Club along with Olympics teammates Sakic and Brendan Shanahan.

After 322 games with the Avalanche in which he scored 62 goals and 208 points, Blake rejoined the Kings, signing as a free agent in July 2006. He spent the last four years of his career on the west coast—two in Los Angeles and two in San Jose—before announcing his retirement.

Steve Reinprecht was a fourth-line centre who saw limited action playing on a team with tremendous depth down the middle in Sakic, Peter Forsberg, and checking specialist Stephane Yelle. Reinprecht registered 104 points in Colorado and was traded in a three-way deal involving Calgary for Keith Ballard on July 3, 2003.

In Deadmarsh, the Kings acquired a gritty forward who had already won a Stanley Cup in Colorado in 1996 and was also a part of the American team that won the World Cup of Hockey later that same year. In 2001-02, his first full season in Los Angeles, Deadmarsh tallied 29 goals and 62 points in 76 games, finishing second only to Jason Allison in team scoring.

Unfortunately, concussions ended Deadmarsh's career prematurely. He suffered his first serious head injury in November 2000 in a fight with Vancouver's Ed

Jovanovski, then sustained a more serious concussion two years later after a collision with teammate Greg Johnson. Despite valiant comeback attempts, Deadmarsh officially retired on September 22, 2005.

Miller was a steady stay-at-home defenceman who missed extended periods of time due to various injuries. Following the trade to Los Angeles, he represented the United States on four occasions, winning a silver medal at the Salt Lake City Olympics in 2002. He also played on the American entries at the 2004 and 2005 World Championships and the 2006 World Cup of Hockey.

THE RESULT GM Dave Taylor couldn't have been expected to replace a player of Blake's stature easily or with just one player, but given that Blake, a Norris Trophy winner, was set to become an unrestricted free agent, the Kings did well in obtaining an impact forward and a solid defenceman.

The unforeseen end to Deadmarsh's career, however, reduced the trade benefit to the Kings in the long-term.

// Large Man Scores—Go Figure

Brian Boyle was selected 26th overall by Los Angeles in 2003 as a result of the Blake deal, and he turned out to be a much better player than what one have first thought. He played the next four seasons at Boston College, but at 6'7" he had to work extra hard on his skating and skill development. He turned pro in 2007 and scored three goals for the Kings in his first four games, but he spent the next two years bouncing between the NHL and AHL. The Rangers stepped in at the 2009 draft and acquired him for a 3rd-round draft choice in 2010 (Jordan Weal). Boyle continued to dedicate himself to skating and footwork, even taking lessons with figure skating champ Barb Underhill. His determination paid off. Boyle had 21 goals in 2010-11 with the Rangers and proved that a big guy can play the game without having to resort to fisticuffs.

JUNE 23, 2001
Sens Rid Themselves of Yashin Drama

The Deal [OTTAWA SENATORS trade **Alexei Yashin**
to the NEW YORK ISLANDERS for **Zdeno Chara, Bill Muckalt,**
and **a 1st-round draft choice in 2001 (Jason Spezza).**

"If a player chooses not to play at all, then that is the player's decision. What the full performance concept requires is that the player renders performance for the full term." —Lawrence Holden

THE DIRT Occasionally a professional athlete will refuse to report to his team until he is able to come to terms on a new contract. In cases where his previous deal has expired and the team is reluctant to trade him, the player is incorrectly—and unfairly—referred to as a 'holdout.' With no agreement in place, there is nothing from which the player is holding out, after all. Other factors such as the absence of an offer sheet, or a disinclined trade market, prolong the stalemate.

But in the case of Alexei Yashin, who took over the captaincy of the Ottawa Senators in 1998-99, the holdout label was accurate. By the end of the season, Yashin had compiled 94 points to finish sixth in the league in scoring. His 44 goals were second only to Teemu Selanne in the race for the Rocket Richard Trophy. Yashin was named to the NHL's Second All-Star team and was a Hart Trophy finalist to Pittsburgh's winner, Jaromir Jagr.

Yashin was one of the best players in the league and understandably wanted to be paid accordingly. However, through his agent Mark Gandler, Yashin insisted that his contract be renegotiated while there was still one year remaining on his current deal. Slated to make $3.6 million in the final year of what was a five-year pact worth $13.5 million, Yashin demanded a two-year extension with a salary of $11 million and $12 million in the two subsequent years.

Ottawa Senators general manager Marshall Johnston balked at the proposal. Yashin, in turn, refused to start the 1999-2000 season with the team, repeating his actions of four years earlier when he was a holdout under similar circumstances. A war of words escalated as Gandler accused the Senators of racism and anti-Russian bias.

In November, Yashin was suspended for the entire season, and the Senators steadfastly claimed that the Russian centre owed the team the final year of service on his contract. The saga lasted well beyond the 2000 playoffs—where the Senators lost a first-round series to the Maple Leafs—and into the summer. Finally in June, arbitrator Lawrence Holden sided with the Senators.

"If a player chooses not to play at all, then that is the player's decision," wrote Holden in his ruling. "What the full performance concept requires is that the player renders performance for the full term of years specified, without illegally holding out if the player wants to obtain the negotiated benefit of free agency."

THE DEBATE Upon returning to the team in 2000-01, Yashin scored 88 points in 82 games but was held to just one point in four playoff games as heavily-favoured Ottawa was swept by Toronto. Although Yashin's reputation in dealing with management had been damaged in the fallout of Holden's ruling, New York Islanders general manager Mike Milbury was unfazed.

"We need somebody with the credentials, somebody with the star power that we can rally around," Milbury said. The trade was consummated at the 2001 Entry Draft in Florida where the Islanders had been slotted to pick in the number two spot. While the Atlanta Thrashers selected Ilya Kovalchuk first overall, Ottawa followed by choosing highly-touted Mississauga, Ontario native Jason Spezza.

Spezza was enjoying a phenomenal junior career, twice having represented

General Manager

Persona non grata in Ottawa, Yashin made a supremely quiet trip to the nation's capital in April 2013 in a most unlikely capacity—general manager of the Russian national women's hockey team. The Women's Worlds were played at Scotiabank Place and the Nepean Sportsplex, and the Russians had won only one medal, a bronze in 2001, since their first WW tournament in 1997. Improbably, the team beat Germany, Czech Republic, Sweden, and Switzerland to advance to the semi-finals, and after being pummelled 8-1 by Canada, the Russians then beat Finland, 2-0, to win a second bronze. There, in the back of the team photo on ice after the stunning victory, is none other than Alexei Yashin.

Canada at the World Junior Championship. On the 2000 edition of the team, he and Jay Bouwmeester became just the fourth and fifth players in Canadian history to play in the tournament as 16-year-olds, following in the footsteps of Bill Campbell, Wayne Gretzky, and Eric Lindros.

At the time of the trade, Spezza was coming off a 2000-01 season during which he collected 116 points in 56 OHL games split between Mississauga and Windsor. When Spezza was cut at the Senators' fall training camp, coach Jacques Martin exacerbated the player's disappointment by saying, "This is a men's league, and he's still a boy."

But the extra year of development paid off in the long run. Spezza earned his third invitation to play on Canada's junior team. By the time he was finally ready to step into the NHL, Spezza was earning ice time as a top-line forward as opposed to grinding among the bottom-six forwards or possibly sitting in the press box.

In 2005-06, Spezza set a club record with 71 assists. The following year, he led all players with 22 points in the playoffs as the Senators advanced to the Stanley Cup finals. A back injury limited him to just five games in 2012-13, but he continued to be one of the league's most dangerous forwards when healthy.

Chara was a towering force on the Senators blue line—both literally and figuratively—for four seasons. The 6'9" defenceman used his extraordinary size effectively on the way to a pair of All-Star selections in 2003-04 and 2005-06. At the end of the latter season, both Chara and teammate Wade Redden headed into unrestricted free agency. Ottawa general manager John Muckler was in the unenviable position of having to choose between the two. He decided to retain Redden, and Chara signed as a free agent with Boston.

THE RESULT Yashin played 346 games with the Islanders over five seasons, registering 290 points. His production was respectable but well below the expectations of a one-time Hart Trophy finalist. As a result of his contract squabbles, Yashin could never shake the reputation of being a floater who was more interested in his salary than helping his team win at all costs. In 2007, he left for the KHL after being bought-out by the Islanders.

The trade was an excellent one for the Senators and could have been even more outstanding had they chosen to keep Chara for the long-term.

/// Yashin Giveth and Taketh Away

Perhaps no player damaged his own reputation in a city more than Alexei Yashin in Ottawa. In 1998, he donated $1 million to the National Arts Centre soon after signing a huge contract with the team, a seeming act of generosity to show "the kind of connection I have with the Canadian people, and especially with the people in Ottawa," he explained at the time. But soon after, Yashin made it clear he expected his family to be paid much of that donation for nebulous consulting services. Indeed, he was scheduled to donate $200,000 a year for five years, but he wanted his family to get $85,000 of that sum. Incredulous, the NAC refused to comply, and Yashin withdrew the donation for "personal reasons," he explained.

JULY 11, 2001

Jagr Too Rich for Mario-less Pens

The Deal [PITTSBURGH PENGUINS trade **Jaromir Jagr** and **Frantisek Kucera** to the WASHINGTON CAPITALS for **Kris Beech, Ross Lupaschuk, Michal Sivek,** and **future considerations.**

"It feels great; he's the top offensive player in this league. We wanted to add offence and this, obviously, is a huge step in the right direction."
—George McPhee

THE DIRT By the time he was just 20 years old, Jaromir Jagr had established himself as the heir apparent to Mario Lemieux in Pittsburgh, and not simply because his first name was, conveniently, an anagram of "Mario Jr." With incredible vision and stickhandling ability, Jagr played on a pair of Stanley Cup winning teams in his first two years in the NHL. He scored his signature goal in game one of the 1992 finals against Chicago when he outmanoeuvred three Blackhawks skaters—Dirk Graham, Brent Sutter, and Frantisek Kucera—before lifting a backhander past a stunned Ed Belfour in the Hawks goal.

In 1994-95, Jagr broke a 14-year stranglehold on the Art Ross Trophy during which the scoring champion had been either Lemieux or Wayne Gretzky. When Super Mario first retired in 1997, Jagr took over the reins of not only the Pittsburgh Penguins, but the entire NHL, as the predominant player. Jagr won four consecutive Art Ross Trophies between 1997-98 and 2000-01, earning recognition as a First Team All-Star on each occasion. He was named Hart Trophy winner as league MVP in 1998-99 and also won a pair of Lester B. Pearson Awards (1998-99 and 1999-2000).

But by the time Jagr was in his third year as team captain, 2000-01, his enthusiasm for the team had waned. He attended, or skipped, practices on his own schedule. He bickered with teammates and coaches. Making his departure out of Pittsburgh all the more imminent, Jagr was contracted to earn $20.7 million over the next two years, beginning in 2001-02. The Penguins had 17 free agents to re-sign, and keeping Jagr was out of line with the team's budget.

"He wanted to move on, so he's glad at this point that it's over with," said Pittsburgh general manager Craig Patrick after the trade. "It's difficult to trade someone who has been here eleven years and accomplished so much."

The Capitals were obviously elated with acquiring a player of Jagr's skills and reputation. "It feels great; he's the top offensive player in this league," Capitals general manager George McPhee said. "We wanted to add offence and this, obviously, is a huge step in the right direction."

Jagr's comments, which he provided by phone from his home in the Czech Republic, were brief. "I have something to prove. I want to be the best player in the world," he said.

THE DEBATE The transaction immediately gave the Capitals a pair of potent forwards in Jagr and Peter Bondra, who combined for 70 goals in 2001-02 (Jagr 31, Bondra 39). But while Jagr's output was decent by an average player's standards, his 31 goals were his lowest total since his rookie year (27 in 1990-91), and his 79 points represented a 48 point drop-off from the previous season in which he had won his fourth straight scoring title.

Unfortunately for Washington, its second-place finish in the weak Southeast division was good enough only for ninth overall in the Eastern Conference, and the Capitals missed the playoffs. Jagr headed to Sweden to play in the World Championships, finishing fifth with the Czech Republic while teammate Bondra won the gold medal with Slovakia.

Bruce Cassidy replaced Ron Wilson behind the Capitals bench for the 2002-03 season, but once again Jagr was constrained by a defensive system, and he occasionally butted heads with the new coach. Jagr finished the year with 77 points. Washington returned to the playoffs but was eliminated by Tampa Bay in the first round. The Capitals attempted to trade Jagr, but his salary was too rich for potential suitors.

"I know that hockey is a business," Jagr said. "You can't expect me to have the same numbers I had in Pittsburgh. If you expect me to score 120 points here, I don't think anybody could do that, not even Mario Lemieux, and I think he's the best ever. There are not many players who could win a scoring title with some teams."

By the time the 2003-04 campaign was underway, Jagr was at the lowest point in his career. Mired in a five-game scoring drought in October, Jagr had also recently ended a relationship with his long-time girlfriend, a former model and Miss Slovakia beauty contest winner. The animosity between Jagr and Cassidy increased. With only eight wins in their first 28 games, the Capitals fired Cassidy and replaced him with Glen Hanlon. A month later, Jagr was traded to the New York Rangers for Anson Carter. The future Hall of Famer's career was rejuvenated in Manhattan, and Jagr won the Lester B. Pearson Award in 2005-06, earning his eighth First Team All-Star selection.

The Kucera File

Like Jagr, Frantisek Kucera started in 1990, with Chicago, but over the course of 14 years he played with seven teams. After four years with the Hawks, he played with Hartford for three seasons, Vancouver for parts of two seasons, and two games with the Flyers in 1996-97. After three years in the Czech Republic, he was lured back to North America by the expansion Columbus Blue Jackets, but soon he was traded to Pittsburgh. Kucera played all of seven games with the Pens before being sent to the Capitals, his last NHL team in a career that consisted of 465 regular season games and only 12 playoff games.

The Penguins received three of Washington's first four 1999 draft picks in the transaction. None of them lived up to their billing. First-rounder Beech, a centre, scored 27 points in 91 games for Pittsburgh before being traded to Nashville in 2005 for a fourth-round draft choice. Sivek lasted just 38 NHL games, eventually moving to the Czech Republic. Defenceman Lupaschuk played only three games in the NHL, spending four seasons with Wilkes-Barre in the AHL before heading to Europe.

Meanwhile Kucera, one of Jagr's victims on the famous 1992 goal against Chicago, lasted one season in Washington, scoring 14 points in 56 games.

THE RESULT The Jagr trade wasn't as much of a surprise as the relative lack of return that Pittsburgh received for one of the most dynamic players in the league's history. Jagr's years in Washington were forgettable, yet his numbers still dwarfed the combined production of the Capitals' prospects that the Penguins received in return.

At age 41, Jagr still showed his effectiveness playing on a Bruins team that advanced to the 2013 Stanley Cup finals after eliminating the Penguins in a four-game sweep in the conference finals under the watchful eye of Pens owner Mario Lemieux.

Twenty-Three Years On

The 2013 Stanley Cup playoffs were surreal for Jaromir Jagr. He won the Stanley Cup in each of his first two seasons, 1990-91 and 1991-92, with a Pittsburgh team led by captain Mario Lemieux. In 2013, Mario long retired and Jagr now a trade-deadline acquisition by Boston, Jagr faced the Penguins in the conference finals. The Penguins were led by Sidney Crosby, who played half his rookie season with Lemieux, who was also the team's owner. Now it was all Crosby, while Lemieux watched the games from the press box, his own protégé facing off against a former teammate who learned so much from Lemieux 23 years ago. The Bruins shut down Crosby, sweeping the Pens in four games to advance to the Cup finals.

FEBRUARY 27, 2007
Tearful Farewell as Smyth Leaves Oil

The Deal [EDMONTON OILERS trade **Ryan Smyth**
to the NEW YORK ISLANDERS for **Robert Nilsson, Ryan O'Marra,**
and **a 1st-round draft choice in 2007 (Alex Plante).**

"I never thought it would come to this day. I've got to turn the page and start a new chapter in life. The New York Islanders have given me that opportunity, and I thank them for this." —Ryan Smyth

THE DIRT Eight months after coming within a game of winning the Stanley Cup, the Edmonton Oilers were a shadow of the team that had made an unexpected run to the finals the previous spring. The anchor of their defence, Chris Pronger, had been traded to Anaheim in July after demanding out. Forwards Michael Peca and Sergei Samsonov had signed as free agents with Toronto and Montreal, respectively.

As the 2007 trade deadline approached, the gap between the Oilers and the eight playoff-bound teams in the Western Conference was widening. Smyth, the face of the franchise, was in the final year of his contract and eligible for unrestricted free agency on Canada Day. Oilers fans held out hope that the man dubbed "Captain Canada" in recognition of his frequent national team representation would be signed to a much-deserved extension.

Instead, general manager Kevin Lowe did the opposite. On the same day that Mark Messier was honoured with a banner-raising ceremony at Rexall Place, Lowe and his Islanders counterpart Garth Snow completed the transaction, effectively transitioning the defending Western Conference champions into rebuilding mode.

In an emotional news conference at the Edmonton airport, Smyth said good-bye to the city in which he had played for eleven years. "I never thought it would come to this day," said Smyth, fighting off tears. "I've got to turn the page and start a new chapter in life. The New York Islanders have given me that opportunity, and I thank them for this."

Snow was eager to insert his new acquisition into the Islanders' lineup as the team geared up for a playoff push. "He's a warrior," sad Snow of Smyth. "He's a play-off performer. He's a hockey player with a big character, and he can score big goals. He'll be perfect in front of the net on the power-play, in that high-traffic area."

THE DEBATE Following the trade, the Islanders went 8-7-4 in their last 19 games of the season. They clinched the eighth and final playoff seed in the Eastern Conference in dramatic fashion on the final day, winning in a shootout over New Jersey when goalie Wade Dubielewicz foiled the Devils' final shooter, Sergei Brylin, with a pokecheck. Smyth was a huge contributor, missing only one game in the final five weeks and collecting 15 points in 18 games. The Islanders faced the Buffalo Sabres in the conference quarter-finals where they were eliminated in five games. Smyth had one goal and three assists.

The Oilers went into a tailspin in March and April, winning just two of their final 19 games to finish with the fifth-worst record in the league. If there were any solace in Edmonton at the time of the trade, it was in that small glimmer of hope that Smyth would return in the off-season. But even that hope was dashed on July 1 when Smyth signed a five-year, $31-million contract with the Colorado Avalanche.

Smyth played two years in both Colorado and Los Angeles, where he was later traded, before returning to the fold in Edmonton in June 2011 when the Kings traded him for Colin Fraser and a 7th-round draft choice. As of the end of the 2012-13 season, his 376 career goals place him in tenth place on the NHL's all-time list among active players. Spending most of his time in Edmonton on teams that, except for 2006, had relatively little playoff success, Smyth is more renowned for his international achievements: one Olympic gold medal (2002), two World Championship gold medals (2003 and 2004), and one World Junior Championship gold (1995).

Nilsson's first full year in an Oilers uniform appeared promising. The son of former NHL player Kent, a four-time 100-point scorer, the younger Nilsson registered 41 points in 71 games in 2007-08. But his point totals decreased over the next two seasons. Altogether Nilsson played 199 games for Edmonton before leaving for the KHL in the summer of 2010.

O'Marra, like Nilsson, had been a first-round draft pick of the Islanders. Playing the bulk of his junior career with the Erie Otters, O'Marra won consecutive gold medals at the World Junior Championship in 2006 and 2007. Although he was a member of the Oilers' organization for five seasons, O'Marra played just 31 NHL games for Edmonton. He spent the bulk of those years in the minors, in Springfield, and then Oklahoma City when the Oilers' AHL affiliate relocated. He was traded to Anaheim for Bryan Rodney on February 26, 2012.

The Oilers also received a first-round pick in the transaction, which they used to select Alex Plante (15th overall in 2007) from the WHL's Calgary Hitmen. Plante played ten games in Edmonton between 2009-10 and 2010-12, used sparingly as a recall from either Springfield or Oklahoma City.

/// From Tokyo to Finland

Ryan O'Marra is a perfect example of a player whose career peaked in junior hockey. He has the distinction of being born in Tokyo, Japan, moving to Canada with his family when he was just a year old. He helped Canada win gold at the 2006 and 2007 U20 World Championships. But O'Marra couldn't keep up as he got older. He went from the ECHL to AHL, landing in the NHL with Edmonton and Anaheim for a total of only 33 games over three seasons. He ended up in Finland, a fine league, to be sure, but below his own—and many scouts'—expectations.

THE RESULT The trading of Smyth wasn't the sole reason for the decline of the Oilers after their run to the Stanley Cup finals. It wasn't even the catalyst for the demise; the Pronger trade was. But it was the punctuation mark to the belief that the team could at least be competitive, if not contend. The anger of Oilers' fans was only further incited after reports surfaced that Smyth and Lowe had been only $100,000 apart on a new deal.

Edmonton missed the playoffs the year of the trade and the next six years. The team didn't finish higher than ninth place in the west over that time and ended in the basement of the NHL standings two years in a row.

The only consolation is that the run of futility, plus a lucky draft lottery win, earned Edmonton the first-overall pick in 2010 (Ryan Nugent-Hopkins), 2011 (Taylor Hall), and 2012 (Nail Yakupov). The lop-sided result of this trade should be forgotten by the time any, or all, of these prospects develops into established stars.

/// Captain Canada

Ryan Smyth was often called "Captain Canada" in international circles for his dedication and long affiliation with his national team, which lasted 15 years. He started at the 1995 U20, winning gold, and he played in his first World Championship in 1999. Between 1999 and 2006, he played in every major event for Canada, including the 2003 and 2004 Worlds when he captained Canada to gold both years. Smyth also played at the gold-medal Olympics in Salt Lake, as well as the 2006 Olympics, and he was also a member of Canada's championship team at the 2004 World Cup of Hockey. He made his last appearance at the 2010 World Championship, playing one game as a late addition to the team.

ACKNOWLEDGEMENTS

///

The authors would like to thank the people at Indigo for their support and enthusiasm for the project, notably Ed Wilkinson, as well as to designer Kathryn Zante for both her creative input and her deft organizational skills.

Andrew Podnieks would like to thank the people at the Hockey Hall of Fame, notably Craig Campbell, Phil Pritchard, and Steve Poirier for their support and assistance. As well to family—mom, Liz, Ian, Zac, Emily, and wife Jane, whom he would never trade for any number of first-round draft choices even if one of them were Sidney Crosby.

Rob Del Mundo would like to thank Rick Couchman, who got me to where I am today, and Stan Fischler, for giving me the opportunity to be a long-time contributor to "The Fischler Report." I also appreciate the professional advice given to me by colleagues and friends Kevin Shea, Debbie Elicksen, Mark Zwolinski, and Joe Warmington. Thanks to Kristen Lipscombe for the 'lippy' laughs. My strongest support group is my family: Dad, Mom, Mel, Jim, Justin, Megan, and Butch. Love you all.

PHOTO CREDITS

///